Social Equity and the Funding of Community Policing

A book in the series:

Criminal Justice Recent Scholarship
Edited by Marilyn McShane and Frank P. Williams III

Social Equity and the Funding of Community Policing

Ricky S. Gutierrez

LFB Scholarly Publishing LLC
New York

First published 2003 by LFB Scholarly Publishing LLC.
First printing in paperback, 2005.
All rights reserved.

Library of Congress Cataloging-in-Publication Data

Gutierrez, Ricky S., 1953-
  Social equity and the funding of community policing / Ricky S.
Gutierrez.
      p. cm. -- (Criminal justice recent scholarship)
Includes bibliographical references and index.
  ISBN 1-59332-001-9 (alk. paper)
  1. COPS Program (U.S.)--Appropriations and expenditures. 2.
Federal
aid to law enforcement agencies--United States. 3. Community
policing--United States--Regional disparities. I. Title. II. Criminal
justice (LFB Scholarly Publishing LLC).
  HV7936.C83G88 2003
  363.2'3'0973--dc22
                                    2003018749

ISBN 1-59332-001-9 (casebound)
ISBN 1-59332-096-5 (paperback)

Printed on acid-free 250-year-life paper.
Manufactured in the United States of America.

Table of Contents

List of Tables

List of Figures

Preface

When I decided that a social equity oriented policy impact study of the community policing program administered by the federal government would be an important contribution to scholarship on contemporary law enforcement, I first became intrigued by the way money for this project was being allocated, as it was the largest federal subsidy of record. Reaching close to a decade of testing the waters, I also became interested in the changes in the organization as well. Pulling together resources available from the 1990 Census, the Uniform Crime Reports, multiple years of Law Enforcement Management and Administrative Statistics (LEMAS) data, and information available from the Office of Community Oriented Policing Services (OCOPS). However good the idea may have been, compiling data from these diverse reports makes for a large data set.

When thinking about the evolution of policing, it is important to consider the social, political, and organizational variables that bring about change in the law enforcement profession. The level of impact a particular major reform policy has and whether it meets the goals and objectives of intended change are of concern to legislators, planners, administrators, and citizens alike.

This analysis of social equity and the solicitation and granting of federal funds will examine how police agencies have changed in lieu of the receipt of these funds authorized by the 1994 Federal Crime Bill championed by the Clinton administration. In the first part of the study, an analysis of the recent history of federal funding aimed at improving law enforcement capabilities will be examined. Being the first major federal subsidy of law enforcement in recent history, the Law Enforcement Assistance Administration funding program will be examined in some detail. Next, the community oriented policing (COP) movement will be analyzed by detailing the types of programs subsidized by the 1994 Crime Bill funding, their original intent, and how they were to be operationalized will be discussed. A theoretical framework will be presented that will use empirical assessments of the number of community (or proactive) programs in place in each agency, degrees of organizational change noted in a three-year review of each department's structure as reported in the LEMAS survey of police departments, the levels of economic inequality present in the jurisdictions that received COP funding, and the ethnic composition of these jurisdictions. The information gleaned from this research will might entice studies in criminal justice programs to examine the law enforcement policy in a way that explores issues outside the realm of institutional control as police agencies strive to enlist citizens in the co-production of order. It will also be interesting to continue tracking the COP phenomenon over the next few years, as priorities for law enforcement make another shift, one that may include training and recruitment of global police officers. The reorganization of the Department of Justice will most likely have some effect on local subsidies in the near future. The past twenty years have seen significant changes in law enforcement and the next twenty may prove even more interesting.

I would like to acknowledge my mentors at Washington State University, specifically Dr. Nicholas P. Lovrich, my colleagues at California State University Sacramento, and my students. The students deserve some acknowledgement for their support and for their persistent queries about the direction of policing in America. Some of the conversations that evolved (both in and out of the classroom) forced a reassessment of how to approach this study of change in policing. Finally, my mother Nita, my wife Debbie, and my sons Ricky, Rudy, Anthony, and Justice all deserve thanks for their support of my work and tolerance for my absence while compiling the results for this study. I dedicate this book to families and the strength that they bring.

CHAPTER ONE

Introduction

LAW ENFORCEMENT CHANGE AND FEDERAL SUBSIDIES: AN OVERVIEW

The past decade has witnessed the widespread, federally subsidized dissemination of community oriented policing (COP) as a major reform of law enforcement practices in the United States. The fundamental concepts underlying COP are that public order is a joint responsibility of citizens and law enforcement and that the creation and sustaining of a cooperative, mutually supportive relationship between citizens and the police ought to motivate a wide range of law enforcement activities and inform democratic police practices (Bayley, 1994; Toch and Grant, 1991; Walker, 1992).

Two principal justifications for placing an emphasis upon building relations between the police and their respective communities have been cited in the literature on COP. First, a strong positive relationship between police and community is arguably an important factor in the efficacy of law enforcement with respect to the apprehension of offenders and their effective monitoring upon release from correctional supervision. Second, this relationship can be a powerful factor in crime prevention and the engagement of the community as co-producers of public order (Skogan and Atunes, 1979). Alpert and Moore (1993:113) have described the changing role of the police in this new relationship as the following: "the essence of this new paradigm is that police must engage in community-based processes related to the production and maintenance of local human and social capital." Since the enactment of the *Violent Crime Control and Law Enforcement Act* (or Crime Bill) of 1994, substantial funds (over $7.5 billion) have become available to police agencies that have engaged in the following COP-sanctioned activities: (1) to employ new police officers (100,000 nationwide) with the intent to implement COP objectives; (2) to facilitate collaborative problem-solving efforts between police and citizens; (3) to measure the outcomes of these efforts in a systematic manner; (4) to provide training in COP philosophy and methodology; and (5) to study public reactions to COP practices (Office of Community Oriented Policing Services, 2001; Trojanowicz and Bucqueroux, 2001).

The present study investigates the outcomes of this major investment in COP with respect to its effects upon **distributional equity**[1]. In particular, it investigates these questions: Are federal government grants for COP implementation being directed to communities where bridges between the police and the citizens they serve are the most in need of repair—i.e., where income inequity is greatest and criminal activity most prevalent? Or, instead, is federal support for COP sought and granted mainly in areas where social equity is present and crime rates are relatively low, and the bridges between the police and the citizens they serve are already in relatively good condition?

Relying upon scholarship dealing with the COP movement with the persistence of income inequality in the U.S. as a major backdrop, and with organizational change in police settings as a focus of concern for outcomes of reform, this study will first address the societal role policing has played over time in the course of U.S. history. This relatively brief overview will be organized in terms of the major "eras" of policing identified in the policing literature: the **political era**, the **reform era**, and the **community era**. The manner in which policing has changed over time in relation to officially reported statistics (e.g., FBI Uniform Crime Reports [UCR], U.S. Bureau of Census data, and Law Enforcement Management and Administrative Statistics [LEMAS]) provide background to an analysis of how contemporary COP programs have changed over the period 1994 to the end of the major granting of federal COP funds in 2001.

A study of the factors that are distinctive to the organizations and communities that have tended to adopt COP strategies is valuable in the promotion of the general fund of knowledge concerning policing in the United States. Information of this type will allow a deeper understanding of how American law enforcement agencies function, and whether the newly expressed interest in COP reflects a genuine engagement of law enforcement agencies in the task of promoting the co-production of public order and citizen safety in this country. An alternate skeptical view is that this **apparent** change in U.S. law enforcement philosophy is more related to the large sums of money offered by the federal government to implement COP-related activities than it is to the genuine desire of U.S. law enforcement authorities to pursue progressive change in policing practices.

AN HISTORICAL BACKDROP TO THE STUDY

An overview of the historical changes which have taken place in American law enforcement is a necessary preface to even a partial understanding of the COP phenomenon. A progression of thought (or regression) over time with regard to preferred crime control strategies in the U.S. gave rise to COP. A brief retelling of this history is a major part of the COP training component of the federal government's efforts to promote the COP philosophy of policing[2].

Prior to the colonization of the United States, highwaymen in the United Kingdom were employed by crime victims and were charged with apprehending suspected criminals. In 1692, passage of the Highwaymen Act provided rewards to citizens who were willing to offer assistance in apprehending criminals, which in turn led to numerous cases of blackmail and false accusations (Gaines, Kappeler and Vaughn, 1999). Prior to the development of formalized policing in the U.S., agents of social control in common law states most often worked for the courts and were compensated by the victims of crime who sought the apprehension and adjudication of offenders. In the United Kingdom, King George II allowed the city council to levy taxes for the purpose of a paid watchman system, which is thought to be the first instance of formal taxation for the provision of law enforcement services (Gaines, Kappeler and Vaughn, 1999). Some scholars have noted that in many instances, these early agents of social control (bounty hunters or thief takers) may have also had criminal histories and were apparently primarily motivated by the prospect of monetary gain (LaGrange, 1998). In U.S. colonial times, police functions were performed by the constable and the watch, whose origins can be traced back to the middle ages (Monkkonen, 1992).

In colonial America, constables were often ineffective and sometimes were characterized as "drunken, snoring fools" who were as apt to join crooks in the commission of a crime as confront them (Bittner, 1970). With only minor modifications, these practices continued until 1829 when Sir Robert Peel revolutionized the function of social control because of his advocacy for the passage of the *London Metropolitan Police Act*. According to Miller (1977), the legitimating of the London police was carefully orchestrated by Peel and his associates. Peel's vision entailed adopting a new model of law enforcement featuring a philosophical foundation midway between that of a military regime and the watch system. Peel envisioned a non-threatening police force able to relate to the public (e.g., less coercion and more emphasis upon utilitarian and normative power), and one that appeared to "win by losing" (LaGrange, 1998). The philosophies espoused in the COP model echo these principles, and represent a rather radical departure from what in time became the prevailing doctrine commonly labeled the "reactive" or "professional" approach to crime control requiring police to work with their respective communities to "develop and implement unified, information-based efforts to solve problems in the community rather than only to react to events or incidents" (Ford and Morash, 2002:1).

INNOVATIONS IN POLICING

With regard to the evolution of policing in the U.S., Monkkonen (1992) identifies four important innovations in American law enforcement which occurred during the 19th Century. The first of these is concerned with the establishment of a hierarchical organization and use of a military model to provide police organizational boundaries and set goals ensuring public order and assuring centralized control over police agent conduct. The organizational control structure of the professional model established the practice that when a crime was reported to the police, that information was relayed to headquarters, and headquarters filtered the information back down the line via a newly established communication system. This system of telephone line communication is well illustrated in a cartoon series entitled "Top Cat." In Top Cat officer Dribble was charged with keeping a neighborhood of felines in order, some of which were perpetually up to no good. It was implied that the neighborhood was co-responsible for order maintenance in an elaborate system of intelligence networks (or system of informants who would provide Officer Dribble with information about the antics and whereabouts of Top Cat and his group of wayward felines). Even with the benefit of this special network of informants, Officer Dribble was seldom able to ascertain the identities of the wrongdoers, and most situations requiring some form of social sanction were handled informally. Some believe that the police have abandoned the community-based tactics portrayed in this depiction of borough policing with precinct-walking cops assigned to specific neighborhoods (Gaines, Kappeler, and Vaughn, 1999). Many scholars argue that the centralization of command in law enforcement was further entrenched by the introduction of the radio patrol car, which served to decrease the functionality and use of the local station house and displaced the accepted and trusted local patrol officer (LaGrange, 1998). In-depth critical analysis of the factors involved in U.S. social change and the evolution of the American democratic process in the administration of justice reveals an additional dimension to this account of the adaptation of American police to their societal environment.

The second innovation in American policing is the progressive placement of the police as subordinate to the executive branch of government as opposed to elements of the courts deserves special attention in this regard (Monkkonen, 1992). This change in organizational placement served to free the police from civil court activities and placed far more emphasis on patrol functions aimed at controlling disorder and crime (Monkkonen, 1992). It can be said that this shift contributed to the need for police to be paid fixed salaries, as they no longer collected their compensation from the victims in crime (Steinberg, 1989). Unfortunately, elected executives during the early era of policing too often used the police in their pursuit of a variety of partisan political interests (LaGrange, 1998). Parties in political power often fortified police forces with personnel who espoused and promoted their preferred partisan concepts and political agendas. This practice had the unfortunate consequence of alienating the police from a substantial portion of the public they served, and brought into question their honesty and fairness (Johnson, 1981)—ultimately forcing the police to change how they select their officers, perform their duties, and develop relationships with the community.

The third innovation in American policing according to Monkkonen (1992) is the uniform. The uniform made the police more visible and accessible to members of the community and visitors alike. Although uniforms were resisted by many officers who viewed them as derogatory, they have become a mainstay for American law enforcement. Common terms such as "men in blue" have been used to denote the camaraderie within the ranks of law enforcement. According to Monkkonen (1992:551), this enhanced visibility in combination with a "centralized communication system, accounted for the sudden turn to police by parents of lost children; prior to police availability, parents had had to conduct frantic, random community searches to locate them." In addition, the uniform also made it easier for supervisors to monitor the actions of their subordinates.

Monkkonen (1992) identifies the fourth development in the evolution of law enforcement as the creation of police as a line item in the city budget. Because police were now expected to be active in their pursuit of crime and deviance, regular salaries, lines in the city budget, and the free prosecution of criminal offenders mandated bringing a more regular and effective mechanism for managing crime and public order in communities across the nation (Monkkonen, 1992).

PROGRESSIVES AND PROFESSIONALISM

As the police profession has progressed through the three eras of policing and has now become comfortable with the concept of COP, Thayer and Reynolds (1997) believe that the concept of community policing (above and beyond the strategies first espoused by Sir Robert Peel and his crime control orientation for police) can be traced to the ideas of Arthur Woods, police chief in New York City from 1914-1919 in response to the widely held view that the New York Police Department (NYPD) had become corrupt and unprofessional during the political era.

The Progressives and their agenda sought to transform policing from an arm of the political machine to one that was oriented towards much more sophisticated and evenhanded responses to problems of crime and disorder. The Progressive reformers viewed "rapid industrialization and the extreme class differentiation that accompanied it as a main source of problems for the criminal justice system, as well as what they called heterogeneity of the American population and the lack of a strong tradition of obedience to constituted authority." The Progressives felt that these were factors that law enforcement must begin to deal with (Center for Research on Criminal Justice, 1975:21). A key idea in their approach was that since modern society was complex and highly diversified, it required more restraint and regulation (Pound, 1922). This more diversified society created a much greater potential for conflict and disorder. It was the job of the criminal justice system (according to the Progressive reformers) to harmonize and adjust potential class and ethnic conflicts within the existing system. During the reform era, there was an attempt to streamline police organization and practices in the service of class interests and business values and to turn the police into a technically proficient and politically neutral agency of social service. The two main major results of the reform era were "(1) the development of a conception of police as professionals that served to insulate police from any significant political and community influence; and, (2) to promote new technologies and new strategies to enable the police to exercise a higher level of surveillance and control of oppressed communities" (Center for Criminal Justice Research, 1977:28). Due to the widespread perception that the police reform era had not accomplished its goals to make police more accountable to local constituents and oppressed communities, law enforcement agencies were forced to once again alter existing strategies and organizational arrangements.

With the development of the professional model of policing, the Federal Bureau of Investigation (FBI) came to be held in high esteem and many local agencies sought to replicate the organization and strategies employed by this federal police agency (LaGrange, 1998). The approach to law enforcement employed by the FBI was that of a hard-core, crime fighting response to deviant behavior in society. The view held at the federal level emphasized the belief that such deviance should be well publicized and documented, and fugitives from justice should be hunted down at virtually all costs (LaGrange, 1998). This message was translated in practice into a mandate to local law enforcement that the apprehension of dangerous criminals was the definitive trait of real police work. "Police leaders such as O. W. Wilson and J. Edgar Hoover cultivated the public perception of police as crime fighters" (Gaines, Kappeler and Vaughn, 1999:90). In response, President Herbert H. Hoover established the list of the Top Ten Most Wanted suspects who were then relentlessly pursued by federal agents with the assistance of local law enforcement. Motels were raided, homes of relatives were crashed, and leads were vigorously pursued by the newly formed FBI, largely irrespective of the credibility of the tip (Center for Research on Criminal Justice, 1975).

Law enforcement was using information from the public to track criminals over a growing and expanding nation. Public safety was elevated to a heightened level of importance during the reform era, and law enforcement made strides to accomplish many goals relating to this important societal role primarily by the use of its coercive power during the professional era.

One of the consequences of this approach to crime control was that little effort was made to bridge existing gaps between the police and the disadvantaged in America's local communities. Far too often, those at the bottom of the socioeconomic scale were the targets of intense police intervention. In their zeal to make communities safer from the hardened criminal, police tended to use their technology to pursue, identify, and monitor their suspects. In addition, innovations in communications and transportation technologies allowed the police to become highly mobile and provided the means to assess more types of criminal activities than ever before. At the same time, the ability to communicate via wireless devices centralized police as never before, often removing law enforcement from direct contact with local residents (Gaines, Kappeler and Vaughn, 1999). Police now moved about in high-speed units and maintained continuous communication with command central—much like military units during wartime campaigns. With the spread of information technology and computerized record keeping, proactive police agencies began to arm themselves with an intimate knowledge of community demographics and computer-generated crime information.

THE FEDERAL GOVERNMENT'S PROMOTION OF CHANGE IN LOCAL LAW ENFORCEMENT

A final phase of police evolution to be reviewed occurred in the context of federal subsidies to local law enforcement and the purposes to which these federal funds were directed by local police agencies. The first of the substantial federal subsidies for local law enforcement took place with the creation of the Law Enforcement Assistance Administration (LEAA). During the LEAA era (1960-1970), U.S. law enforcement agencies were given substantial federal funds (through a competitive categorical grant process) to initiate planning and undertake problem-solving efforts. In addition, LEAA funds and guidance were used to provide the law enforcement organization a basis for putting both sides of the modern police strategy into practice. In the legislation originally establishing the LEAA, crime was considered a national catastrophe (Center for Research on Criminal Justice, 1975). Although Congress agreed that crime control was a local responsibility, the state of affairs in law enforcement at this time was seen as being overly decentralized and haphazardly administered. LEAA was designated to lead the "war on crime" (Center for Research on Criminal Justice, 1975). Unfortunately, most of the funds for fighting the war on crime were used to procure new guns, high speed automobiles, riot control equipment, helicopters, computers, and sophisticated intelligence gathering systems (Center for Research on Criminal Justice, 1975). Although the LEAA also supported the so-called softer approach to crime by encouraging police-community relations and sensitivity training for officers as well as a promoting greater community involvement in policing, the vast majority of the LEAA funds were used to purchase equipment and to establish "communications, information, and intelligence systems" (Center for Research on Criminal Justice, 1975). In addition, the LEAA was responsible for initiating efforts that would develop nationwide standards and goals for the criminal justice system, but fell short in this area as well (Center for Research on Criminal Justice, 1975).

By 1980, a growing number of social science researchers began to study the police from a number of theoretical perspectives during the LEAA period (Feeley and Sarat, 1980; Uchida, 1997). A number of analyses of how these funds were used suggested that a significant proportion of agencies chose to use the funds for conventional crime suppression activities unrelated to the realm of planning and problem solving. Given this record of accomplishment of local uses of federal grant funds, the analysis of commentaries on the LEAA and the series of annual crime bills that sustained it reveal pertinent information relative to the study of contemporary federal efforts to promote COP through a similar process of competitive grants. The LEAA experience instructs us that sometimes federal assistance to local government is operationalized in ways that are inconsistent with the goals and objectives of the stated policy.

STATEMENT OF NEED—THE IMPORTANCE OF EXAMINING THE DISTRIBUTION OF COP FUNDS AS A POLICY ISSUE

Observation of changes that have occurred in policing (e.g., an organizational anthropology view[3]) as a result of the adoption of a COP philosophy is essential to the study of contemporary change in public service organizations engaged in the "reinvention of government." Because the reinvention of government movement has called for enhancing the performance of public services agencies, it should be emphasized that few roles in society are regarded as having a more extensive ability to improve community well-being than the second line of defense[4] in the realm of social control represented by the police. It is equally important to consider how these organizational changes affect the way police interact with the community. Further, there are many scholars of the democratic process who believe that a strong sense of community is an integral wire in the conduit of democracy (Etzioni, 1993; Putnam, 1995a; Putnam, 1995b; and de Tocqueville, 1966).

In viewing policing from an embedded system organizational perspective, the work of Talcott Parsons is instructive as a conceptual tool. Parsons (1960) defines four problems that any bounded social system must manage: **adaptation** (coping with demands originating from the environment); **goal achievement** (defining objectives and mobilizing resources to accomplish them); **integration** (unifying member units into a single entity); and **latency** (maintaining motivational and cultural patterns over time). An organization charged with maintaining public safety in a community (e.g., law enforcement) is engaged in all of these areas of work, and the adoption of a COP philosophy would dictate the approach and methods used in accomplishing all those functions. If Parsons (1960) is correct in the assumption that all social systems are concerned with adaptation, goal achievement, integration, and latency, a functional model may be devised using these components to compare data concerning the extent to which police agencies have adopted the philosophies and practices of community policing. Further, these concepts of organizational adaptation are related to other variables that can be explored in a thorough analysis of COP implementation.

When considering anticipated changes in the way police operationalize their crime control functions, it is in turn helpful to consider a set of concepts developed by Amitai Etzioni (1961) to explore power and influence phenomena. Etzioni posits that there are three basic types of power that can be used to achieve organizational goals—namely, **coercive**, **utilitarian**, and **normative**. These three types of basic power have traditionally been used in police agencies as organizational tools (Brooks, 1997). It is also important to note that police have traditionally employed primarily coercive forms of social control to achieve public order (Bittner, 1970). In contrast to the coercive means used by police agencies over the course of the past 50 years, COP programs embrace strategies that result in more utilitarian and normative forms of power being added to a police agency's range of options for assuming a place at the second line of defense in social control. This entails developing proactive, citizen-engaging strategies that address problems of public safety.

The COP philosophy that has guided the allocation of federal funds to police agencies across the nation is supported by many scholars of policing who tend to share the view that enlightened law enforcement activities and democratic police practices are inherently linked (Bayley, 1994; Bureau of Justice Assistance, 1994; Rosenbaum, 1994; Toch and Grant, 1991; Walker, 1992). While the philosophical argument may be compelling, the truest test of COP is to be found in the pattern of implementation of COP philosophies by law enforcement agencies and the degree of efficacious use of the funding provided. The breadth of innovative programs present in departments which have received public funds to implement COP will illuminate what efficacious use is. Have the beneficiaries of these funds made use of those resources in a way that promotes public safety, enhances the co-production of public order, and promotes social equity? This is an empirical question that warrants careful study.

The purpose of a policy impact analysis is to ascertain whether a particular policy is an effective instrument for the accomplishment of its stated objectives. It is perhaps the case that the contemporary COP effort at the federal level represents a repeat of the LEAA experience— that is, it may be the case that COP funds are often diverted to support conventional, coercive methods of law enforcement rather than being used to promote an increase in the use of utilitarian and normative forms of power associated with community building and collaborative problem-solving.

In this regard, it is also important to look at the social equity aspect of COP implementation. Given the long-established and persistent inequities in American society associated with institutional racism, discrimination, economic exploitation, and the maldistribution of wealth, it is particularly important to assess major public policies with respect to their impact on social equity. Is the quality of life already high for those residents who reside in demographically homogeneous jurisdictions with large (in per capita terms) COP awards? Or, instead, is the level of COP award directly associated with the breadth of utilitarian and normative programs present in departments serving demographically heterogeneous communities? If substantial COP dollars have been awarded to communities that feature high levels of economic inequity, what types of programs have been implemented to improve the quality of life for those citizens at the lower end of the socioeconomic scale? What types of agencies typically use COP awards to develop strategies intended to strengthen the sense of community, and what types of agencies use these funds to supplement patrol allocations? These are all interesting questions for scholars who are tracking changes in contemporary American law enforcement, and seeking to understand the relationship between these changes and broader societal change.

A concurrent analysis of the relationships among income inequality, crime rates, and COP allocations in U.S. cities should provide an insightful assessment of how well federally assisted change in policing practices is being accomplished. It is unfortunate that large federal monetary grants for public agencies are too seldom analyzed for their efficacy in addressing problems of social equity. At this point a nagging question persists: Does this substantial federal subsidy for local law enforcement serve to make positive changes in the social fabric in America's larger cities? Or is it the case that federal money is being used primarily to bolster the number of traditional crime control personnel and support conventional forms of coercive social control? The systematic assessment of the distribution of COP grant funds and the uses made of those funds in the context of the following three-level table (Table 1.1) should provide a powerful insight into these questions.

Table 1.1: Pattern indicating favorable policy impact

Level of Income Equity	Incidence of Crime	
	Below Average	**Above Average**
Below Average		High per capita COP High Implementation Activity
Above Average	Low Per Capita COP Low Implementation Activity	

If the federal COP grant program is effectively addressing the need to build bridges between the police and the citizens they serve, then it should be the case that the most in need jurisdictions (high crime, socio-economically heterogeneous) receive the highest per capita allocation of funds and use those funds for bridge building (utilitarian and normative influence) ends. Alternatively, if the federal grant program serves to accord advantage to "good grant writers" as opposed to those whose need is greatest, it should be demonstrable that the high crime, low social equity jurisdictions do not receive high per capita allocations of COP funds and do not apply those funds to community bridge-building ends.

CHAPTER TWO

Review of the Literature

INTRODUCTION TO THE COMMUNITY POLICING FUNDING INITIATIVE

The *Public Safety Partnership and Community Policing Act of 1994* earmarked nearly $9 billion to support the tandem objectives of substantially increasing the number of police officers employed by local law enforcement agencies around the United States and promoting the adoption of "community policing" by those same agencies. Known colloquially as the Federal **COPS Program** (after the Office of Community Oriented Policing Services in the U.S. Department of Justice), Title 1 of the 1994 Violent Crime Control and Law Enforcement Act was heralded by its proponents as a means for effectuating a virtual revolution in the "business" of American policing. As even its most strident critics would admit, given the magnitude of Washington's funding commitment, the nation-wide scope of its coverage, and the ambitious character of its aims the COPS program clearly represents a significant public policy initiative. Indeed, in terms of its potential importance as a federal law enforcement initiative, it ranks alongside—and perhaps even surpasses—the Omnibus Crime and Safe Streets Acts of 1968 that occasioned the creation of the Law Enforcement Assistance Administration (LEAA) . Administered through its own agency located within the U.S. Justice Department, the COPS office has already distributed grants to more than half of the nearly 20,000 local, county, state and "special" police agencies responsible for the maintenance of law and order in America's communities.

15

Whether, in fact, the COPS program has attained its primary goals is a matter of substantial debate among politicians and scholars alike. At the very least, however, it has created the equivalent of comprehensive and ongoing experiment in law enforcement, one that promises to yield lessons that can be extended to other areas of public policy beyond policing. Since the inception of COPS some eight years ago, there has been a dramatic expansion of published research on the subject of community policing. Many of these recently published works are essentially evaluation studies of COPS grantee agencies. Among them stands what is by any yardstick the most comprehensive investigation of community policing undertaken to date (Roth et al., 2000). Jointly sponsored by the National Institute of Justice (NIJ) and the Urban Institute, this multi-study evaluation of the COPS program as a whole was conducted by a research team working under the co-direction of Jeffrey Roth and Joseph Ryan.

The researchers who contributed to Roth and Ryan (2000) constructed the project's database through the use of both quantitative and qualitative information-gathering methods. These methods included the analysis of statistical data gathered from the COPS Office, mail surveys and questionnaires sent to randomly selected grantee agencies, telephone interviews conducted with select informants, and on-site case-study field visits to purposively chosen law enforcement departments. The qualitative field research was intended to generate a richer body of information than could be captured through the use of any single quantitative method of analysis. In addition, as several of the research teams stated in their respective studies, the field visits were also meant to get at the "ground truth" about aspects of community policing activities being reported under the COPS initiative. As one such team put it, the "reality check" aspects of the project were necessary in light of severe difficulties in "separating the rhetoric of community policing from the reality of what law enforcement agencies actually do" (Roehl et al., 2000:236).

As to what law enforcement agencies receiving COPS grants are supposed to be doing under the banner of community policing, we gain some initial grasp of that from the mission statement of the COPS Office. In that declaration of purpose, the term "community policing" is defined as "a policing philosophy that promotes and supports organizational strategies to address the causes and reduce the fear of crime and social disorder through problem-solving tactics and community-police partnerships" (Cited in Roehl et al., 2000:190). Upon initial inspection, this appears to be a cogent and cohesive change. True, alternative definitions have been put forth, but such nuances aside, the COPS Office definition of "community policing" describes it as (1) a "philosophy" that is linked to (2) "strategies" that are to be operationalized through (3) certain "tactics," most notably problem-oriented policing and community-police partnerships. As another Roth and Ryan (2000) research team has noted, in addition to being construed as a law enforcement "philosophy," a group of organizational "strategies," and an aggregation of working "tactics," "community policing" has also been approached as a "rhetoric" (Gaffigan, Roth, and Buerger, 2000:32-33). According to Gaffigan, Roth and Buerger (2000:33), the community policing concept or model espoused by COPS "has played all four roles at various times and in various endeavors."

Before and after 1994, several critics of community policing have charged that it is, at bottom, merely a rhetorical device. In 1988, for example, as the core ingredients of the COPS paradigm were coming together, David Bayley (1988:225-226) asserted that community policing is best viewed as "a trendy phrase spread thinly over customary reality...another attempt to put old wine in new bottles." Three years later, another prominent critic of community policing, Carl Klockars (1991:239), characterized it as "the latest in a series of circumlocutions whose purpose is to conceal, mystify, and legitimate police distribution of nonnegotiable coercive force."

This survey of the literature will necessarily address the "rhetoric or reality" dimension of the community police studies debate. At this introductory juncture, it is appropriate to highlight two quandaries encountered in attempting to delineate this area of study. First, because community policing exists on multiple levels (as rhetoric, philosophy, strategies, and tactics), its relation to and location within any particular theoretical framework cannot be conclusively determined. Arguably, as a set of operational tactics, community policing belongs to that corpus of criminal justice literature known as law enforcement or police studies. As a "strategy," however, community policing is better approached from the standpoint of organizational dynamics studies; as a "philosophy" it connects to the disciplines of public administration, political science, sociology, and group studies; as a "rhetoric" it may be located within policy studies. Trying to limit and locate the context of "community policing" is akin to the task of attempting to nail Jell-O to a tree.

The second dilemma facing any researcher in this field is how the issues of community policing reflected in the literature fit with the concept of "equity" at large and, more specifically, to questions about how "equitable" the results of implementing community policing have been and are likely to be. Although a handful of researchers, most notably David Thacher (2001), have analyzed community policing through the application of "equity" criteria, most of what has been written concerning the outcomes of community policing and the COPS program employs efficiency (or effectiveness) and/or responsiveness measurement constructs. These values, of course, touch upon equity, but they are by no means adequate surrogates for it. Thus, this literature review will be structured around four inter-penetrating but distinct levels (i.e., the levels of rhetoric, philosophy, strategy, and tactics[5]).

COMMUNITY POLICING AT THE LEVEL OF "RHETORIC"

An Overview of the COPS Program

Title I of the $30 billion 1994 Violent Crime Control and Law Enforcement Act, the *Public Safety Partnership and Community Policing Act of 1994* was signed into law by President William Jefferson Clinton on the 13th of September, 1994. Shortly thereafter, the Office of Community Oriented Policing Services (COPS) was established within the Department of Justice to administer the grant-funding program. The broad aims of what would become known as the COPS program were to effectuate a net increase of some 100,000 in the number of sworn officers working on patrol in communities around the country, and to stimulate (or accelerate) the adoption of community policing practices by those newly financed police officers. Toward that end, Congress authorized nearly $9 billion in grants to local (municipal, county, state, and "special") law enforcement agencies. Under an array of specific programs, these funds were to pay 75 percent of the direct costs of hiring and paying salaries for new officers for a period of three years, of hiring and paying civilians to replace sworn officers as full-time equivalent (FTE) personnel, and to upgrade agency technologies to free up additional officers for patrol.[6]

When approached from the standpoint of "rhetoric," the policy devised by the Clinton Administration, with the assistance of what John Kingdon (1995) would call "policy entrepreneurs," came about through a highly partisan political process. Although some scholars, notably those of the "reinventing" government and "communitarian" schools, tend to assume that public policies are rather rationally related to value ends, critical post-modern theorists such as Kingdon (1995) and Deborah Stone (1997) have elaborated on the "garbage can" model of government policy formulation as proposed by Cohen, March and Cohen (1972) to highlight the often "irrational" basis of public policy. In this context, the COPS program can be conceptualized as the ultimate result of a highly partisan political process, such that the inequitable outcomes noted above can be understood as manifestations of some irrational elements of the American democratic policy process.

Virtually all local law enforcement agencies in the United States were eligible to apply for COPS grants, conditional upon their acceptance of certain responsibilities and rules (see below) and, most importantly, conditional upon demonstrating a willingness to commit themselves to adopt strategies and tactics associated with the philosophy of community policing. At the outset of the program, a total of 19,175 law enforcement agencies were eligible for COPS grant funding. Between 1994 and the end of 1997, 10,537 such agencies actually applied (55 percent of those eligible), although 761 (7 percent of all applicants) withdrew their applications (Roth and Ryan, 2000:8).

In addition to the community policing conditions, a local contribution equivalent to 25 percent of the direct remuneration of new hires during the three-year grant period, as well as all of the collateral costs for new hires and FTEs was required of local agencies participating in the program. Two other important rules with significant fiscal implications were built into the program. First, participating agencies were to commit themselves to keeping (and thus paying for) the hired officers/FTEs after the end of the three-year grant period. Second, agencies were to abide by the federal doctrine of non-supplanting. The controlling principle here was that "federal funds were meant to increase total resources dedicated to the purpose of the grant, not to replace local resources diverted from that purpose in anticipation of the grant award" (Gaffigan, Roth, and Buerger, 2000:53). In essence, local agencies committed themselves to picking up the full tab of the COPS hires/FTEs after three years, and they could not use COPS funds to hire personnel or purchase technology that they would have acquired had they not received these federal funds.

Surveying both agencies that withdrew from the application process and those who decided not to apply, Roth, Johnson, Maenner, and Herrschaft (2000:73) reported that "objections to the community policing objectives of Title I were of negligible importance as a barrier" to participation in COPS. Instead, the vast majority of both non-applying agencies and rescinders cite the fiscal obligations attached to COPS, most notably the 25 percent local matching requirement and the outlays required for staff integration and other collateral costs (Roth et al., 2000:64). These findings suggest that the distribution of COPS funds was likely skewed toward those jurisdictions that could afford to meet the immediate and/or long-term obligations associated with COPS grants.

Beyond this, as part of the political compromises that attended passage of the bill through Congress, the 1994 Act specified that at least half of all COPS funds would be distributed to law enforcement agencies serving communities with populations of less than 150,000. The policy concern here was that large urban departments would receive an inordinate share of COPS funds, with rural (and suburban) jurisdictions suffering as a consequence. The political concern was that the COPS bill could not pass the U.S. Senate without some support from states with dispersed populations (e.g., the Midwest farm belt and the sparsely populated states of the West).

In his 1995 testimony before a committee of the House of Representatives, Joseph Brann, the first Director of the COPS Office, stated that the community policing requirements of Title 1 reflected three primary objectives:

> (1) building crime fighting partnerships among the police, community, and other governmental resources; (2) developing effective problem-solving tactics that involve all three of these stakeholders so that officers no longer respond to recurring incidents at the same location; and (3) refining organizational structures and improving deployment tactics to enhance the overall community policing strategy (Brann, 1995, n.p.).

Although Brann did not include "crime prevention" as a distinct element, others (including representatives of the COPS Office) have cited this to be an implicit goal of the program. The two paramount goals of the community policing principles of the 1994 Act, however, were "(1) an emphasis on problem-solving, also known as problem-oriented policing...and (2) community involvement and the building of partnerships among police, citizens, city agencies, and others..." (Roehl, Johnson, Buerger, Gaffigan, Langston and Roth, 2000:183). Among others, Skogan and Hartnett (1997) have highlighted "problem-oriented policing" and "community partnerships" as the twin pillars supporting the community-policing edifice.

Virtually all discussions of the origins of community policing present its roots in the perceived shortcomings of the so-called "professional" model of law enforcement (Ford et al., 1999). The "professional" model originally promoted by Progressive Era reformers in the first decades of the twentieth century featured a high degree of administrative centralization, extensive departmental specialization, a precisely-defined "crime fighting" police agency mission, and the strict imposition of both organizational and individual standards on the conduct of officers and personnel in leadership positions. In operational terms, "traditional" policing emphasized departmental efficiency, effectiveness, and speed of response in handling calls for service from the public (Goldstein, 1987:11). In the 1960s, reformers advocating a professional model of policing charged that this orientation was overly reactive, with patrol officers generally waiting for explicit information about violations of the law to direct their activities. It was argued that this approach to policing led to a sharp division between the reactive police, on the one hand, and their potential crime-stopping allies— namely the public at-large and other public agencies and community-based, nonprofit agencies and civic organizations (Thurman, 1995).

It is essential to note that before the current community policing movement gained substantial momentum in the late 1980s and early 1990s, many law enforcement agencies had initiated community crime prevention measures (Feins, 1983:5). By the 1970s, neighborhood watches and citizen patrols were fairly widespread programs entailing active police/community collaboration. At the same time, local police departments participated in longer-term efforts to deter crime at its source through youth socialization programs such as the Police Athletic League, classroom school visits by uniformed officers, and in more recent years the anti-drug DARE program. Finally, in the early 1980s, inspired by an article in the *Atlantic Monthly* by James Q. Wilson and George Kelling (1982), some urban police departments began to cooperate with other agencies of local government such as building code enforcement personnel in addressing signs of urban disorder (e.g., fixing broken windows and cleaning up vacant lots and buildings). These efforts were meant to repair overt manifestations of physical decay that were believed to undermine public order and generate the impression that "anything goes" in some neighborhoods (Gaffigan, Roth, and Buerger, 2000:39).

Perhaps the most well known tactics of the community crime prevention era can be seen in various experiments in preventive patrolling and beat deployment. Particularly in the wake of the foot patrol demonstration project in Flint, Michigan (Trojanowicz 1982), law enforcement agencies began to experiment with taking officers out of their patrol cars and placing them on the street—either on foot, on a bicycle or in some other non-traditional transportation mode. Team policing (Skogan and Hartnett, 1997) and permanent beat assignments were instituted by several large progressive departments such as Chicago and Philadelphia (Kane, 1999 and 2000) as crime prevention measures were initiated and neighborhood substations were opened up in high crime areas (Gaffigan, Roth and Buerger, 2000). These tactical changes were intended to "bring the police closer to the public, instill a sense of beat ownership and accountability in police officers, and, perhaps most importantly, to reduce the public's fear of crime and disorder by increasing the visibility of law enforcement in their neighborhoods" (Kane, 2000:259-260).

The main driver behind the current community policing movement overlaps with these fear reduction tactics but goes significantly deeper into the manner in which law enforcement personnel typically address crime and disorder. Most closely associated with Herman Goldstein (1977, 1979, 1990), "problem-oriented" policing seeks to reverse the traditional concentration of police attention on implementing the means or techniques of law enforcement and redirecting it toward a focus on the ultimate ends of police work. Problem-oriented policing begins with the recognition of a problem within the community, defined in the Newport News (VA) experiment as "a group of incidents occurring in a community that are similar in one or more ways, and that are of concern to the police and the public" (Eck and Spelman, 1987:42). Thus, for example, if police authorities receive a pattern of complaints from citizens about noisy, late-night revelers on a neighborhood's streets, rather than respond to these as individual incidents, with proper crime analysis data available they might trace it to a common source (e.g., a local bar's closing time) and then solve the noise problem through restrictions on that source. A specific and widely disseminated procedural model for conducting problem-oriented policing was proposed by the Newport News experiment in the form of Scanning, Analysis, Response and Assessment (or SARA). It is, in fact, the SARA model that the COPS Office has promoted as an effective approach to problem-oriented" policing. It is noteworthy that the SARA construct calls upon law enforcement to undertake a systematic assessment or evaluation of its responses to community problems.

Formal Evaluations of the COPS Program

To date, the central focal point of COPS program evaluation studies has been on two principal outcomes—namely, its impact upon crime and its fulfillment of President Clinton's 1992 campaign promise to place 100,000 more police officers on America's streets. In a statistical study carried out under contract to the COPS Office, Jihong Zhao and Quint Thurman (2001) attributed a decline in reported national crime rates since the mid-1990s to that program's acceleration of the community-policing model's dissemination. According to Zhao and Thurman (2001:20), "COPS hiring grants had a significant negative effect on both violent and property crimes in cities with populations greater than 10,000 and innovative grant programs have had a significant negative effect on the entire population of grantees." This positive outcome assessment has since been challenged by researchers who ascribe the decline in crime rates to external factors such as the favorable demographic trends of an aging national populace. Zhao and Thurman (2001:19) acknowledge that their conclusions about the influence of the COPS program on crime rates were in conflict with research studies sponsored by other evaluation teams, most notably the politically conservative Heritage Foundation.

The Heritage Foundation, an ideologically "minimalist government," Washington-based think tank has come to a very different assessment of the extent to which COPS fulfilled President Clinton's campaign rhetoric. Contrary to Zhao and Thurman, the Heritage Foundation research team of Davis et al. (2000:2) concluded that when "natural growth" rates for police officers are taken into account, the COPS program fell well short of President Clinton's announced goal of placing 100,000 more officers on the beat. In their estimate, due largely to a widespread "supplanting" phenomena, the actual net influence of COPS by 1998 was the addition of between 6,231 and 39,617 more officers than would have been the case without the existence of the COPS grant program. Indeed, Davis and his associates (2000) noted that among 147 departments pre-identified by the COPS Office itself as "at risk" of supplanting, 41 percent did in fact engage in the substitution of federal dollars for local funding rather than adding COPS grants to their personnel budgets.

For their part, the Roth and Ryan study team (2000) falls between these two estimates. They note that when the Clinton Administration "celebrated" the milestone of surpassing the 100,000 "new" cops target in May 1999, the "real" figure, taking both new hires and MORE program FTEs into account, was closer to 80,000. They noted further that this figure would peak at 84,600 officers and equivalents by 2001, and then decline and stabilize at around 83,900 by 2003 (Roth and Ryan, 2000:17). The main reason for this disparity, according to Roth and Ryan, was that as three-year COPS grants expired, some recipient agencies would essentially renege on their commitment to personnel retention.

The equity dimension of COPS has generally been subordinated to crime reduction/force increase outcome measures. It should be noted in this context that Zhao and Thurman (2001:10) developed three measures of community "heterogeneity" (i.e., the percentage of minority residents in communities, a socioeconomic status variable, and a community "mobility" factor) in their statistical exercises. Surprisingly, Zhao and Thurman briefly report in their conclusions that their "community heterogeneity" variables did not yield statistically significant results regarding the equity dimension of COP (2001:20).

By contrast, the Davis et al. (2000) study encompassed an intensive investigation of equitability in the distribution of COPS grants. They noted that among the 315 largest jurisdictions (by population) in the United States, 276 received some COPS funding. However, the top 10 recipient agencies received almost half (47.7 percent) of the monies allocated by the COPS office to these 315 jurisdictions even though these ten agencies served only 21.3 percent of the populace and reported 24.3 percent of crimes among the 315 largest jurisdictions (Davis et al., 2000:13-14). Moreover, in terms of crime rates, 5 of the 20 largest police agencies receiving the largest grants between 1993 and 1997 were below the average for comparable jurisdictions (Davis et al., 2000:3). In terms of specific comparisons, Davis et al. (2000) found that the Sacramento Police Department, with 1,488 violent crimes a year per 100,000 residents, received $4,400 per crime from COPS. By contrast, the Nashville Police Department with a rate of 5,321 violent crimes a year per 100,000 residents, received less than 10 percent of that amount, i.e., under $400 per violent crime (Davis et al., 2000:11).

Such disparities have not escaped the attention of the popular press. In an article appearing within a 2000 issue of *United States News and World Report*, Jeffrey Glasser (2000:22) reported that "COPS officials insist that most of the new police officers are on the front lines, preventing crime, even though more than half of the federal grants have gone to halcyon jurisdictions with low crime rates and fewer than 10,000 residents." It is imperative to note that this is a reported distribution of grants, not verified funding amounts. Nevertheless, there were some glaring anomalies, including a $554,000 grant to the Beverly Hills Police Department, and the hiring of eight new COPS-funded officers by the Potsdam, Ohio Police Department, a law enforcement agency serving a community with a populace of around 250 residents (Glasser, 2000:23).

On the equity front, the researchers associated with the Roth and Ryan (2000) project first noted that:

> To a degree rare among Federal grant programs, local decisions drove the distribution of COPS funds. Beyond the broad statutory requirement that funds distributed to jurisdictions of less than 150,000 population equal funds awarded to jurisdictions exceeding that size, no Federal formula governed the allocation of funds (Roth, Johnson, Maenner and Herrschaft 2000:63).

Like Davis et al., Roth and his colleagues (2000) reported that some large, primarily urban jurisdictions (e.g., New York City) received a disproportionately large share of all COPS grants. Summarizing these results, Roth and Ryan (2000:10) stated the following:

> Of all agencies selected for awards by the end of 1997, only 4 percent served core city jurisdictions (i.e., central cities of Census Bureau Metropolitan Statistical Areas), which are home to 27 percent of the U.S. population. They received 40

percent of all COPS dollar awards for all programs combined, and 62 percent of all COPS MORE funds. On average for the United States as a whole, core cities received substantially larger awards per 10,000 residents ($151,631) than did the rest of the country ($86,504). However, their average award per 1,000 index crimes ($184,980) was less than two-thirds the average of the rest of the country ($299,963).

In other words, when gauged in terms of dollars per resident, large urban grantees received more than their fair share of COPS monies. When measured in terms of dollars per crime, however, large urban departments received less than their fair share of COPS disbursements.

A THEORETICAL APPROACH TO INEQUITIES IN THE COPS PROGRAM

The framework for analysis employed in this study is based upon the theoretical tenets that have been examined in a plethora of writings on the types of arrangements one can expect in departments that attempt to implement COP (c.f. Bayley, 1994; Buerger, 1994; Cordner, 1997; Goldstein, 1979; Greene and Mastrofski, 1988; Rosenbaum, Trojanowicz and Bucqueroux, 1990; Thurman, Zhao and Giacomazzi, 2001; Wilson and Kelling, 1982; Zhao, 1996) . Each of these works has identified specific dimensions of COP that are related to rhetoric, philosophy, strategy, and tactics associated with COP. For the purpose of this analysis, the main theoretical grounding can be found in the work of Zhao (1996). Zhao examined change over time in a sample of 281 Municipal Police agencies using three waves of data examining the internal dynamics of municipal police departments as reported by police chiefs and municipal clerks. In addition, Zhao used data from the 1990 Census of the Population and the 1990 Census of Population and Housing to enumerate social, economic and housing characteristics for these same jurisdictions.

The principal findings of Zhao's research revealed that externally and internally focused change efforts tended to produce a group of boundary spanning units that operate independently of the agency's technical core, one that remains relatively unchanged from the accumulated experiences of the past 50 years (Zhao, 1996). Using this theoretical orientation, it is possible to examine the degree of organizational commitment to COP in terms of the development of specialized "units" to address local problems rather than adopting an agency-wide COP. This study will examine COP in terms of the level of commitment by each department in response to funding allocations provided under the 1994 Crime Bill, and whether the level of commitment is related to specific need in each jurisdiction.

The evidence cited above suggests that some inequities may have been present in the allocation of COPS funds. When the COPS program is viewed as "rhetoric," the examples of non-engagement and disinvolvement cited above are not indicative of intentional discrimination against high-crime, predominantly minority communities. Instead, they illustrate a more fundamental discrepancy between the manner in which we normally conceive of policy formulation and the manner in which policies actually come about.

As exemplified by the "communitarian" school of public policy associated with Amitai Etzioni (1995), the primary and traditional approach to policy is "rationalist" in orientation. Viewed within this paradigm, societal needs arise and commonly shared problems exist, and policy decision-makers work together to devise responses to them. There is, to be sure, a political contest reflecting variations in values, ideologies, and partisan interests, but at base the programs that policies generate are primarily rational responses to perceived needs and/or problems.

In 1972, Cohen, March, and Olsen presented their "garbage can" model of organizational decision-making. Contrary to all rationalist assumptions about public policy formation, Cohen et al. (1972:1-25) asserted that the preferences of key policy participants are either unclear or, if defined, typically in conflict with each other. In most instances, none of the participants fully comprehend the policy-making processes, and they tend to drift in and out of the scene.

Post-modern students of the policy process have embraced this view of the policy process. For example, in *Agendas, Alternatives, and Public Policies* (1995:2) John Kingdon asserted that public policies tend to be generated through a "particularly untidy" process that does not unfold in tidy stages, steps, or phases. Rather, a close examination of how policies come about suggested to Kingdon (1995:19) that they are typically the result of three independent streams:

We conceive of three process streams, flowing through the system—streams of problems, policies, and politics. They are largely independent of one another and each develops according to its own dynamics and rules. But at some critical junctures, the three streams are joined, and the greatest policy changes grow out of that coupling of problems, policy proposals, and politics.

The "coupling" process is facilitated by what Kingdon refers to as "policy entrepreneurs," persons and groups that typically develop alternative proposals and then wait for a problem to be defined as a cause for action by trends, events, and changes in decision-making personnel. Kingdon's key point is that the policy process as a whole does not unfold in a unified manner analogous to the logical cognitive/behavioral processes that (presumably) govern an individual's pursuit of a valued end. Instead, throughout the public policy process we "encounter considerable doses of messiness, accident, fortuitous coupling and dumb luck" (Kingdon, 1995:206).

A similar, but by no means identical, view of the policy process has been put forth by Deborah Stone in *Policy Paradox: The Art of Political Decision Making* (1997). In Stone's view, the notion that public policies are "rationally" and "apolitically" related to fixed goals (e.g., reducing crime) is woefully erroneous. Instead, Stone maintained that goals are strategically constructed in the very process of policy formation, writing that "the concepts of equity, efficiency, security, and liberty are continuously constructed" (Stone 1997:37). Stone (1997:155) asserts that:

Problems...are not given out there in the world waiting for smart analysts to come along and define them correctly. They are created in the minds of citizens by other citizens, leaders, organizations, and government agencies, as an essential part of political maneuvering. Symbols, stories, metaphors, and labels are all weapons in the armamentarium.

Although Stone's deconstructionist approach differs somewhat from Kingdon's critical approach, the broad point is the same: rather than representing rational responses to perceived problems, public policies are typically the result of a process that is complex, fluid, and in many respects irrational.

Applying a post-modern perspective to the COPS program construed as an expression of political rhetoric, we note along with Gaffigan, Roth and Buerger (2000:42) that "the political climate helped to shape not only the (1994) act itself, but how the newly created COPS office would execute its mandate."

The principal driving force behind the COPS program was the increasing salience of crime and disorder in the collective mind of the American voting public. As Gaffigan and his colleagues (2000:30) apprise us, in the 1980s and early 1990s, "the national debate on criminal matters came to be dominated by a 'get tough' approach, and criminal justice system reform took an increasingly punitive direction." A prime example of the federal response to this demand for "tougher" treatment of criminals can be seen in the federal government's support of stiff mandatory minimum sentences for narcotics distribution and possession offenses. The public perception that stronger enforcement is required to meet the threat of crime and disorder still prevails today. According to a recent survey (Johnson et al., 1999), Americans overwhelmingly want the criminal justice system to "get tough" on criminals, and 90 percent believe that increasing the number of police on the streets is either a very or a somewhat effective way of reducing crime.

In his 1988 presidential campaign, Democratic candidate Michael Dukakis was soundly defeated by George H. Bush, and many analysts pointed to the former's reputation as being "soft on crime" (e.g., the Willie Horton incident) as a major factor in the election's lopsided results. Mindful of his party's vulnerability to such charges, Democratic Party presidential candidate Bill Clinton adopted an aggressive stance on crime control, pledging to extend hiring grants/subsidies to local law enforcement agencies to put "100,000 new cops" on the beat. At the same time, however, the Clinton team recognized that it had to respond to criticism of law enforcement and demands for greater responsiveness by police departments to civilian concerns (Gaffigan, Roth and Buerger, 2000:31-32). The "solution" was to link force increases to a new approach to policing, one that had a grassroots or communitarian ring to it. As a form of reinventing government, community policing clearly fit that bill.

By 1992, moreover, the community policing philosophy had garnered the support of many highly influential law enforcement professional associations which functioned, in Kingdon's terminology, as "policy entrepreneurs" (Roth and Ryan, 2000:6). These associations tend to be dominated by the opinions of big city police chiefs, many of whom had initiated experiments in community crime prevention and/or problem-oriented policing within their jurisdictions. Precisely how influential this group was in the passage of Title 1 of the 1994 Act cannot be determined definitively. Nevertheless, according to Roth and Ryan (1996:5), it was at the behest of certain high-profile police chiefs that the MORE program based on hiring civilians to "free sworn officers for patrol work became part of the COPS legislation, and it was this same group that championed the cause of technology upgrades paid for with federal funds." As Roth and Ryan (2000:13) have noted, to date the purchase of mobile computers and management/administrative computers by local law enforcement agencies represents the predominant form of use of COPS technology grants.

The newly installed Clinton Administration recognized that Congressional Republicans had their own proposals for assisting local police departments lying in the wings in the form of unconditional block grants distributed from Washington based on local crime rates. Faced with rival legislation, the architects of the COPS program intentionally left the details of the program, including allocation formula, uncommonly open-ended. According to Gaffigan et al. (2000:43):

> As a 'new' and desired policing strategy, the abstract and ambiguous term 'community policing' offered the flexibility needed to gain the necessary political support for the Crime Act. The term also allowed wide latitude to State and local police agencies in the application of this concept within their agencies.

From the outset, the COPS office described its conception of the generic elements of community policing in very broad terms, and left the task of determining how those broad elements would be operationalized to the individual grant applicant agencies (Roehl et al., 2000:179).

Concurrently, recognizing that a Republican alternative to COPS was still afoot in Congress and that there was a political need to show results as quickly as possible, the Clinton Administration's Attorney General, Janet Reno, established the COPS Office in a matter of days after the legislation was enacted and directed it to expedite first-wave applications as quickly as possible. As part of the streamlined grant process established, the application forms themselves were uncharacteristically brief, initially consisting of one or two pages for jurisdictions of less than 50,000 residents (Gaffigan, Roth and Buerger, 2000:47). As Gaffigan and his colleagues (2000:49) point out, in reviewing these streamlined applications, "evidence of insufficient knowledge or commitment regarding community policing did not result in rejection of grant applications." Instead, such evidence was met with the offer (but not the requirement) that the applicant(s) undergo training and technical assistance in community policing from trainers recommended by COPS Office staff. At the same time, COPS Office representatives became engaged in "an aggressive marketing and dissemination" campaign, to apprise local law enforcement agencies of the existence of their grants and to encourage them to apply for them" (Gaffigan, Roth and Buerger, 2000:48).

The net result of the streamlined grant process and the active marketing of COP was a rush to approve grants largely without regard to underlying need. The individual who wrote the first COPS grants briefing books, Kalee Kreider, later commented that during its first year in operation at least $1 billion of the budgeted $2.1 billion in COPS funds was "misspent" (cited in Glasser, 2000:22). So sloppy was the administration of the COPS program that Kreider left her position, asserting in retrospect that the manner in which funds were disbursed was "criminal" in its negligence (cited in Glasser, 2000:22). Looking at the COPS program five years later, the highly regarded criminologist Samuel Walker proclaimed: "There's no accountability...It's a wholly politically driven process" (cited in Glasser, 2000:23). As for program accountability mechanisms, during the first five years of its existence, a total of five different agencies shared the responsibility for determining whether COPS grantee agencies were in compliance with the "retention" and "non-supplanting" conditions of the program (Gaffigan, Roth and Buerger, 2000:52). Moreover, until the year 2000, no agency actually checked the extent to which COPS grant recipients were translating community policing principles into working strategies and tactics.

At the level of rhetoric, then, the COPS program appears to conform rather closely to the model of irrational policy-making delineated by post-modern scholars of the governance process. Plainly, political considerations drove the linkage between increased federal grants to local law enforcement agencies and the adoption of a community-policing model by the federal government. Prominent law enforcement professional associations bolstered this linkage, and key aspects of the program (e.g., MORE and the technology enhancement grants) were the handiwork of these same community-policing advocates. Moreover, there was a concerted effort on the part of the COPS Office to induce departments to buy into the community policing philosophy. How this philosophy of policing would be translated into operational terms, however, was left very open-ended. Indeed, even when uncharacteristically brief applications betrayed ignorance of community policing strategies and tactics, COPS Office staff nonetheless approved grants to local jurisdictions. Accountability over the retention/non-supplanting requirements of the program was fragmented at best; accountability for faithful implementation of the community policing philosophy was virtually non-existent when the program began. Under these particular circumstances, it would seem that inequities in the allocation of COPS funds were bound to arise and planned change in policing practices would only sometimes result from the infusion of COPS funds into a local police agency.

COMMUNITY POLICING AT THE LEVEL OF PHILOSOPHY

The relationship between the public and private spheres has been examined by a number of scholars. More specifically, the work of Amitai Etzioni is widely cited when exploring the connectivity between public agencies and the communities they are charged to serve. According to Correia (1998:18), the prevalence of "hyperindividualism and materialism has inhibited the necessary development of social capital and civic virtues, which communitarians believe are necessary for effective and enriching community life." To this end, the community aspect of community policing exerts a powerful appeal to the traditional political philosophy of the United States since its inception (i.e., democratic pluralism). In addition, Correia (1998) further relates the concepts of communitarian thought to the relationship between the private and public spheres of communal life.

When the COP philosophy is embraced by law enforcement agencies, there appears to be a likelihood that an integrated and healthy sense of community is present in the community at large (Wallach, 1988; Sandel, 1982 as noted in Correia, 1998).

On the level of philosophy, the United States has traditionally been described as a pluralist democracy, and in the 1950s and 1960s the "group" theory approach to understanding governmental processes, based upon pluralist assumptions, was espoused by David Truman (1951) as well as pluralist community studies scholars such as Robert Dahl (1961). Despite its initial popularity in Political Science, starting in the early 1960s this pluralist paradigm of the group process came under heavy and effective criticism from those who challenged the notion that interest group politics as practiced in democratic America is inherently "fair." Indeed, in *The Logic of Collective Action* (1965), Mancur Olson argued that group-based political outcomes are necessarily biased toward the interests of some individuals/groups possessing certain advantages. This "exchange model" of group influence upon public policies has been examined by David Thacher (2001) in application to community policing. As will be explained in this literature review, the community policing precept of responsiveness to the interests, demands, and inputs of the community can easily lead to inequitable results owing to the inordinate power of "squeaky wheel" elements within a given jurisdiction to partner with law enforcement. In conjunction with the correlative weakness of other elements in the community (e.g., residents who are unorganized and/or confront additional handicaps that undermine their capacity to partner with the police) this model can generate inequitable results.

As Jeffrey Berry (1997:3-4) apprises us, in the 1950s and 1960s pluralist scholars "argued that many (that is, plural) interests in society found representation in the policymaking process through lobbying by *organizations*. The bargaining that went on between such groups and government led to policies produced by compromise and consensus." According to Edwards, Wattenberg and Lineberry (2000:339), there are at least five working assumptions common to pluralist scholars:

(1) groups provide a key link between people and government; (2) groups compete; (3) no one group is likely to become too dominant; (4) groups usually play by the `rules of the game'; and, (5) groups weak in one resource can use another.

Although pluralism suffered a decline as a paradigm for American Political Science during the first half of the twentieth century as legalism came to rule the day, following the publication of David Truman's *The Governmental Process: Political Interests and Public Opinion* in 1951 the group approach to the policy process came newly to the fore in the discipline. As Baumgartner and Leech (1998:48) elaborate:

> Group theory...relied on the pluralistic assumption that the best political outcomes would arise as a result of group conflict. Free and active group life was seen as crucial to the functioning of a democracy. The role of the state was not to dictate outcomes, but rather to arbitrate among various interests.

It is through the activities of the interest group, defined by Truman (1951:33) as "any group that is based on one or more shared attitudes and makes certain claims upon other groups of organizations in the society," that equitability in policy outcomes necessarily arises.

The philosophy of democratic pluralism found its expression in various community studies conducted in the 1950s and 1960s. For example, in *Who Governs?* (1961), Robert Dahl investigated the local power structure of Hartford, Connecticut. Dahl attempted to determine precisely "who" had the power to influence policy in three key issue areas—political party nominations, urban redevelopment, and public education. He found that power was not concentrated in the hands of any single elite, whether construed as a few key individuals or a handful of privileged groups. Power in New Haven, Dahl reported, was distributed across complex combinations of many groups, officials and government structures operating in loose, shifting coalitions. The general impression that emerged from Dahl's research (like that of many, but not all, community power studies of the 1960s), lent support to the pluralist model of the process through which private actors influence public policy outcomes.

But at this juncture, critics of democratic pluralism as an explanation of how policy decisions are made in the United States began to proliferate. In 1960, E. E. Schattschneider fired one of the first salvoes in *The Semi-Sovereign People*, asserting that "the flaw in pluralist heaven is that the heavenly choir sings with a strong upper-class accent" (p.35). Thereafter, Theodore Lowi proclaimed in *The End of Liberalism* (1969/1984) that the pluralist game is not fair "because once government officials began to bargain with a given set of interest groups, they tend to favor them at the expense of others" (Lowi, 1984:60). By the early 1980s, even former pluralist exponents such as Dahl were forced to issue major qualifications of their previous endorsements. For example, in his 1982 textbook, Dahl observed that "unequal resources that allow organizations to stabilize injustice... enable them to exercise unequal influence in determining what alternatives are taken seriously" (Dahl, 1982:47).

One of the most serious criticisms of the democratic pluralism paradigm was presented in Mancur Olson's *The Logic of Collective Action* (1965). In that work, Olson demonstrated that some groups, notably well-organized small groups with well-defined interests, have overwhelming advantages over large and relatively unorganized interest groups. If a given interest group is small enough, Olson asserted, higher rates of mobilization and participation among its potential members can be expected because the benefits of securing desired outcomes are shared by fewer individuals. As Baumgartner and Leech (1998:67-68) have observed, Olson's theory of collective action exposed the critical flaw in the pluralist assumption that all potential groups have a relatively equal chance of participating in the public policymaking process. Some groups, notably small, business-oriented ones, had great advantages in organization and were likely to mobilize in the manner Truman described. Other groups, notably those with many potential members and seeking only collective benefits, were at a considerable disadvantage and were unlikely to mobilize to even a fraction of their potential influence.

In a recently-published study, David Thacher (2001) examined the equity dimension of community policing and community-police partnerships. Thacher argued that "the ideal of being responsive to individual community groups often conflicts with the equally important ideal of equity, which directs police to provide fair service to all segments of the public" (Thacher, 2001:3). In practical terms, Thacher noted:

> The source of the dilemma is quite simple: The whole community never shows up at police-community meetings, and it is often especially difficult to find neighborhood groups and other willing partners in poor neighborhoods compared with wealthier ones. As a result, if the police are responsive to

the community groups that do organize they run the risk of winding up with skewed priorities that benefit the better off at the expense of the poor (p.3).

This is, in essence, a variation on the old adage that the squeaky wheel gets the grease, that in forming collaborative partnerships that are responsive to the input of the community, the police run the risk of neglecting those elements in the community that are poor, unorganized, and relatively inarticulate.

To illustrate this point, Thacher presented three case studies of police-community partnerships undertaken in the context of community policing. The first of these took place in Seattle, Washington's Chinatown International District. In 1995, a well-established middle-class group, the Community Action Project, formed a coalition with a community development corporation (PDA) for the purpose of persuading the police to deploy additional officers in an area the corporation planned to develop. More particularly, this well-organized group sought bicycle patrols and permanent beat assignments from the Seattle Police Department. For their part, the relevant decision-makers in the Seattle PD were assiduously aware that this coalition was a "squeaky wheel" with an apparent set of narrow interests. Thacher cited the remarks of the Chinatown International District's precinct captain, Tom Grabicki:

> The people that tend to be the most vocal are the people who have their own interests at stake, and often it is a financial interest, and they want to use the police or police resources to affect their financial interests in a positive way. And I am not too sure they are overly concerned with police service to the broader spectrum of the community (cited in Thacher 2001:5).

With other neighborhoods in the district in far greater need of additional patrol, the police initially resisted this call from the coalition's upper-middle class and business constituents. The result was that for a period of two years the police-community partnership was locked in an acrimonious stalemate.

The logjam in the development of the partnership was broken when a group of three high ranking officers met with representatives from the CAP/PDA without any other interests in the community in attendance. As Thacher (2001:5) tells it, "the three ignored concerns that their attention to the Chinatown-International District left other more-deserving neighborhoods slighted, as well as concerns that the PDA did not adequately represent the opinions of the entire district." In the end, the "squeaky wheel" succeeded in its objective: additional bicycle patrol resources were deployed in the area under commercial development. But the community-police partnership was discredited in the eyes of the broader community and in the view of other police officers, and the three community policing liaisons assigned to the area in question were viewed with derision within the department.

Thacher's accounts of the Lowell, Massachusetts and Fremont, California cases provide further evidence of how inequities can arise through police responsiveness to the most vocal and richly-endowed elements. However, in these instances the police departments in question took extraordinary steps to ensure a degree of equity in the police-community partnership. In Lowell, upper-middle class residents of the Cupples Square neighborhood within the Highlands District attempted to persuade the police to locate a sub-station within their neighborhood's boundaries. On the basis of need (i.e., high crime rates and disorder), the police were drawn to citing the sub-station in Centralville, an area in which the populace was comprised primarily of low-income and unorganized Cambodian immigrants. Prior to a police-community meeting on the issue, the police community relations department actively recruited Cambodian residents and encouraged them to voice their interests in the upcoming dialogue. The police used statistical data to demonstrate the greater potential effectiveness of a Centralville sub-station, and all sides came to a mutual agreement that this was the superior choice.

In the Fremont, California case a set of middle-class community groups insisted that the police take enforcement action against offenders among the predominantly Mexican-American residents of a low-cost housing complex, believing that it was a hotbed of rampant narcotics dealing and blatant prostitution. Instead of accepting this accusation at face value, the Fremont PD performed a SARA analysis. They found that the building in question was not an epicenter of crime and disorder, and that most of the residents were members of intact working class families. These findings were then presented to the middle-class groups at a police-community meeting at which minority neighborhood residents of the housing complex attended at the express invitation of the Fremont PD.

Commenting on the Lowell and Fremont experiences, Thacher (2001:10) noted that, "these departments engaged the "vocal groups" in a dialogue that transformed their demands rather than subordinated them. They did so by reaching out to absent publics, however imperfectly; by ensuring that relevant information was considered; and by focusing debate firmly on the question of the public good." But to ensure a balance of responsiveness and equity in these instances, "the respective police departments were compelled to go well beyond merely listening to demands raised in community-police forums, actively organizing absent "publics" and shaping the conditions of the dialogue itself." Whether these "success" stories can be replicated in many settings elsewhere is an open question. Thacher's study demonstrates that the COP emphasis on increased responsiveness of the police to community input can either ameliorate or exacerbate pre-existing inequalities, depending on the level of sophistication and collaborative skills of the police department in question. As noted earlier, a strong presence of communitarian thought could serve to strike a better balance in a decidedly pluralistic society that tends to neglect certain aspects of community when attempting to implement new public policies.

COMMUNITY POLICING AT THE LEVEL OF STRATEGY

At the level of strategy, community policing embodies the adoption of problem-oriented policing supported by key organizational changes. As Gerasimos, Giankis and Davis (1998:485) have written, community policing can be viewed as a manifestation of the "reinventing government" movement; on a strategic level, community policing is strongly associated with decentralization of decision-making authority within law enforcement agencies and a reduction of barriers separating these organizations from their external constituents or clients—that is, the public at large.

As a strategy, community policing involves the flattening of organizational hierarchies through organizational decentralization, the delegation of discretionary authority down the chain of command, etc., in addition to the opening of organizational decision-making to external influences (e.g., input from the community). But as John Crank and Robert Langworthy (1996) have argued, community policing can be approached as an example of "fragmented centralization." The upshot is that COP strategies tend to reinforce existing policies and power arrangements—in effect, to support the status quo rather than promote change. Examining the several evaluation studies in the Roth and Ryan report (2000), we find evidence of this precise phenomenon at work. In an introduction to their compendium, Roth and Ryan (2000) observe that many COPS grantees have "stretched the definition" of community policing to include "traditional quick-fix enforcement actions, draconian varieties of zero tolerance, long established prevention programs, and citizen advisory councils that are *only* advisory" (original italics, Roth and Ryan, 2000:21). Other social science researchers have reported that organizational changes that have been undertaken under the community-policing banner (e.g., "decentralization") have in fact been shallow in regard to the depth of change undertaken. The most critical manifestation of such gaps has been witnessed in the area of community partnerships. Thus, on the basis of their study of 30 grantee agencies, Roehl et al. (2000:213) reported that:

> Although many segments of the community and other agency partners are involved in problem solving, true collaboration was evident in only a handful of sites. Problem solving appeared to be a police-determined activity in most of the jurisdictions, and in several jurisdictions, it was explicitly preferred.

Worse, regarding the ten agencies that were chosen for in-depth research because they were considered to have made superior progress in implementing community policing strategies, Mark Moore et al. (2000:257) reported:

> Particularly troubling is the fact that success in establishing working partnerships with minority communities was spotty at best... Apparently, establishing effective partnerships with community groups remains more challenging to police departments than the development of a proactive capacity for problem solving, and it remains particularly challenging to establish working relationships with poor minority groups— just as it has always been.

At the level of strategy, there appears to be a significant difference between the community policing philosophy and its implementation, and this gap seems to have the most adverse consequences for communities in which "poor minority groups" are predominant.

According to John Crank and Robert Langworthy (1996), most cases of organizational changes undertaken under the name of community policing are not an example of decentralization, but instead represent what they term "fragmented centralization." Congruent with the foregoing analysis of community policing as political rhetoric, Crank and Langworthy asserted that the community policing concept did not come to prominence through the labors of "grass roots" proponents, but rather from the dedicated activities of well-placed policy entrepreneurs. "Community-based policing is a special case of fragmented centralization. Though community-based policing is intended to look local, Crank and Langworthy (1996:223) observed, "it is centrist in origins, sponsorship, and intellectual leadership." One of the inevitable results of fragmented centralization, these scholars apprise us, is "inconsistency, cross-purposes, and lack of coordination among powerful constituencies horizontally and vertically across levels of government" (Crank and Langworthy, 1996:215).

The relevance of this conceptual framework for the analysis of equity in community policing at the level of strategy is evident when we consider the gap between the goals of the community policing philosophy and the limited degree to which authentic organizational changes have been undertaken by departments which have embraced it. As Maguire et al., (1997:368) have recently noted:

> Despite the attention that community policing is receiving, there is still a fundamental concern about the degree to which its basic precepts are actually being implemented. Research indicates that community-policing implementation is uneven across both individual agencies and various cross sections of agency and jurisdiction types (p.368).

In 1994, prior to the initiation of the federal COPS program, Robert Trojanowicz reported that 42 percent of all police departments serving populations of 50,000 or more persons that he surveyed indicated that they had implemented some form of community policing. In that same year, however, Mark Moore (1994:286) concluded that "in practice, no department has yet fully implemented community policing as an overall philosophy."

Returning to the Roth and Ryan research project, we find with them that much of what has been implemented under the rubric of "community policing" by COPS grant recipients actually concerns support for traditional prevention programs (DARE, Neighborhood Watch), "now subsumed under the community policing label" (Roth and Ryan, 2000:21). In like manner, Roth and Ryan (2000:20) have found:

> In some jurisdictions, traditional enforcement and investigative activities are called problem solving under the community-policing umbrella when these activities are directed toward problems the community had identified as concerns. Problem-solving projects dominated by enforcement actions, however, rarely advance the objectives of community policing because they are unlikely to either fix underlying causes or attract the community support needed to maintain solutions.

Indeed, one manifestation of this phenomenon is the implementation of "zero tolerance" directives as "community policing" under the justification that the public at large wants local departments to get tough on crime. "What might have been called a crackdown 5 years ago is now implemented under zero tolerance or order maintenance policies and classified as part of community policing" (Roth and Ryan, 2000:20). Roth and Ryan proceed to observe that such policies may be inimical to the spirit of community policing when they are undertaken without opportunity for the community to register opposition or articulate objections. They may, in fact, "directly undercut the objective of partnership building by alienating potential community partners" (Roth and Ryan 2000:21).

To gauge the extent to which community policing was actually being operationalized into working strategies, Breci and Erickson (1998) first identified 10 principles of community policing and then surveyed 89 law enforcement agencies in the Minneapolis-St. Paul SMSA. Breci and Erickson (1998:20-21) reported that:

> Seventy percent of responding agencies had incorporated at least five of these ten principles. The most common changes among the sampled departments were: (1) giving officers discretion and authority; (2) freeing up officers to work COP; (3) training all personnel regarding COP; (4) establishing

community partnerships; and (5) increasing participation of citizens. On the other hand, the principles that were not widely implemented were: (1) internal changes within the agency; (2) changes in personnel evaluation procedures and criteria; (3) refocusing of expectations; (4) integration of the entire agency into COP; and (5) development of a department-wide strategy to implement COP.

Taking a "glass half-full" stance toward these mixed results, Breci and Erickson (1998:16) suggested that since it requires "at least ten years" to implement community-policing principles, "the controversy over whether or not a department is, in fact, using COP may be more a reflection of time rather than definition."

As one of the Roth and Ryan studies, Roehl and her colleagues (2000) undertook in-depth examinations of thirty law enforcement agencies that had received COPS funding. Of paramount interest, Roehl et al. (2000:235) found that only six of the departments in their sample had taken steps "to decentralize policy-making and (to) give officers more discretion to tackle problems as they saw fit." The finding that only a minority of agencies purporting to implement the COPS philosophy reported by Roehl and her colleagues was consistent with the results of a study conducted by Giankis and Davis (1998). They examined the degree to which organizational changes supportive of community policing were being implemented by Florida law enforcement agencies that identified themselves as committed to community policing. While two-thirds of the departments in their study indicated that they had implemented some type of decentralization program, Giankis and Davis (1998) found these did not go to the structural core of the command hierarchy.

> Virtually no contemporary law enforcement agency, however, has affected existing operational policies and administrative procedures across the board, and even those professing structural change and geographic decentralization seem to focus on changing the beliefs and behaviors of officers rather than altering the organization (Giankis and Davis, 1998:507). Although several departments cited the establishment of sub-stations as a form of decentralization, Giankis and Davis (1998:503) reported that these were invariably "storefront operations that did not house command responsibilities."

Instead of effectuating deep organizational changes in the direction suggested by the community policing philosophy, "the majority of these agencies are seeking to implement community policing by changing the officer rather than the organization" (Giankis and Davis, 1998:485).

In many instances, moreover, "changing the officer" was equated with intensifying the attention of community patrol officers to signs of disorder (for example, persistent vagrancy). Considering their results, the researchers cautioned, that "the penetration of these (poor, minority) urban areas by a better bureaucracy wielding new bureaucratic tools…can only serve to exacerbate social alienation" (Giankis and Davis, 1998:509). At the very least, Giankis and Davis concluded that required "operational and structural changes" directly associated with the "reinventing government" movement "cannot be mandated through legislation like the 1994 anti-crime bill…" (Giankis and Davis 1998:510).

In terms of organizational changes supportive of community policing, the implementation of decentralized structures of decision-making authority among COPS grantee agencies and other departments purportedly committed to the community policing philosophy has been spotty at best and, on the whole, rather superficial where it has occurred. Turning to the dimension of making organizational boundaries more porous with respect to community input, the findings of Roehl et al. suggest a continuum with these two end-points:

(1) Partnerships that involve true collaboration in all phases of the work among police, community residents and organizations, local service providers, and other criminal justice agencies; and, (2) Partnerships that include the mere involvement of such parties (2000:194).

A majority of the 30 agencies examined by Roehl and her associates had created and/or bolstered citizen advisory committees. According to these researchers:

The key word in most of these community partnerships is the word 'advisory.' Although police departments are opening up to community input and influence, most police executives remain reluctant to give the community real authority and responsibilities (Roehl et al., 2000:196).

It is noteworthy that in most of the far broader sample of COPS fund recipient agencies surveyed by Roth and his associates (2000), the decision to apply for federal grants was seldom presented to communities per se. Instead, this decision was typically made by "police chiefs in conjunction with the chief executives (mayors) and budget/financial officials of their respective communities" (Roth et al., 2000:63-64). Moreover, in terms of community participation in decisions about how COPS funds would be utilized, site visits conducted by Roth et al. (2000:73) indicated "substantial variation in the local meaning of participation."

Delving yet more deeply into problem-oriented policing and police-community partnerships, researchers Mark Moore, David Thacher, Catherine Coles, Peter Sheingold, and Frank Hartmann (2000) associated with the Kennedy School of Government at Harvard University carried out extensive field observations of ten COPS grant recipients. These police departments were selected because they were believed to be among the most advanced in translating the community policing philosophy into working practice. On the basis of their observations, they reported the following:

Although many departments seemed to move pretty far in the direction of increasing the *quantity and quality of problem-solving efforts*, they did less well in developing their *capacity for establishing and maintaining community partnerships* (original italics, Moore, Thacher, Coles, Sheingold and Hartmann, 2000, p.255).

Moore et al. (2000) continued on to find that community policing partnerships were weakest (or non-existent) within those neighborhoods that had the highest crime rates, the greatest resource deficits, the highest proportion of minority group residents, and a shared legacy of police-community conflict.

A particularly troubling finding derived from these evaluations is the observation that success in establishing working partnerships with minority communities was spotty at best (Moore et al., 2000). The only clear success stories here were found in the work of the St. Paul Police Department with respect to the city's Hmong community. In addition, the Lowell, Massachusetts and Portland, Oregon police departments made solid gains in working with their respective minority communities. Spokane, Washington has also made a major effort to strengthen its relationships with its minority communities, but it remains unclear whether that effort has produced a lasting change in the attitudes of the city's minority community.

Further evidence that law enforcement agency decision-making processes remained closed to the full range of community interests was found among the thirty COPS-funded departments examined by Roehl et al. They noted that when police officials were asked about crime prevention strategies, most departmental spokesman enumerated a laundry list of programs (e.g., DARE, Neighborhood Watch, and other similar programs) rather than identifying a comprehensive strategy. "They did not articulate any philosophy of prevention, the logical end product of true collaboration and problem solving focused on underlying causes" (Roehl et al., 2000:214). Consistent with Thacher's description of the Seattle case, the Roehl team stated that police-community partnerships for problem-solving frequently involved ongoing contacts with only a few individuals from the community. To illustrate this point in the extreme, Roehl and her colleagues alluded to the police-community partnership in the River Bend community near Des Moines, Iowa in which the "partnership" was confined to exchanges between the Chief of Police and a single community activist, the chief's brother-in-law (Roehl et al., 2000:213).

From the Roth and Ryan studies and the other investigations cited, then, we gain the strong impression that in general the adoption of community policing philosophies has not been accompanied by supportive organizational changes in terms of decentralizing the decision-making structure and opening up departments to genuine community input. In addition, we have strong cause to suspect that the weakest records of partnership building are found in communities in which poor, minority group members comprise the majority of the populace. Lastly, we note that in some cases "tough on crime" crackdowns and zero tolerance policies directed against "undesirable" elements (typically the poor, often minority group members) have been initiated under the banner of "community policing." Of course, such policies are inimical to the building of genuine partnerships between the police and the "whole" community they are obligated to serve.

COMMUNITY POLICING AT THE LEVEL OF TACTICS

Lastly, at the level of tactics, patterns of uneven community policing can be explained through Crank and Langworthy's (1996) concept of "loose coupling." Loose coupling generates disparities between what organizational leaders such as those preferred by police department chiefs committed to community policing want on a tactical level, and what those under their authority actually do. At this level, we find widespread opposition to community policing among the middle managers (captains, lieutenants, and sergeants) as well as the rank-and-file sworn officers. More importantly, as Roger Parks et al. (1999) have reported from their extensive "ride along" observations with "regular" patrol and "community" police, the latter tend to interact less with citizens. At the same time, the community police in the Parks et al. study tend to voluntarily associate with some elements in the community (e.g., white, middle-class business owners and members of community associations) while limiting their interactions with others (e.g., poor, minority group members). In combination with resource deficits common to many predominantly poor, minority neighborhoods, and the historical antagonism existing between the police and the latter, the net outcome may be a community policing regime that is less equitable than the "911" response system that it is intended to complement and partially replace.

Returning to Crank and Langworthy's (1996) analysis of community policing as an example of "fragmented centralization," we find that their operational concept of "loose coupling" is germane to this study's interests in the equity dimension of COPS and community policing in practice. According to Crank and Langworthy (1996), fragmented centralization at the strategic level is strongly associated with loose coupling at the tactical level. By "loose coupling," Crank and Langworthy (1996:217) denote a "loosely articulated relationship between the formal goals and purposes of the organization, and the day-to-day behaviors of line personnel."

In this context, we recall the observation made by Roehl et al. that the impetus for the adoption of a community policing model has usually come from the apex of the agency hierarchy, and that "most law enforcement agencies adopt community policing principles due to internal desires, led by the chief...to improve policing service" (Roehl et al., 2000:186). The Roehl team also found that as upper management attempted to implement deeper organizational restructuring such as decentralization of command, they encountered mounting resistance from their subordinates, particularly middle management captains, lieutenants, and sergeants (Roehl et al., 2000:233).

This observation of middle management opposition to change is by no means novel. More than two decades ago, Lawrence Sherman (1973:107) wrote that "pioneering" efforts to implement community policing (or community crime prevention techniques) often ran up against "mid-management of the departments (studied) who (saw) team policing as a threat to their power, subverted and, in some cases, actively sabotaged the plans." Herman Goldstein recognized this roadblock to the implementation of community policing, asserting that for many police sergeants, lieutenants and captains "the mere suggestion that police officers operate with greater flexibility is viewed as an anathema" (1987:13). More recently, George Kelling and William Bratton (1993) have identified middle management resistance as a key "administrative problem" in the adoption of community policing models in American law enforcement agencies.

Resistance to community policing is not limited to middle management, however. As Rohe, Adams and Arcury (2001:80) have noted, "line officers often have difficulty accepting the shift from enforcing laws to resolving community problems." Paoline, Myers and Worden (2000:577) have argued that although police organizational culture is not monolithic, the "traditional" values of the law enforcement profession "idealizes a hard-nosed approach to law enforcement and crime." Indeed, consistent with this emphasis upon stringent enforcement of the law, officers typically are rewarded when they go by the book and make arrests, and often are reprimanded for engaging in innovative activity not completely sanctioned by superiors. Thus, Paoline, Myers and Worden (2000:578) opine that "the police culture stresses law enforcement or *real* police work over order-maintenance or service roles" (emphasis in original). Among the departments visited by Gaffigan, Roth and Buerger (2000:26), "routine" patrol officers frequently voiced the view that community policing is "soft policing" and "not real police work." Roehl et al. (2000:233) reported resentment by "regular" police officers towards the release of community cops from having to respond to 911 calls, particularly during those periods when incoming caseloads are high.

In one of the most widely cited studies of rank-and-file attitudes toward community policing, Arthur Lurigio and Wesley Skogan (1994) conducted a survey among the uniformed members of the Chicago Police Department immediately after the Chicago Alternative Policing Strategy (CAPS) was launched in five pilot districts. Lurigio and

Skogan administered an author-constructed survey instrument to a total of 1,045 sworn officers on the first day of their participation in an orientation workshop aimed at preparing them for their new roles in CAPS. They reported that while the majority of the subjects in this sample either strongly agreed or agreed with the statement that "the prevention of crime is the joint responsibility of the community and the police" (87 percent of those queried), most did not agree that officers can learn more about the neighborhood problems on foot patrol than in patrol cars (36 percent), and most disagreed with the statement that "police officers should try to solve non-crime problems" (28 percent). Moreover, a majority of the subjects in this study indicated that the implementation of CAPS would have a number of negative effects upon their work, most notably in terms of community group and citizen demands upon police officers and police resources. On the whole, Lurigio and Skogan's results suggested that these officers were not particularly enthusiastic about community policing, nor did they believe that it would enhance their capacity to perform either traditional or non-traditional patrol tasks. Many of the officers selected for CAPS were concerned that the implementation of the program would reduce departmental autonomy and place a heavy burden of demands upon them.

To be sure, the attitudes of uniformed officers toward community policing tend to vary according to individual officer characteristics. From a study conducted with members of the Fort Worth, Texas Police Department, Yates and Pillai (1996:203) concluded that, "police attitudes toward community policing are not uniform and will vary with the presence or absence of job induced strain...Officers exhibiting more strain were found to be less supportive in their attitudes toward community policing." In the Lurigio and Skogan (1994) study and in an update of same (Skogan and Hartnett, 1997), it was reported that minority group officers and older, more seasoned officers tend to have more favorable attitudes toward community policing than their respective non-minority and less seasoned counterparts. Nevertheless, we can reasonably surmise that among the rank-and-file of many police agencies which have officially embraced community policing, attitudes toward community policing likely remain rather mixed.

Shedding additional light on this topic, researchers Paoline, Myers and Worden (2000) surveyed officers in two metropolitan police departments—Indianapolis, Indiana and St. Petersburg, Florida—in an effort to determine how their priorities compared with the broader mission of community policing. Eighty percent of the subjects in this study stated that law enforcement remained their most important responsibility, and 50 percent indicated that law enforcement was "their most important responsibility *by far*" (original italics, p.589). Paoline, Myers and Worden (2000:592) also reported that "officers vary widely in the extent to which their role conception includes a responsibility for addressing conditions that give rise to or signify disorder," such as broken windows, trash, graffiti and the like.

Although police chiefs are typically more enthusiastic about community policing than those whom they command, Zhao and Thurman's (1997) national survey of police chiefs casts some doubt upon the depth of their commitment. In the aggregate, the responding police chiefs "ranked the crime control function at the top and the provision of service at the bottom of the prioritization hierarchy." Zhao and Thurman noted that "a similar prioritization has been observed by police scholars since the inception of the bureaucratic model many years ago" (1997:353). Zhao and Thurman concluded their study with the statement that on the whole, "those persons charged with administering police functions...view protecting the public from crime in the streets as the agency's top priority, with much less interest in deploying police personnel to provide other services or engage in order maintenance" (1997:354).

Jeffrey Roth et al. (2000) conducted a line officer, questionnaire-based study to determine how much time COPS-funded community police actually spend doing non-traditional, COP-type activities. The vast majority of "community cops" responding to this questionnaire indicated that they spent at least some of their time working with community groups (95.9 percent) and engaged in problem-solving (95.5 percent) (Roth et al., 2000:114). Indeed, from a separate questionnaire sent to law enforcement departments, more agencies reported that COPS-funded officers were 'spending most or all of their time doing' problem solving (43 percent) and working with community groups and residents (39 percent) than any other activity" (Roth et al., 2000:113).

A decidedly different view of what community police officers do in the field can be found in research conducted by Roger Parks et al. (1999) in the same urban locations where Paoline et al. did their work—namely, Indianapolis and St. Petersburg. Rather than relying upon self-report data from individual or agency informants, Parks and his colleagues (1999) actually rode along with both regular patrol officers and designated community policing officers. They hypothesized that the latter would spend more time in contact with members of the community than the former. In fact, they reported that the opposite was the case, noting that "unexpectedly, however, community policing specialists in both sites spent less time in encounters with citizens than did the patrol generalists" (Parks et al., 1999:500).

Much more significant in terms of this literature review's central interest, Parks and his associates (1999:513) reported that the patrol generalists spent 95 percent of their citizen contact time with individuals described as suspects, disputants, or victims/complaints who were far more likely to be "male, minority, and younger" than the population at large. By contrast, freed from the responsibility of responding to 911 calls, the community specialists spent half of their citizen contact time with citizens categorized as "acquaintances" by the researchers (Parks et al., 1999:510). Many of these "acquaintances" were associated with "local businesses, government or non-profit agencies, and neighborhood groups" (Parks et al., 1999:513). Indeed, community policing specialists spent more time in contact with local business owners than with any other group. Hence, Parks and his colleagues concluded that given the opportunity to select civilians for interaction, officers assigned to community policing positions tend to gravitate toward those with whom they identify and share values, and "those who were more receptive to police and whose problems may have been more tractable" (1999:515).

Parks and his associates framed their argument by first noting that,

A number of research projects in the 1970s suggested that the ("911," traditional or reactive) system distributed services to neighborhoods and citizens with no strong relationships to race or socioeconomic class.... In this sense, 911 policing exhibits a rough egalitarianism in the distribution of public service, although it is governed by bureaucratic decision-making rules (Parks et al., 1999:484).

By contrast, community policing gives officers the discretion to associate with whomever they wish and, in general, "these people are frequently identified as residents, businesspeople, members of neighborhood organizations, and others invested in the area, such as those who work in schools and belong to churches and other collectivities" (Parks et al., 1999:486). That being the case, "911 policing, characterized by central dispatch and a more structured work environment, may provide more egalitarian service, or at least may bring the police to the scene of those situations which seem most likely to require immediate intervention" (Parks et al., 1999:513).

The conclusions of Roger Parks and his colleagues concerning the reduced equitability entailed in shifting from a 911 system to community policing tend to support the idea that community policing tends to be biased toward "established" elements within any given community. Thus, one of the findings from Sherman's (1997) review of the effects of community policing is that its benefits are concentrated on "white, middle-class homeowners" (p.52). As Buerger (1993:112) has elaborated, when choosing partners in the civilian community, line officers tend to seek alliances with the "property-owning taxpayer, usually the white middle class voter who has very little need of direct police services." Moreover, such alliances are implicitly arrayed against "inner-city residents, typically black, Latino and other recognizable minorities, who are often dependent on tax-funded public assistance of one form or another and who have regular contact with the police" (Buerger, 1993:114).

Compounding the inherent inequities in the preferences of community police for "upstanding" citizens who share their values, as Wesley Skogan (1988) remarked upon the community crime prevention programs that preceded current community policing, "anticrime organizations are often most successful in communities that need them least" (p.42)…(and) least common where they appear to be needed most—in low-income, heterogeneous, deteriorated, renting, high-turnover, high-crime areas" (p.45). Prior to the COPS program, the first Bush Administration advanced its own federal anti-crime initiative under the title of Operation Weed and Seed. The "weed" portion of the operation referred to "weeding" out criminals through aggressive law enforcement, while the "Seed" part connoted "a broader governmental effort to sustain order through social services and community redevelopment" (Gaffigan, Roth and Buerger, 2000:31). As Gaffigan, Roth and Buerger (2000:31) have stated, the "seeding components proved difficult to mount, in part because the infrastructure needed for service delivery was lacking in some neighborhoods." Finally, as one of the key determinants of community policing success, Moore et al. (2000:258) stated that "community policing also gets a boost where there is a strong local tradition of neighborhoods, joined with a tradition of neighborhood governance...It is weaker when it is hard to find these coherent communities..."

It requires very little documentation to establish that within America's inner-city or "ghetto" neighborhoods, the social infrastructure associated with community policing "success" is seldom in evidence. As Brain Duffy (1992) stated at the time of the Rodney King riots in Los Angeles, within the nation's inner city ghettoes, "the institutions—families, schools, workplaces, even churches—that once exercised some control and proffered some hope for change have disintegrated or disappeared" (p.21). Relatedly Alex-Assensoh (1995) noted the following:

> The exodus of (minority group) middle- and working-class families from concentrated poverty neighborhoods has adversely contributed to the concentration of poor people in inner-city neighborhoods. Undesirable behaviors have emanated from concentrated poverty neighborhoods because residents are out of touch with mainstream role models who have moved to other neighborhoods (p.13).

Within these "dysfunctional" and "disorganized" communities it is nearly impossible to garner a consensus about how the police can address problems of crime and social disorder (Mastrofski, 1991:63). As community-policing critic Carl Klockars (1991:257) has declared, "police can no more create communities or solve problems of urban anomie than they can be legalized into agents or the court or depoliticized into pure professionals." Indeed, within some of these communities, the few remaining activists often hold a highly unfavorable view of law enforcement as an instrument of "racist oppression" (Rudovsky, 1992:467).

As suggested in passing above, race has been, and continues to be a factor in citizen perceptions of law enforcement agencies and their personnel. Public opinion polls clearly demonstrate a high degree of antagonism toward the police on the part of many African-Americans. According to W.S. Wilson and Michael Vaughn (1996), race remains one of the strongest predictors of public attitudes toward the police in the United States. Many African-Americans believe that Whites receive preferential treatment, while Blacks are subject to frequent discrimination at the hands of the police. In a 1993, nationwide poll of 840 subjects, 74 percent of White respondents stated their belief that the police did a "good job" as compared to 48 percent of African-Americans (Wilson and Vaughn 1996:32-33). More recently, Ronald Weitzer and Steven Tuch (1999:499) reported from a broad-based survey that 80 percent of African-Americans (as opposed to 56.4 percent of Whites) believe that racism among police is either "fairly common" or "very common."

Quint Thurman and Michael Reisig (1996) have added a key qualification concerning race and public attitudes toward the police to this overall picture. They have noted that in a study conducted in Atlanta, Georgia in 1990, African-American residents living in high crime areas were twice as likely to hold negative attitudes toward the police as black residents of lower crime neighborhoods (Thurman and Reisig, 1996:575). Additional research studies suggest that it is not "race" per se that is determinative of attitudes toward the police, but rather it is the prevailing "neighborhood culture" that is critical (Thurman and Reisig, 1996:581). It is in precisely those communities that are in most dire need of police-community partnerships to prevent crime and uphold order (i.e., low-SES African-American and Latino inner-city neighborhoods) that the prospects for finding willing community "partners" are least favorable.

In their text *Above the Law*, Jerome Skolnick and James Fyfe (1993:258) asserted that community policing is "far less likely to generate police violence than traditional patrol policing." Nevertheless, several law enforcement scholars have expressed reservations about projected reductions in police brutality cases through community policing. For example, David Bayley (1988:237) has speculated that community policing may "weaken the rule of law in the sense of equal protection and evenhanded enforcement...lessen the protection afforded by the law to unpopular persons...and even encourage vigilantism" by mobilizing one segment of the community against another.

As a collection of tactics, then, community policing at the level of citizen interaction appears to illustrate the "loose coupling" phenomenon. There is widespread opposition from line officers to community policing and the new roles that they must take on in addition to their traditional law enforcement responsibilities. In carrying out their missions, community police specialists may not interact as frequently with members of their communities as their titles would suggest. Even more disturbing, there is evidence that they tend to seek out and ally themselves with established interests and with individuals who share their values, background, and social status. Even if they were to reach out to the entire community, including to "disadvantaged" groups, both the capacity and the willingness of poor, minority group members to forge alliances with the police present barriers that may well generate further inequalities.

With regard to the public administration and policy scholarship, a study of the implementation of COP must draw heavily on the theoretical constructs proposed by H. George Frederickson (1990). When looking at the overall development of the New Public Administration that came about during the late 1960s, emphasis on the necessity for public agencies and public administrators to begin to explore policy implementation as it relates to social equity emerged as a central issue for both scholars of public administration and for public administration practitioners alike (Frederickson, 1990). According to Fredrickson (1990:228), "social equity began as a challenge to the adequacy of concepts of efficiency and economy as guides for public administration. Over the course of time, social equity has taken on a more broad meaning." In an earlier treatment of the social equity concept, Frederickson (1980:6) explained social equity in the following terms:

> Social equity is a phrase that comprehends an array of value preferences, organizational design preferences, and management style preferences. Social equity emphasizes responsibility for decision and program implementation for public managers. Social equity emphasizes change in public management. Social equity emphasizes responsiveness to the needs of citizens rather than the needs of public organizations. Social equity emphasizes an approach to the study of education for public administration that is interdisciplinary, applied, problem solving in character, and sound theoretically.

Given these concepts and constructs, there appears to be a strong link between public administration with regard to the theory of social equity and the accountability issues that are to be examined in this analysis of the implementation of COP. Even further, Fredrickson (1993:251) believes that central to the practice of government administration (as in the COP funding allocations) is the issue of accountability. Before the policy-administration dichotomy was exiled to the realm of myth by the New Public Administration, Fredrickson (1993) posits that it might have been possible for public administrators to fall back on the rhetoric and substance of neutrality. This means that policy should be administered in a neutral format, where social equity during the public development and implementation phases of the policy process is considered at the forefront of the policy process.

According to Frederickson (1993:252) "there is evidence in the existing research revealing that bureaucrats tend to be responsive, within the law and their appropriations, to executive direction" rather than to principles of social equity (citations are made to Seidleman and Gilmour, 1986; Moe, 1987; Weingast and Moran, 1983; Wood and Waterman, 1991). In addition, Frederickson indicates that strong examples of this can be found in cases where there is an absence of accountability or where there is a violation of the law or standards of ethics. One example drawn from the law enforcement arena is the experience with the FBI under J. Edgar Hoover, where both congressional and presidential oversight and controls failed to make any significant changes in the way the FBI was managed for decades (Hart and Hart, 1992). Administrative agencies and their leaders are both experts and advocates for their tasks or missions, and they will seek support among legislators and elected executives to ensure their agency perspective is considered during the policy making process (Kelman, 1987). In addition, interest groups and clients will support the programs and budgets of agencies supporting their interests (Thompson, 1967; Zhao, 1996).

CONCLUDING OBSERVATIONS ON THE COP PHENOMENON

At all four levels of analysis—rhetoric, philosophy, strategy, and tactics—there is good cause to believe that community policing as it is currently practiced in the United States may actually reinforce and/or exacerbate existing socioeconomic inequalities. Paradoxically, while community policing has been extolled as a means of "bridging the gap" between law enforcement and the community at large, its implementation could, in fact, divide communities still further. To be sure, the philosophy of community policing is by no means inimical to the precept of social equity. However, in working practice, there is the strong potential for factors that have been well-documented in the literature of policy, policing, and social equity that would tend to favor the hypothesis set forth in this exploration of federal funding allocations: there is the strong potential for inequality embedded in the present model.

In sum, we first observe that in the view of at least some COPS researchers, the distribution of funding under the 1994 Crime Act has not been equitable. Davis and his colleagues (2000) have argued, for example, that COPS grant monies have not been allocated in proportion to actual need when defined, for instance, in terms of community crime rates per capita. As will be explained in the subsequent chapters, there may be a strong element of self-selection at work here. Some otherwise eligible agencies have either foregone COPS funding altogether, or they have withdrawn their funding program applications due to the fiscal obligations that adhere to the acceptance of these federal funds. This, of course, suggests one degree of inequitability; law enforcement agencies in fiscally constrained communities may have balked at a "Trojan Horse," their relative lack of financial resources indirectly skewing the COPS fund allocations toward those communities that can afford to pay for the strings attached to the grants.

Given the present status of COP in the literature that was reviewed for this study, the COP model (as it presently exists within the realm of policy debate) might serve to worsen rather than bridge gaps supporting the advantaged and disadvantaged minorities and non-minorities and law abiding and law challenging elements of American society. The data that will be analyzed in this study will help determine the extent of which COP implementation has disproportionately benefited areas that experience low crime rates, where degrees of racial and ethnic variation are low, and in areas where family incomes are relatively ample and equally distributed.

CHAPTER THREE

Assembling Data From Diverse Sources

TYPES OF DATA ASSEMBLED AND RESEARCH HYPOTHESES: LINKING THE DATA TO THEORETICAL CONSTRUCTS

In attempting to examine the degree of impact a program/policy has upon its intended targets, one method of impact analysis is that of assessing the presence or absence of predicted results using data on outcomes experienced by program participants and/or persons or entities affected by the policy in question. For the purposes of this policy impact assessment, a set of 202 U.S. municipal law enforcement agencies employing 100 or more commissioned officers is used to test the several research hypotheses set forth above.

The testing of these several hypotheses relating to the distribution of Community Oriented Policing grant funds will entail the examination of the extent of COP implementation present in each department studied, the amount of change in organizational factors reported over the course of the grant period by those 202 departments, the character of crime statistics reported for the jurisdictions in question, and municipal population demographics. This research effort will make use of: 1) data on COP grant awards made to each municipal law enforcement agency over the period of the COPS Office grant program; 2) archival data from the 1993, 1997, and 1999 Law Enforcement Management and Statistics (LEMAS) surveys conducted by the U.S. Department of Justice; 3) data on ethnic diversity derived from the 1990 U.S. Census Bureau Report; 4) Uniform Crime Report

(UCR) statistics from 1993, 1997, and 1999; and, 5) a computation of income inequality (Index) based on the reported incomes for families and households derived from the 1990 U.S. Census Bureau Report. It should be noted that considerable social science research has been conducted with each of these sources of data in the past.

For example, LEMAS data have been used by researchers such as Maguire (1997) and Worrall (2001) to analyze the changing demographics of law enforcement agencies, the alteration of hiring practices of these agencies, the patterns of allocation of agency resources, the number and type of organizational subunits in operation, specific features of training programs made available to commissioned personnel, and related information used in the assessment of the attainment of the main goal of law enforcement—namely, the protection of public safety. In a study conducted by Maguire (1997), data from successive LEMAS reports were used to determine whether structural changes were occurring in American law enforcement agencies as a consequence of the broad adoption of Community Oriented Policing. Similarly, Worrall (2001) used LEMAS data to conduct an analysis of the connection between COP and the presence of citizen review boards. Likewise, Correia (2000) made use of LEMAS data to make his selection of cases for his six-city study of how the character of COP implementation constitutes a reflection of community factors. LEMAS variables were also used to assess differences between accredited and non-accredited law enforcement agencies in the U.S. (McCabe and Fajardo, 2001).

With regard to the use of Census information and the study of the effects of income inequality in American communities, for the purposes of this study it is important to review research that explores theories regarding how the gap between the rich and poor finds its way to the public policy analysis sphere. In one of the first published studies on income inequality effects upon public policy and institutional performance, Kuznets (1955) argued that once a threshold level of economic development occurs within a particular region, further economic development will be associated with additional reductions in income inequality. His research demonstrated that per capita income and income inequality tend to be negatively related in advanced contemporary market economies.

In a study conducted by Levernier (1999), income inequality in metropolitan counties was examined to identify major factors affecting family income inequality in the U.S. Levernier carefully explored the possibility that state-level societal characteristics may affect county-level income inequality using data from the 1990 Census of the Population in an OLS regression model where income is regressed on a variety of demographic, economic, and geographic characteristics of U.S. counties. Levernier noted that income inequality is strongly affected by demographic factors such as proportion of households that are female-headed, and the presence of dependent populations (i.e., youth under the age of 18 and seniors who are above the age of 64). In addition, Braun (1988) used multiple measurements of U.S. income inequality to exact a test on the effects of income inequality on employment rates and uncovered an inverse relationship between an area's income inequality and its level of gainful employment. In a similar mode of research, Nord (1980) examined the effects of city size on income inequality and concluded that in smaller cities (under 50,000 in population) income inequality tends to decline as the population increases.

This study will use evidence from the Uniform Crime Reports (UCR), 1990 Census of the Population, COPS Office grant funding information, and data from the LEMAS survey to examine the pattern of allocation of COPS Office funds to law enforcement agencies in 202 jurisdictions employing more than 100 sworn officers. The examination of ethnic diversity within a community and its relationship to the role minorities play in the development of policy is also an important concept to examine to enhance our understanding of how policies regarding public safety issues are implemented. Political scientist Rodney Hero has examined the effects upon public policy of the presence of ethnic minorities in a community. Hero (1988) compares his "social diversity" framework with the political culture framework of Daniel Elazar in the course of his analysis. Hero sets his own theory apart from Elazar's by including the migratory changes that affect local demographics (as reflected in the Report of the Census and in the rate of voter registration/participation) that build upon the "historical legacy" concepts first explored in the widely read work of Elazar (1966, 1972, 1984). Further, when looking at how policy is enacted in areas populated by diverse cultures, Tolbert and Hero (2001:571) report empirical findings regarding the strong relationship between voting behavior and the social context (high racial/ethnic diversity) and institutional context (frequent use of direct democracy). They demonstrate that these social and institutional settings are associated with the adoption of public policies directly affecting minority groups.

According to Hero, within the policy realm, social diversity explanations are more powerful accounts of majority-minority gaps in social policy outcomes than most rival accounts. In sum, Hero believes that ethnic diversity (particularly in the context of the presence of white ethnics)[7] is a major predictor in the explanation of local government policy and policy processes that affect minorities. Given the "community bridge-building" and promotion of "active community partnerships" for public safety at the heart of COP, it is clear that the Hero-type analysis of ethnic diversity effects on COP program implementation is an important area to be explored in this analysis.

In sum, it will be argued here that the public policy research literature strongly suggests that income inequality and ethnic diversity constitute important elements of context in public policy formation and analysis. This study will draw on previous research in an attempt to discern whether COPS Office resources have been appropriately allocated to urban areas that are in the greatest need, and where the need to address income inequality and build bridges between the police and racial and ethnic minorities is the most evident. These data will allow us to observe how federal COPS Office resources were distributed in large cities, in medium sized cities, and in small cities that employ more than 100 sworn police officers. In addition, this study will examine factors that affect the varying degrees of COP implementation in 202 municipal police departments with 100+ sworn officers spread across the entire nation.

A primary goal of the 1994 Crime Bill was to employ 100,000 additional law enforcement officers. According to the COPS Office, COP is a progressive policing philosophy that promotes organizational strategies to address the causes of crime, to reduce the fear of crime, and to reduce social disorder through problem-solving tactics and the formation of community-police partnerships (USDOJ, 2002). In addition, at the heart of the COPS Office effort is the intention to award grants and underwrite cooperative agreements that can assist communities in tackling the social problems underlying crime and disorder (e.g., domestic violence, teenage pregnancy, social incivility, etc.). While most COPS Office funds have been earmarked for the hiring and redeployment of community policing officers, the COPS Office has also provided assistance to directly address numerous quality of life issues. It is important, consequently, to review the levels of funding allocated to each of the 202 police departments featured in this study to ascertain whether change experienced within these agencies is associated with budgetary enhancements awarded through grants and cooperative agreements provided by the COPS Office—as opposed to being the consequence of the adoption of COP as an organizational philosophy without COPS Office grant funds. Concerning the considerable degree of difference that exists between these jurisdictions in relation to income level and equity of distribution, and with regard to ethnic variation, scholarly works reviewed for this study suggest that the participatory government aspect of public safety brings with it many channels for the penetration of the policy implementation process by "political" factors (see Bayley, 1988; Buerger, 1993; Eck and Spelman, 1987; Goldstein, 1977, 1979, 1987, 1990; Trojanowicz, et al., 1998; Wilson and Vaughn, 1996; and Yates and Pillai, 1996).

Policy makers and politicians responsible for the enactment of major programs and policies are quite naturally rather eager to have the general public believe that their major policies of significant magnitude (such as COP) are well monitored, and that every reasonable attempt has been made to ensure equity in the distribution of program benefits and even-handed implementation in program or policy operations (see Berry, 1997; Giankis and Davis, 1998; Lowi, 1979; Olsen, 1965; Stone, 1997; and Truman, 1951). As previously noted, the critical assessments that have been presented concerning the COPS Office grant award process, and the overall history of police relations with ethnic minorities in the U.S., would seem to suggest that the American police profession is disinclined to make use of resources and new opportunities such as the COPS grants and awards to implement lasting change within the architecture of their organizations.

COPS FUNDING DATA

Using information originally provided to the author under the *Freedom of Information Act*, archival data on federal awards for COP grant applications were later acquired from the annual reports presented by the COPS Office from their official website (http://www.usdoj.gov/cops/home.htm). In order to assess the policy impact that COP funding has had on change in law enforcement, this study will use information about the levels of monetary award allocated to police agencies and the number of sworn officers that have been acquired as a result of the funding for the hiring/redeployment grant programs (as per figures provided by the COPS office). In addition, this study will explore the level of commitment to COP reported in departmental survey data provided in the 1999 LEMAS study.

Beyond just documenting the size of the COP awards and the number of COP officers funded, it is also important to understand the conceptual premises upon which each of these forms of assistance (as noted by the COPS Office in their description of each funding goal and opportunity) is based. One answer that may emerge from the analysis of these data is whether the presence of these programs is simply "window dressing," or is it the case that substantial police agency resources have been committed to the success of these innovative ventures by the municipal police departments included for careful study in this study. As previously noted, the COPS Office grants can be divided into two broad categories: COP commissioned officer hiring grants and innovative program grants. A complete list of each grant award and total amount for innovative and hiring programs can be found in Appendix Table 3. A description of each of the hiring grants is as follows:

Making Officer Redeployment Effective[8] (*MORE*) and **MORE Renewal** (*MRENEWAL*)—This grant program—commonly referred to as the "civilianization" grant—provides for communication technology and equipment, as well as additional support personnel with the intent to decrease time spent on paperwork and other bureaucratic activities, and increase time spent by officers in the engagement of COP-related activities. The MORE award program was available in 1995, 1996, 1998, 2000, and 2001. Of the 202 agencies included in this study, 155 received funding (76%) under at least one of these MORE programs. Ninety agencies received MORE 95 funding, totaling close to $71 million for the hiring of 4322.7 officers. Seventy-one law enforcement agencies received MORE 96 funding, receiving more than $89 million for the hiring of 3385.8 officers. Eighty-four police agencies received MORE 98 funding, totaling awards of just over $122 million for the hiring of 4581.1 officers. Thirty-five agencies received MORE 2000 funding, totaling almost $6.5 million in grants for the hiring of 238 officers. Twenty-two agencies received close to $13 million in COPS Office grants and added 510.7 new officers under

MORE 2001. Finally, 72 police departments received funding under the MORE Renewal award, totaling just over $60 million in grant funds. In sum, the MORE grants totaled $361,974,741 for the acquisition of 13,038 new officers in the 202 cities studied here. The distribution of these funds is detailed in Appendix Table 6.

Universal Hiring Program[9] (*UHP*)—The goal of this COPS Office program is to provide direct funding directly to local, state, and tribal jurisdictions for salaries and benefits of line officers engaged in community policing in addition to the provision of funding intended for the hiring of additional community policing officers and to assist law enforcement agencies in establishing partnerships with other public agencies and with community-based organizations in their communities. There have been 57 announcement rounds for UHP grants. Of the 202 agencies included in this study, 132 (65%) received funding for 9,280 COP officers with monetary awards totaling in excess of $881 million (see Appendix Table 6).

Cops in Schools[10] (*CIS*)—CIS provides law enforcement agencies assistance in the form of direct support for hiring school resource officers (SROs) for the purpose of engaging in COP-related activities adjacent to local middle (junior high) schools and in the vicinity of senior high schools. The overall goal of this grant program effort is to assist with the development of collaborative problem solving networks within the community directed toward the reduction of violence in the nation's secondary schools. Announcements for the CIS program resulted in awards to over 2,100 grantees and the allocation of grant funds in excess of $567 million. These funds were used to hire more than 4,900 School Resource Officers across the country. Sixty-five municipal police agencies included in this study were awarded grant funds under this grant program, allowing for the hiring of 424 school resource officers with awards totaling more than $52.79 million (see Appendix Table 6).

Small Community Grant Program[11] (*SCGP*)—This grant program was designed to help small communities retain patrol officers hired with COPS funds (which last for three years) for a fourth year of support. For the limited purposes of this particular piece of research, there are nine communities with a population smaller than 50,000 residents included in this study. Of those 9 municipalities, only one (Linden, New Jersey) agency in this study was awarded funding under this particular grant program at the rate of $90,000.

Distressed Neighborhoods Pilot Project[12] (*DNP*)—This grant was meant to provide timely assistance in the form of a team of community policing officers in neighborhoods that are shown to be among the most in need of external support. Eighteen cities were targeted for this program, with the underlying assumption upon which the program was created being that high crime associated with grinding poverty can be significantly alleviated through appropriate COP interventions. Of these eighteen cities designated for support under this COPS Office program, ten will be examined here. Police departments selected for this grant project received 100% funding for an entry level officer's salary and benefits over the course of a three-year period of service. Neighborhoods that experienced high levels of crime (both violent and property UCR crimes) and featured significant proportions of poor people were to receive the services of a team of experienced COP officers. The intent of the grant program was for each selected neighborhood to be the beneficiary of a 6- to 12-month intensive problem-solving intervention. The 18 cities selected for the program received approximately $116 million to fund 784 new COP officers. Six hundred, forty-nine of these officers were hired in ten cities featured in this study. In addition, more than $101 million dollars were awarded to these ten U.S. cities (see Appendix Table 6). This set of grant awards was specifically intended for impoverished and high crime areas, and therefore inequality, diversity, and COP implementation in these ten cities will be examined quite closely in the results and conclusion sections of the book.

COPS AHEAD[13] (Accelerated Hiring, Education, and Deployment—*AHEAD*)—This COPS Office program provided for the expedited hiring of commissioned officers to engage in community policing activities and to foster partnerships with other public agencies and community-based organizations in the community. This program related directly to the goal of placing 100,000 new officers on the streets by the end of 2000 by accelerating the process of grant application review and award announcement. The AHEAD program provided an outright subsidy of 75% of the officers' salary/benefits or $75,000 per officer hired, whichever amount is less. The grant recipient police department was required to provide the remaining 25% in local matching funds. The program constituted a one-year opportunity (1995), and estimates provided by the COPS Office reveal that a total of approximately $284 million dollars was spent on hiring nearly 4,000 new officers across the country. One hundred sixteen agencies in this study received funding from this grant program, totaling more than $136 million in grant funds and resulting in the addition of 1,805 new commissioned officers to the swelling ranks of local law enforcement (see Appendix Table 6).

COPS FAST[14] (Funding Accelerated for Smaller Towns— *FAST*)—This COPS Office grant program targeted smaller communities (populations of less than 50,000). This program was designed to foster the development of COP in smaller communities, and to provide for the deployment of new law enforcement officers to engage in COP-related activities in the nation's rural areas. Local matching requirements and grant fund allocations are the same for this program as was the case for COPS AHEAD (the lesser of 75% of an officers' salary or seventy-five thousand dollars). Because the majority of jurisdictions in this study are relatively large agencies employing 100 or more commissioned officers, only 4 of the ten departments in this study with populations lower than 50,000 residents received an award from this grant program totaling $825,000 in grant funds and resulting in the hiring of 11 new police officers.[15]

Phase 1[16] (*PHASE1*) and **Police Hiring Supplement Program** (*PHSP*)—These two programs were created to help meet the need for more officers in American cities where serious shortages of police resources could be documented. In 1993, Congress provided funds for the Police Hiring Supplement Program (PHSP); a competitive program that awarded grants to law enforcement jurisdictions to hire additional officers upon such a showing. This particular grant program was administered by the Bureau of Justice Assistance (BJA) rather than by the COPS Office, and it permitted the funding of only one out of every 10 applications. Built on the foundation of the PHSP grant application program, the COPS: Phase 1 program operated by the COPS Office was established in order to fund the 2,506 eligible jurisdictions which could not be funded under the PHSP program. The grant recipient law enforcement jurisdictions which benefited from this program were required to demonstrate a public safety need for more officers, a community policing strategy in place to address the public safety need in question, an implementation plan for the community policing strategy, and a fiscal plan for retaining the additional officers after grant funding runs out. Of the 2,506 grant applicants, 392 were awarded grants that either funded up to 75 percent of the total salary and benefits of each officer over three years, up to a maximum of $75,000 per officer, or provided for 50 percent of the covered costs. The remaining costs were paid by state and local matching funds. Forty-one agencies included in this study received funding from this COPS Office grant program (see Appendix Table 6) totaling just over $49 million and allowing for the hiring of 597 officers. Fifty-four agencies received funding under the BJA's PHSP program in the sum of $71.5 million and allowing for the acquisition of 957 new officers (see Appendix Table 6).

While the hiring of new COP officers was one important goal of the COPS Office, another was the promotion of a systematic reform of police practices in the direction of the COP philosophy of policing that draws upon problem solving strategies, the development of community partnerships, and involving citizens in the co-production of public order. The following programs reflect this second goal, and they are classified as being directed toward the promotion of innovative COP practices:

Advancing Community Policing[17] (*ACP*)—This two-dimensional grant program was designed to help police agencies further develop an organizational infrastructure to institutionalize and sustain community-policing practices for the long-term future. All eligible law enforcement agencies with an established background in community policing could apply for an ACP grant, either under the Demonstration Sites rubric (see below) or under the Advancing Community Policing (Organizational Change focus) category. Police departments which were awarded grants under the Advancing Community Policing program were those that could demonstrate they were developing strategies and initiatives designed to change their existing internal structures in order to accommodate community-policing practices on a long-term basis. Advancing Community Policing grantees were required to focus on one of the following five priority areas: Leadership and Management, Organizational Culture, Modifying Organizational Structures, Research and Planning, and Re-engineering other components of the organization. Ninety-six agencies were awarded grants under Organizational Change, totaling $16.4 in funds. No local match was required for this program; however, each law enforcement agency grant recipient's local government was strongly encouraged to contribute an in-kind match to their project. Forty-six municipal police agencies included in this study received funding under the Advancing

Community Policing program, totaling more than $20.8 million in grant dollars allocated (see Appendix Table A7).

Anti-Gang Initiative[18] *(GANGS)*—The Anti-Gang Initiative represents an innovative grant program designed to assist law enforcement agencies in addressing gang-related violence, gang-related drug problems, and the public's fear of gangs in the cities and the neighborhoods most adversely affected by gang activity. In 1996, the COPS Office identified 15 urban municipal and county police departments across the nation as having significant gang problems in their jurisdictions. Funding was provided to these jurisdictions to assist them in acquiring the necessary resources to implement strategies supportive of community policing and problem solving practices to address gang-related issues. These law enforcement agencies developed a variety of innovative programs and strategies under the auspices of this initiative, including: building partnerships with the community, schools, social service agencies, and local city agencies; utilizing geographic information systems (GIS) to identify gang hot-spots; enforcing curfew and truancy regulations; and using civil remedies, such as building code enforcement and civil abatement. Funding was also provided to these 12 agencies to evaluate the effectiveness of the various strategies employed under this grant program. Of the fourteen agencies selected to receive this COPS Office funding, 12 are part of this study and received close to $8.5 million dollars.[19]

Community Policing to Combat Domestic Violence[20] *(DV)*— The COPS office promotes a philosophy that supports organizational strategies to address the causes and reduce the fear of crime and social disorder through problem-solving tactics, the building of community policing partnerships, and the promotion of the co-production of public safety. In 1998, Congress appropriated approximately $12.5 million to create a new program entitled "Community Policing to Combat Domestic Violence." This program was established pursuant to section 1701(d) of part Q of the *Omnibus Crime Control and Safe Streets Act of 1968*. Seventy-three agencies included in this study received funding from this grant program, totaling just under $13 million in grant funds (see Appendix Table 7). In addition, assistance to study the domestic violence problem was provided to test sites (DVTS), of which ten are detailed in this study receiving $3.7 million dollars in assistance (see Appendix Table 7).

Comprehensive Communities Program[21] *(CCP)*—It is the intention of the Comprehensive Communities Program to promote local and state governments, the private sector, and neighborhood associations in reducing violent crime, drug use and abuse, and improving the quality of life in local communities. The Comprehensive Communities Program is a community-based crime prevention and crime control program that is currently in operation in sixteen jurisdictions in the nation. The COPS office coordinates budget clearances with the Office of the Comptroller relative to the community policing component of this grant program, conducts occasional site visits to review community policing activities, organizes and is a participant in BJA-sponsored conferences, and is represented at monthly CCP-TA Providers Consortium meetings. Of the 16 jurisdictions receiving funding from this grant program, 6 are included in this study, and the total award received was slightly less than $6 million in grant funds (see Appendix Table 7).

Demonstration Sites Program[22] *(DEMO)*—The Demonstration Sites Program is a 3-year grant program intended to promote broader access to a comprehensive, department-wide community-policing prototype in a few selected law enforcement agencies and communities for agencies wishing to adopt and/or further enhance their own Community Policing activities. This program is also linked to the ACP program described above. The goals of the DEMO program also include the dissemination of findings of the demonstration project to the police profession generally. The role of the COPS Office in the implementation of the Demonstration Site grants has included coordinating budget clearances with the Office of the Comptroller, notifying grantees of changes in budgets, reviewing technical proposals, conducting site visits to examine community policing activities and other compliance matters, and performing any administrative duties on an as-needed basis. Of the 13 sites funded under this program, 12 are included in this study and were awarded $3.98 million in grant funds (see Appendix Table 7). Law enforcement agencies funded under the Demonstration Centers grant category consisted of police agencies that have taken the lead in implementing the philosophy of community policing throughout their respective organizations. Grantees were required to develop strategies and tactics intended to expand and enhance their internal community policing practices, as well as develop methods to disseminate information about their community policing activities to other law enforcement agencies across the nation.

Methamphetamine Initiative[23] *(COPSMETH)* and **Other Methamphetamine** *(OTMETH)*—The purpose of these grant programs is to develop and implement innovative community-policing programs that address problems associated with methamphetamine production, distribution, and use. The COPS Methamphetamine Initiative (and other methamphetamine funding) builds on previous innovative COPS programs that allow law enforcement agencies to use advanced technologies and employ creative strategies to implement solutions to persistent crime problems associated with the manufacture and distribution of methamphetamines. It provides innovative community policing grants to a limited number of law enforcement agencies in jurisdictions with significant numbers of methamphetamine lab seizures, frequently reported deaths attributed to methamphetamine abuse, large percentages of those arrested testing positive for methamphetamine, and high numbers of reported arrests for drug dealing and possession. Grant site agencies were encouraged to develop partnerships with other local government agencies to enhance the effectiveness and sustainability of local initiatives. In FY01, funding for Methamphetamine initiatives totaled $48.3 million for this national effort. Project planning has predominantly focused on combating methamphetamine problems through training intended to help prevent trafficking in methamphetamine and detect methamphetamine operations, intelligence gathering and effective prosecution preparation, equipment purchase to develop needed infrastructure, and clean-up efforts upon the discovery of methamphetamine manufacturing by-products. Ten jurisdictions received funding under this COPS Office program are featured in this study, with the total awarded funds being just under $12.8 million (see Appendix Tables 7 and 9).

Problem Solving Partnerships[24] *(PSP)*—The Problem Solving Partnership (PSP) grant provided police agencies and their community partners the opportunity to work in collaboration to address persistent crime and disorder problems. The PSP program promoted the use of problem solving to identify crime problems, analyze why (and where) they occur, develop tailored responses based on this analysis, and assess the impact of the countermeasures adopted. All grant applicants were required to focus on one specific crime or disorder problem. Specific problems targeted included the following: Residential/

Commercial Burglary, Auto Theft, Larceny, Homicide, Assault, Rape/ Sexual Assault, Alcohol-related Problems, Street-level Drug Dealing or Drug-related Problems, and Vandalism, Prostitution or Other Disorder Problems. Additionally, an important goal of the program was to promote "learning what worked" from collaborative problem solving; consequently, agencies taking part in the program were required to select a community-based entity with which to work as their learning partner in their problem-solving effort. The PSP grants funded a variety of resources intended to enhance a community's ability to do creative problem solving, such as: computer technology, including geographic information (GIS) and mapping systems; crime analysis personnel; subject matter experts; neighborhood and environmental surveys; victim and offender interviews; community organizers; and training and technical assistance in collaborative problem-solving. All grant recipients were required to provide for an independent evaluation of their projects through a partnership with an established college or university located in their area. A total of 470 agencies were awarded grants totaling more than $39 million for the Problem Solving Partnership Program. Of those 470, 46 are included in this study, with the total awarded funds approaching $5 million (see Appendix Table 7).

Regional Community Policing Institutes[25] *(RCPI)*—Regional Community Policing Institutes[26] provide comprehensive and innovative community policing education, training and technical assistance to law enforcement agencies, local government agencies, and community members throughout a designated geographic region.

The regional institutes are intended to provide a national network of supportive technical assistance to local law enforcement agencies and to accelerate the dissemination of innovative community policing training throughout the country. A national cadre of community policing trainers, electronic dissemination of training, teams of trained police officers and citizens, and the use of multi-media approaches for training serve to provide direct access to innovative learning approaches and technical assistance for smaller jurisdictions in particular. Regional institutes have been experimenting with cutting edge ideas to challenge and improve traditional training curricula, and to develop curricula that support and sustain community-policing implementation into the future.

The areas of training provided by the regional institutes include, but are not limited to, involving community organizations in local problem solving efforts, improving delivery of technical assistance services to patrol officers, supervisors, middle managers, chief executives, civilians, and community groups, and introducing organization-wide learning opportunities in order to emphasize a range of specialty training related to the promotion of organizational change. The areas of specialty training include the topics of collaborative problem solving, partnership development, managing the stress of organizational change, developing flexible change implementation strategies, training in ethics and integrity associated with enhanced discretion for problem solving, exploring rural community policing, serving special populations (e.g., the aged, mentally ill citizens, immigrant groups), and making effective use of technology in the promotion of public safety.

It is prudent to develop the mindset that the COPS Office envisions community policing as a philosophy that promotes and supports organizational strategies intended to address the causes of crime and reduce the fear of crime and enhance public safety through problem-solving tactics and community-law enforcement partnerships. This philosophy has brought about unprecedented change in the way policing services are delivered to the community in many jurisdictions that are not likely to be successful in competing for federal grants. The development of the regional institutes has greatly expanded the reach of COP by providing localized access to COP training and technical assistance (including applied research).

One of the more critical needs often cited by law enforcement agencies is that of funding to provide for the ongoing training needs of officers. The resources available to most local law enforcement agencies fall far short of the level needed to match the scope of training necessary to advance and sustain progressive community policing programs. By establishing regional training institutes, the intent of the COPS Office was to dedicate a portion of their "discretionary" funds (resources left to the agency to allocate as opposed to being line-item entries in the agency's budget) to the effort to provide easy access to locally-based and locally-known exemplary practitioners of Community Oriented Policing. Twenty-eight grants were allocated for these regional training institutes, and of those 28 institutes six agencies in this study tallied a share of more than $12.3 million as a Regional

Center for administering COP training (see Appendix Table 7). The COPS Office claims to have trained over 77,000 individuals through the efforts of these 28 institutes.

School-Based Partnerships[27] *(SBP)*—The School-Based Partnership grant program provides police agencies the opportunity to work with school districts and community-based educational organizations to address persistent school-related crime problems. All grant applicants are required to focus on one primary school-related crime or disorder problem occurring in or around a middle or secondary school. Specific problems targeted may include the following: Drug Dealing or Use on School Grounds, Problems Experienced by Students on the Way to and from School, Assault/Sexual Assault, Alcohol Use or Alcohol-Related Behavioral Problems, Threat/Intimidation, Vandalism/Graffiti, Loitering and Disorderly Conduct Directly Related to Crime or Student Safety, Disputes that Pose a Threat to Student Safety, and Larceny. It was intended that applicants would use COP problem-solving methods to gain an understanding of the causes of the problem; develop specific, tailor-made responses to that problem; and assess the impact the responses have had in reducing the crime or disorder problem in question.

In order to help communities make use of creative problem solving to address school-related problems, this COPS Office grant program was intended to provide resources such as: computer technology; crime analysis personnel; the cost of conducting student surveys and victim/offender interviews; the cost of community organizers, school personnel and/or students involved in analyzing or coordinating the project; and training and technical assistance in collaborative problem-solving. During the 1998 grant year, School-Based Partnership funds were awarded to 155 law enforcement agencies with a total of $16.5 million being allocated to these school/police collaborative efforts. An additional 124 police agencies received supplements to their existing grants, totaling $1.9 million.

There were over 320 applicants for this program from across the nation. No local match is required under the School-Based Partnerships program, although each applicant law enforcement agency was strongly encouraged to contribute an in-kind match to their project. In 1999, School-Based Partnerships grant announcements for this program took place in August. The award period was for one year, and the official start date for these grants was August 1, 1999. The School-Based

Partnerships program awarded more than $13.2 million to 120 law enforcement agencies in 1999. Of these 319 police agencies, 31 are included in this analysis totaling just over $5.2 million in grant funding (see Appendix Table 8).

Troops to Cops[28] *(TROOPS)*—The Troops to Cops 1999 program is designed to encourage the hiring of recently separated military veterans to serve as law enforcement officers. The ultimate goal of the program is to help ease the transition of eligible members of the armed forces into community policing positions across the nation. The Troops to Cops 1999 program was sponsored by the U.S. Department of Justice. This one-year grant provided reimbursement of up to $25,000 per veteran to defray the cost of hiring expenses for eligible military veterans selected for employment as local law enforcement officers. The program is designed to complement the COPS Universal Hiring Program (UHP), which funds 75 percent of an officer's three-year entry level salary and benefits, up to a maximum of $75,000.

Under Troops to Cops 1999, law enforcement agencies that hired qualified veterans with their UHP grant were eligible to receive additional funding for academy and field training, supplemental community policing training, uniforms, and basic issue equipment. In 1999, Troops to COPS grants were awarded to 259 agencies across the country, benefiting nearly 500 veterans. The 1995 Troops to COPS program also funded 500 veterans. Fifty-six agencies in this study received funding under the Troops to Cops grant program in the amount of $2.15 million (see Appendix Table 8).

Youth Firearms Violence Initiative[29] *(YFVI)*—The Youth Firearm Violence Initiative program is designed to assist local law enforcement agencies in developing programs and action strategies to combat the incidence of youth firearm violence. In 1995, the COPS Office provided funding to ten police departments across the nation to support targeted, focused enforcement efforts directed at combating the rise of youth firearm violence. The Youth Firearms Violence Initiative encouraged each of the selected jurisdictions to employ citizen-engaging community policing approaches to develop or enhance programs designed to: 1) decrease the number of violent crimes committed by youth; 2) reduce firearms-related gang offenses; and 3) reduce firearms-related drug offenses in their cities and neighborhoods. The fundamentals of community policing,—i.e., problem solving, community partnerships, and co-production of public safety [crime prevention through citizen-initiated action]—were central in the development of tactics used under this COPS Office grant program. Common strategies that were funded included: developing/enhancing partnerships with schools, community—based groups and associations, probation/parole agencies; using civil remedies at the neighborhood level, such as code enforcement and civil abatement; and utilizing directed patrol and overtime to enforce zero tolerance policies. Funding was also provided to the 10 agencies in question to evaluate the effectiveness of the various strategies employed under this grant.

The formal announcement for this program took place in September of 1995. All YFVI grant awards were made for a one-year period, with no-cost extensions granted on a case-by-case basis. A total of $10 million was made available under the YFVI program, and each selected site was eligible to receive up to $1 million. There was no local match required; however, each agency was encouraged to contribute an in-kind match. Eight agencies included in this study received funding under this grant program, totaling more than $6.7 million in grant funds (see Appendix Table 8).

Value Based Initiative[30] **(*VBI*)**—Faith community partnerships and innovation in outreach efforts are the key components of VBI grant program. The key idea lying behind the VBI program is that the drawing together of the law enforcement and the religious communities offers many benefits to a community concerned over public safety issues. Additionally, VBI is intended to provide enhancements to local COP efforts by establishing additional links between citizens and existing community resources and services, allowing the community to participate in the dialogue that can develop regarding social issues that hinder quality of life in communities, developing and coordinating community crisis plans, and allowing the community to take the lead as a major participant in efforts to reduce crime. COPS Office awards totaling more than $2.1 million were allocated to nine cities included in this study (see Appendix Table 8).

Alternative to 911[31] **(*ALTEMERG*)**—Developing an alternative to the established 911 systems has been seen as one way to improve customer service and more effectively manage the deployment of uniformed officers and other crisis intervention units. The "311" access number for non-emergencies grant program allows funding for agencies to implement an easy to remember hotline for citizens to call when their situation does not warrant immediate response because of a life threatening incident, but nonetheless represents an important message to pass on to law enforcement authorities from a concerned citizen. The 311 number was reserved as a national non-emergency use number by the Federal Communications Commission (FCC) in 1997, and it is used on a voluntary basis in communities deciding to adopt the access number. Twelve jurisdictions received COPS Office funding in the amount of $5.5 million to support 311 implementation, and to document whether this effort can alleviate some of the stress placed on their 911 System. Close to $4 million was awarded to seven cities included in this study (see Appendix Table 8) to examine the effects of an alternative to 911.

Justice-Based After School Program[32] (*JBAS*)—This COPS Office pilot program was designed to assist agencies with furthering their collaborative, crime prevention programs relating to youthful offenders. Established in 2000, this COPS Office program has provided just under $3 million in order to assist local law enforcement and community service agencies such as Boys Clubs, YMCAs, Youth Centers, Police Athletic Leagues, etc. with the development of high quality after-school educational and recreational programs. A chief goal of the JBAS assistance program was to reduce juvenile crime and to minimize juvenile victimization in high-crime neighborhoods, and to improve the quality of life in those communities where opportunities for constructive youth activities are particularly limited by socio-economic disadvantage. Two local police agencies included in this study received $664,460 in JBAS assistance under this COPS Office program (see Appendix Table 7).

Problem Solvers/Peacemakers[33] (*PSPM*)—The COPS Office created the *PSPM* funding program to encourage law enforcement agencies to strengthen or expand existing local programs that reflect the "best practices"[34] approach in building trust between the police and their respective communities. In June of 1999, the United States Attorney General convened a national conference entitled "Strengthening Police-Community Relationships." The main focus of this national conference was the examination of the need to identify those police practices in greatest need of reform in order to build public trust in law enforcement. One aspect of this examination included the desire to reduce police misconduct, and to enhance police integrity. One lesson that was learned from this conference was that the police can be most effective in their work when they have the trust and cooperation of the residents they serve. However, in many communities, a disturbing lack of trust in law enforcement among residents continues to surface. Allegations of corruption, racial profiling, and excessive force have exacerbated tension in ethnically diverse communities, in particular.

As a result of the discussions that arose at this national conference, working groups were convened to problem-solve these troublesome issues. The working groups identified some "routine" police-citizen encounters (e.g., traffic stops and pedestrian stops) as a source of potential conflict and tension, especially in communities where citizens believe that police actions are taken based on racial stereotypes or bias. Other themes that surfaced included developing systems for accountability, proper supervision of officers in the field, proactive interventions to reduce crime and disorder, and changing the way police agencies manage recruitment campaigns by targeting racially diverse applicants. The working groups concluded that by developing programs that promote police as problem solvers and peacemakers, law enforcement could demonstrate that police officers can be effective in reducing crime in communities featuring ethnically diverse populations. In addition, the groups resolved that while keeping neighborhoods safe is a primary concern for law enforcement, the achievement of this goal should not come at the expense of disregard for Constitutional rights and the condoning of discriminatory police practices by police managers. It was decided that law enforcement officers should endeavor to treat all citizens in a respectful and dignified manner in the course of the performance of their law enforcement duties.

In Sacramento, CA, COPS Office funds are currently being used to collect and analyze vehicle stop data so that police may address concerns about racial profiling and biased policing. Sacramento will attempt to produce a best practices approach for the collection of vehicle stop data so that this information can be used by other agencies to assess routine interactions between police and citizens. The Sacramento Police Department will also provide technical support and advice for any agency wishing to replicate their racial profiling evaluation model. This type of funding can help police agencies to examine how the level, type, and quality of interaction between police and citizens affects their efforts to develop collaborative partnerships aimed at making communities safe while improving the quality of life for all citizens, regardless of their race, religion, or ethnic background.[35]

Targeted[36] *(TARGETED)*—The targeted police recruitment program was established in 1998 to develop police recruitment programs designed to recruit particular "critical skill" personnel. Targeted police recruitment programs focused on applicants from diverse technical and ethnic backgrounds and special communities (e.g., immigrant groups) by providing advertising assistance and tutorial programs designed to enable these individuals to meet police force academic requirements and to pass entrance exams. It also provided counseling for applicants who encounter problems during the application process, and supported programs designed to retain these officers once they were brought on board. Two cities in this study were awarded more than $159,000 to develop targeted recruitment efforts under this program (see Appendix Table 7).

Integrity[37] *(INTEG)*—The integrity program was designed to assist law enforcement agencies with assessing how the increased discretion that is afforded to officers under COP affects the way officers respond to various ethical decision dilemmas faced in serving the community. In addition, funding under the integrity program provides training in how appropriate discretion should be employed in police supervision. Racial profiling training is just one area of such concern, and numerous police agencies have used grant funds under the integrity program to acquire such training. A total of 17 cities included in this study received $4.29 million in Integrity Program funds (see 3.F).

Cops in Community Prosecution Program[38] *(CICP)*—This program was predicated on the assumption that having full-time sworn officers linked with community prosecutors (such as in the Spokane County Sheriff's Department Edgecliff Problem Solving Partnership) would enable a more efficient medium for victims of crime to participate in the prosecutorial process that is centrally located (e.g., assignment of officer/prosecutor to a community substation). Two agencies in this study received close to $500,000 dollars to implement this type of innovative, victim-oriented approach to criminal prosecution (see Appendix Table 8).

Specialized Training and Technical Assistance Pilot Studies *(TTA)* and **Problem Solving Collaborations** *(PPSECA)*—The COPS Office allocated funding to provide training and technical assistance to agencies engaged in advanced stages of COP implementation. More than 2,500 agencies have received general COP training, but only one agency in this study is identified in the allocations for this training in the sum of $495,592 (see Appendix Table 8). Training and applied research dollars were allocated to Reno, NV in a two-part grant that allowed for the development of a new Field Training Officers (FTO) program that incorporates principles that foster the propagation of COP and promote community collaboration. In addition, a manual was designed and distributed to Charlotte, NC, Lowell, MA, Richmond, CA, San Diego, CA, Savannah, GA, and Colorado Springs, CO with the intent of monitoring whether law enforcement was now approaching "best practice" in educating newly hired officers.

One study that specifically discussed the present state of FTO programs in police agencies was conducted by Langworthy, Hughes, and Sanders (1995). Their study revealed that not only were less experienced officers assigned FTO duties, but that many of the agencies included in their sample rotated officers with insufficient job experience into the role of trainer and evaluator of inexperienced academy graduates. Their research also revealed that the number of FTO hours had changed as well, but not for the better. Research on training can provide scholars with rich information about the effects specific instructional/training modules can have on how police perform their duties. Many COP advocates have argued that an increase in level of educational attainment among police is one important way to enhance the longevity of COP practices. The PPSECA program in Washington, DC represents another innovative effort present in the one agency included in this study. In Washington, DC, the COPS Office awarded $725 thousand dollars with the main goals of this award being to establish problem solving networks in the community. It was very difficult to find any information on the specific goals and objectives of PPSECA. After numerous telephone calls to the COPS Office in DC and with the DC Metropolitan Police, it was still vague as to what type of specific problem or partner is involved with this funding allocation.

Problem Solving Partnership Evaluation[39] (*PSPEVAL*)—The PSPEVAL grants were awarded to study the effects of a subset of the Problem Solving Partnership grants awarded to agencies to explore the relationship between specific problems in the community and the interventions that were designed to reduce the incidence of the problem in question. Four hundred and seventy agencies received PSP grants, and of the 46 PSP agencies included in this study, only six communities received a follow-up award to evaluate the effects of the intervention undertaken (see Appendix Table 6). In addition to these major evaluation studies, the COPS Office mandated that all PSP grant recipients devote 10% of their grant award to evaluating the effect of their efforts by establishing a partnership with a local college or university.

Training and Technical Assistance[40] *(TTA)*—Training and Technical Assistance has been operationalized in many forms, with no single model program being present in any given agency. Six cities in this research study have received $816,326 for training and technical assistance, often found in the form of conferences, workshops, and in-service education regarding COP implementation.

Each of the programs discussed above has been categorized as either an award that fosters traditional police patrol activities by increasing manpower (e.g., hire officers to increase patrol capacity and coverage) or one where the primary purpose of the funding was to implement innovative programs to improve the quality of life for residents in the community. In sum, 13 grants were developed by the COPS Office to foster the hiring of police officers with the underlying premise being that the addition of these officers to the ranks of the police would foster the development of lasting COP programs and practices. Additionally, the COPS Office made funds available to agencies seeking budgetary enhancements to implement proactive strategies that improve community relations and strengthen community partnerships, with the focus of collaborative efforts being to improve the overall quality of life in the broader community. The COPS Office created 23 programs to achieve this goal.

The amount of COPS Office funding for hiring programs totaled $1,654,198,465 and the total funds allocated for innovative programs summed to $138,808,165. This equates to a grand total of $1,793,006,630[41] or 24% of the budget allocated for administering all of the COP grant programs ($7.5 billion). It should be noted that these 202 agencies comprise only 1% of the 17,000+ law enforcement agencies in the United States, yet they received close to 1/4 of the funds allocated to implement and advance COP practices. In the data analysis section of this study, the relationship between the monetary awards made by the COPS Office and the breadth of COP activity within each department will be explored to examine the impact this federal subsidy has had on the development of COP among larger law enforcement agencies and in major urban communities across the United States. The information provided in this study provides a sound foundation to build upon when studying the COP national planned change phenomenon, and when seeking to discern where the architecture of policing has experienced the greatest amount of change as a consequence of the COP movement. More specifically, because this sample of agencies has received a significant portion of the $7.5 million in federal funds allocated to implement COP, examining the evolution of COP will be enhanced by examining the organizational and community dynamics in these 202 agencies.

Data detailed above that was originally acquired through the Freedom of Information Act from the COPS Office, the 1993, 1997, and 1999 LEMAS surveys, and the 1990 Report of the Census were used to create the 13 variables noted in Table 3.1 below. These variables will be used to ascertain the social equity dimension of this policy impact analysis with regard to how funding was allocated across this group of 202 cities.

Table 3.1: Funding and demographic variables

(To be used in the examination of equity)

Dependent variable	Label and method of computation
LEVEL7$	Total monetary award dollar per household

Independent variable	Label and method of computation
PERS93	Total person crimes in 1993 per 10, 000 households
PROP93	Total property crimes in 1993 per 10,000 households
HH	Coefficient for household income per 1990 Census
MEDHH	Median household income per 1990 Census
EDTOTALS	Percentage of population in 1990 with less than HS diploma
EMTPOS93	Percentage of vacant positions in 1993 to authorized full-time sworn positions
BLACKPOP	Percentage of Blacks per 1990 Census
HEROETH1	Rodney Hero measure of white ethnic diversity
HISPPOP	Percentage of Hispanics per 1990 Census
OFFHH93	1993 total sworn officers per 10,000 households per 1990 Census
HH1990	Total households per 1990 Census
ASIANPOP	Percentage of Asians per 1990 Census

LEMAS Data

This periodic survey of police agencies, administered by the Bureau of Justice Statistics' program on Law Enforcement and Administrative Statistics (LEMAS) since 1987, presents information on five types of general-purpose law enforcement agencies: state police, county police, special police (state and local), municipal police, and sheriff's departments. For the purpose of this particular research effort, data will be drawn from municipal agencies exclusively. Variables in the LEMAS studies include size of the population served, demographics of department personnel, spending levels, a listing of various specialized functions that might be performed by the department, average salary levels for uniformed officers, personnel policies, training programs, and other matters related to agency management. Data from three administrations of LEMAS surveys (1993, 1997, and 1999) will be used to measure various organizational factors that are known to be associated with the successful implementation of COP principles. As there are many different views of the proper definition of COP, this study will proceed on the premise that the number of dollars (per capita) received under the 1994 Crime Bill, breadth of operation of COP-type programs, number (proportion of uniformed workforce) of officers assigned to perform tasks associated with COP, and whether community input is sought and used by the department are all organizational variables that can be linked to the COP philosophy and can be used as an effective measure of how COP is being employed in large, mid-size, and small departments. The primary variables that will be used in the assessment of the degree of adoption and implementation of COP in municipal police agencies are as follows:

- Changes in the number of sworn officers over the six-year span
- Percentage of officer resources devoted to COP in 1999
- Total number of officers per household in 1999
- Number of vacant positions as percentage of total authorized full-time sworn officers
- Presence of geographic patrol units
- Encouraged use of the SARA model
- Training of new recruits in COP

- Training of citizens in COP

- Number of officers acquired through COP grants (per 10,000 households)

- Number of COP officers as proportion of total full-time sworn officers

- Number of School Resource Officers (SROs) as a proportion of total full-time sworn officers

- Total number of volunteers as a proportion of population

- Number of fixed neighborhood substations per 100 full-time sworn officers

- The presence or absence of involvement with problem solving partnerships

- Whether the agency has developed a COP plan

In addition, data from each year of LEMAS reporting can be used to explore the number of training hours required (academy training), required levels of education (HS, GED, AA, BA, etc.), and whether the agency offers additional pay as an incentive for police officers to pursue higher education. For a complete descriptive listing of variables taken from the LEMAS data collections, see Appendix Tables 3, 4, and 5.

Grouping agencies into categories that reflect a high level of COP activity, a medium level, and a low level will provide an opportunity to assess the factors associated with an agency's level of commitment to COP implementation. In the 1993 LEMAS survey (the baseline year), there are no specific references to COP programs; however, the LEMAS report for that year does provide information about the existence of special units within a department. The presence of such units will be used to assess the breadth of an agencies' innovation at that point in time. In the 1997 LEMAS report, there is far more information about the levels of COP orientation and there are detailed descriptions of programs included in the reporting of specialized unit activities that exist within a given police department. The fullest portrayal of COP activity is presented in the 1999 LEMAS report. Herein community-based partnerships and the range of contacts maintained with the broader community public are annotated in a special section devoted to exploring the breadth of COP activities. This research will draw heavily on this particular information to determine the various levels of COP activity in operation and the extent of funding received over the course of the past 6 years of major COP promotional activity on the part of the federal COPS Office. In order to create a composite measure of COP activity, indicators for the presence of COP-oriented programs were added together and then scaled to indicate a low, medium, or high degree of involvement in COP.

CENSUS DATA

Census data represent one of the most widely used sources of information to report on the American condition employed by the social sciences. Again, it should be noted that the role of **income inequality** and **poverty** in the production of violent crime has been examined from a wide range of theoretical perspectives, including social disorganization (Shaw and McKay, 1942), anomie theory (Merton, 1938), Marxist theory (Bonger, 1916; Gordon, 1971), and macrostructural theory (Blau and Blau, 1982). Even policy process differences receive attention with regard to race and crime in the form of analysis done by Wolpert (1999), who reports on the relationship between race and crime and the opposing theories that govern the policy formation process. Track-level Census data were used by Kovandzic, Vieraitas, and Yeisley (1998) as critical contextual variables in their exploration of the relationships among the structural covariates of murder rates in urban areas.

When using Census data it has been noted by some researchers that smaller political or geographical areas (such as cities rather than SMSAs) tend to be more homogenous social communities than larger aggregations, and that they prove to be a more reliable units of analysis when investigating issues such as crime, income inequality, and the allocation of public funds (Bailey, 1984; Messner, 1982; Messner and Tardiff, 1986; Parker, 1989). One study of note that deals with the allocation of public funds for the distribution of welfare payments in large metropolitan counties (SMSAs) was conducted by DeFronzo and Hannon (1998). This study employed data from 406 counties that had populations larger than 100,000, that had a metropolitan Census designation, and that had available county-level UCR crime data. The results of this study revealed that the measure cost-of-living-adjusted Aid to Families with Dependent Children (AFDC) payments per recipient person was found to have an independent, direct negative impact on homicide rates and a separate, indirect negative relationship to homicide rates through its association with household status.

All demographic data assembled for this research effort were drawn from the 1990 Report of the Census and will be used to compute racial and ethnic diversity measures within each community, the total number of households present, the total number of families in residence, and the levels of 1989 income for both households and families in each of the 202 cities included in this study. These data will be used to examine whether communities with high levels of racial and ethnic diversity and income inequality, that are arguably the most in need of creating community partnerships through community policing, have received their fair share of COPS Office grants based on the level of grant awards received and on the level of commitment to and implementation of the COP philosophy. A list of census variables (degree of ethnic variation, population, household population, and family unit population) can also be found in Appendix Table 1.

INEQUALITY MEASURES

As previously noted, Census data can be a valuable tool in the analysis of the effects of community cohesion on the implementation of public policy (see Braithwaite, 1979; Giorgi and Pohoryles, 1999; Kelly, 2000; and Tanninen, 1999). Some of the more prominent scholars (Donahue, 1999; Levernier, 1999; Madden, 2000; O'Connor, 2001, Ryscavage, 1999; St. John, 2002) have examined levels of income disparity in communities using the **coefficient**. When looking at some of the important literature on socioeconomic conditions and crime, it can be noted that Thornberry and Farnworth (1982) investigated the social correlates of criminal behavior and the relationship between social status and criminal behavior. In addition, Hirshi (1969:67) found that "if socioeconomic status is unrelated to delinquency, then consistency requires that socioeconomic status be removed from the dictionary of delinquency theory and research." A major question that presents itself in this study is whether social class demographic characteristics of communities are related to the allocation of COP funding and to the pattern of implementation of COP programs and practices in cities. A list of coefficients for each jurisdiction is included in Appendix Table 2.

Within criminal justice scholarship, research on the connection between levels of crime and income inequality has been a ripe subject during the past decade. For example, research done by Wright et al. (1999:175-176) found that low socioeconomic status (SES) promotes delinquency by "increasing individuals' alienation, financial strain, and aggression and by decreasing educational and occupational aspirations, whereas high SES promoted individuals delinquency by increasing risk taking and social power and by decreasing conventional values." This type of analysis reaffirms that there are an array of variables to consider when pressing the assumption that the poor and underprivileged are more prone to criminal activity than their more privileged counterparts.

One of the strongest and most cited pieces of criminal justice research on police and their ability to control crime by enhancing manpower was conducted by Kelling et al. (1973). The Kansas City Patrol experiment found that traditional routine patrol in marked police cars does not affect the level of crime, nor does it have an impact on the public's feeling of security. The experiment further demonstrated that urban police departments can successfully test patrol deployment strategies, and that they can manipulate patrol resources without unduly jeopardizing public safety. The study also revealed that levels of crime, fear of crime, and perceptions of police service delivery were not positively affected by a show of force (e.g., putting more police officers in cars thereby increasing their visibility to the public).

When considering the development of COP, it is important to explore issues other than sheer manpower and fiscal enhancements if we are to get a true picture of what is happening with regard to public safety in communities that received federal COP subsidies. Levels of crime in neighborhoods with little or no vested interest in the quality of community have also been studied in order to assess the types of interventions police should develop to address feelings of disenfranchisement. William Julius Wilson (1998:8) describes the population of disenfranchised inner-city residents (or underclass) being composed of those "groups who have been left behind and are collectively different from those that lived in these same neighborhoods" in different times. In addition, Wilson (1998:30) indicates that "there is no single explanation for the racial or ethnic variations in the rates of social dislocation experienced by poor, inner-city dwellers," but rather "there are several interrelated explanations that represent a comprehensive set of variables—including societal, demographic, and neighborhood variables" that are responsible for high crime rates in the inner city, high rates of joblessness, the presence of many single parent-headed households that contribute to the demise of life for conventional inner-city dwellers.

Apart from the analysis by Wilson in 1980, crime rates in the 1990s have seen the most dramatic sustained decline since data on crime have been collected systematically (Rennison, 2000). In the realm of policing, Eck and Maguire (2000) argue that the areas that have experienced significant reductions in violent crime have not necessarily been exposed to some type of innovation in police services delivery, as the levels of crime were already declining prior to the implementation of COP type police programs. Given this disparity in assessments as to the effects of local demographics, socioeconomic status, and delivery of police services, it is now more important than ever to examine whether funding police-community partnerships is something we should continue to do. This brings us to the literature on organizations and organizational change, and why it is important to make a statement about the condition of agencies that are expanding their operational reach and modifying their beliefs about how best to accomplish their goals of enhancing public safety and improving the quality of life in communities across the nation.

There are several ways to express the degree of income inequality present in a society. One way is to rank the units of measure (e.g., persons, families, or households) from poorest to richest; divide this hierarchy into fifths (quintiles) or tenths (deciles), and compute the average income by quintiles or deciles. Comparisons can then be made between the average wealth of the rich and the poor quintiles or deciles. Results may also be expressed as a ratio of each group's income compared to that of the societal income as a whole. The resultant information is commonly known as the index.

Two indices were used in this study: one pertaining to family income and the other pertaining to household income. Household income refers to income generated by all members of a household, not limited to family relationships. This grouping includes single persons living alone as well as conventional family units. The average income of the nation's 68.1 million families is higher, and their income distribution more equal, than the 28.2 million non-family households, due in part to the fact that the latter group includes a number of poorer persons living alone. Unfortunately, the U.S. Census Bureau only began reporting income data for households in 1967; therefore, longer-term comparisons must use the family income figures. Figure 3.1 represents a graphic depiction of income distribution taken from the index compared with the egalitarian ideal. The quintile divisions are displayed along the horizontal axis, and the cumulative share of income follows the vertical axis. For example, for 1968, the cumulative value for quintile 1 is the share earned by quintile 1, or 4.2%; that for quintile 2, 11.1%+4.2%, or 15.3%; and so on, up to quintile 5, when the sum is 100%. The graph plots these values for 1968 and 1992. These lines are termed "Lorenz Curves" (see Figure 3.1 below).

In a society with perfectly equal income distribution, the cumulative share of income would be equal to the cumulative population share; e.g., the value for quintile 2 would be 40% (20%+20%), instead of the actual value reported in 1968: 15.3%. The unbroken 45° line represents a mythical egalitarian society. The gap between the actual lines and the mythical line of perfect equity is a function of the degree of inequality present in the given society. Utilizing this graphical representation, it is immediately apparent that income inequality was more pronounced in 1992 than in 1968. The index measures the gap between the census information as represented in the broken line and the egalitarian ideal as represented by the unbroken line. In an equitable society, the index would be 0.000, since the Lorenz curve would match the 45° line perfectly. Therefore, the higher the numbers in the index, the greater the degree of unequal income distribution.

Figure 3.1: Lorenz Curve

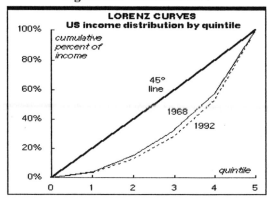

For the United States, indices are computed using a sample of some 60,000 households polled by the Census Bureau every March as part of its Current Population Survey. For this study, indices are computed using the figures reported in 1990 Census data.

UNIFORM CRIME REPORT DATA

Since 1930, the FBI has compiled the Uniform Crime Reports (UCR) to serve as periodic nationwide assessments of reported crimes not available elsewhere in the criminal justice system. By 1985, there were approximately 17,000 law enforcement agencies contributing reports either directly or through their state reporting programs. Each year, this information is reported in four types of files:

- Offenses Known and Clearances by Arrest
- Property Stolen and Recovered
- Supplementary Homicide Reports (SHR)
- Police Employee (LEOKA) Data

Offenses known and clearances by arrest data files include monthly data on the number of UCR Index offenses reported, and the number of offenses cleared by arrest or other means. The counts include all reports of Index Crimes (excluding arson) received from victims, officers who discovered infractions, or other sources. The Property Stolen and Recovered data are collected on a monthly basis by all UCR contributing agencies. These data, aggregated at the agency level, record the nature of the crime, the monetary value of the property stolen, and the type of property stolen. Similar information regarding recovered property is also included in the UCR data. The Supplementary Homicide Reports provide incident-based information on criminal homicides. Further, the data provided monthly by UCR agencies contain information describing the victim of the homicide, the offender, and the relationship between victim and offender. The Police Employee (LEOKA) Data provide information about law enforcement officers killed or assaulted (hence the acronym, LEOKA) in the line of duty. The variables created from the LEOKA forms provide in-depth information on the circumstances surrounding killings or assaults, including type of call answered, type of weapon used, and type of patrol to which the officers in question were assigned.

Crime reporting data have served as an important tool for policy analysts since the inception of the Uniform Crime Reports, and it has been used to analyze injustice, to assess level of crime occurring, and to identify gaps in police crime data (Anderson, 1997; Beckett and Sasson, 2000; LaFree, 1999; Maltz, 1999; and Wolpert 1999). Unfortunately, there are some problematic aspects of the UCR indexing of crimes in this reporting mechanism. One of these problems concerns the systematic reporting and uniform classification of crimes. For example, if the same person committed two crimes, only the most serious crime is reported as a Type One offense. This hierarchy rule is based upon the logic that in a multiple-offense situation (i.e., one wherein several offenses are committed at the same time and in the same place), after classifying all Type One offenses, only the highest-ranking offense is recorded and all others are ignored, regardless of the number of offenders and victims involved. In addition, only crimes known to police are included in Type One offenses of the UCR. This presents a problem for the researcher in terms of the accurate presentation of crime data. People do not report crime for a variety of reasons (i.e., they may feel the crime is a personal matter, they may not want to get involved, they may believe police cannot help, or they may fear personal retaliation from the offender) (LaGrange, 1998). Among some Type One crimes, some offenses are less likely to be reported than others. It has been estimated that approximately 50 percent of robberies, burglaries, and aggravated assaults are never reported to police, and only 32 percent of rapes and 27 percent of larceny-theft crimes are reported (U.S. Department of Justice, 1994).

For purposes of this study, data from the Uniform Crime Reports (UCR) were collected for the years 1993, 1997, and 1999 for Type One offenses (murder and non-negligent manslaughter, forcible rape, robbery, aggravated assault, burglary, larceny-theft, motor vehicle theft, and arson) in each jurisdiction under study (see Appendix Table 5). It should be noted that for practical purposes, the reporting of offenses known is limited to the selected crime classifications because they are the crimes most likely to be reported and most likely to occur with sufficient frequency to provide an adequate basis for comparison. Because the American public develops perceptions of the crime problem in substantial part by taking notice of these top eight offenses, and also because political platforms about proper interventions are built using this data source, the measure of Type One offenses will be useful for this study. In addition, it may be that the public is especially concerned about these eight street-type[42] crimes represented in the index of Type One offenses. It should be noted that although Type One offenses are important in shaping perceptions of crime, they are not the only laws police must enforce or that may concern the public. Type One offenses will be used in this analysis as a measure of "need" in communities related to levels of COP involvement, income inequality, ethnic diversity, and the federal subsidy of COP activities.

As noted above, the types of data assembled for this study have been widely used in the past when discussions of income inequality are brought forward, when discussions of crime and public policy are undertaken, and when discussions of how policy is affected by the level of minority presence within a community. In the subsequent chapters, the police organizational data will be analyzed within the context of income inequality, ethnic variation in communities (and in law enforcement agencies), levels of crime, and the amount of funding received from the federal government to implement COP strategies. As noted earlier, the diverse set of measures assembled for this particular sample of agencies will provide a rich foundation for research efforts beyond the limited scope of this preliminary analysis of the implementation of Community Oriented Policing in law enforcement agencies employing more than 100 sworn officers.

CHAPTER FOUR

Establishing Hypotheses and Analyzing the Data

INTRODUCING THE MAJOR QUESTIONS

This study is concerned with exploring two major questions with regard to the examination of the COP experiment in American Policing. The first deals with issues of social equity and policy implementation. Did the ultimate pattern of distribution of COPS Office grant funds take into account issues of need such as the prevalence of crime and the presence of ethnic diversity in the sample of 202 major municipal police agencies included in this study?[43] In particular, did low crime areas receive a disproportionate amount of federal grant money? Did communities with high levels of ethnic diversity get too little money in comparison to ethnically homogeneous communities? These are important questions for policy makers and policy analysts to be concerned with inasmuch as the large-scale investment of federal government funds in a comprehensive attempt to produce change in law enforcement is a concern both for those who study public policy dynamics and outcomes and those who follow the development of policing practices in the United States.

A second, and equally important inquiry deals with what was done with the funds received by these agencies. Was it the case that jurisdictions that received significant COPS Office funds actually did adopt COP practices and policies? Or, did they instead use those funds to "staff up patrol" while reinforcing the traditional reactive model of American Policing? Did highly grant-funded agencies actually engage in COP development? Did poorly funded agencies adopt COP practices less frequently than their highly funded counterparts? Further, was it the case that the effects of COP grant funding differ among large, mid-size, and small jurisdictions? The data presented in these analyses will address these major questions about the COP experiment in American Policing. In order to appropriately examine the presence or absence of relationships between funding levels and COP implementation, it is important to examine some of the core concepts associated with COP, social equity, and the Rodney Hero "theory of minority representation and policy implementation." The analyses presented in this chapter will attempt to clarify some important policy issues, the first and most important being whether the COP funding effort has been equitable in its distribution and whether agencies which received COP funding are in fact doing COP-type activities within their communities.

The first set of analyses will test the following hypothesis relating to social equity in the operation of the COPS Office grant program:

The level of COP award per household is affected by levels of diversity present in each jurisdiction, where crime problems are a factor, where economic inequalities are present, where the population is generally low on the scale of educational attainment, and where the level of sworn officers per household is low.

SOCIAL EQUITY ISSUES

When looking at how the COPS Office grant program has been implemented over its relatively short lifetime, the data compiled for this research will be used to ascertain whether factors such as high levels of crime, low levels of educational attainment, and the presence of ethnic diversity affect the granting of COPS Office funds to promote COP adoption. In the worst-case scenario, low crime, economically prosperous and socially homogenous communities received a disproportionate amount of COPS Office grant money. In the best-case scenario vis-à-vis social equity, high diversity and high crime areas containing economically disadvantaged people received disproportionate amounts of COPS Office money. In addition, in keeping with contemporary theories of social diversity in the context of social order and crime control, Rodney Hero (1998) argues that diversity issues are strongly related to the means used to achieve social order. A more detailed discussion of the Hero theory is presented below.

With respect to social equity concerns, H. George Frederickson (1990) also believes that good public policy and fair planning practices should include dimensions of social equity when examining how policy is designed, implemented, and analyzed with respect to ultimate societal outcomes. More importantly, according to Frederickson, it is the duty of public agency planners and public administrators to ensure that the social equity dimension receives adequate attention when providing public service and administering public policy. Because the COPS Office funding program represents a very large-scale federal public policy initiative, social equity becomes an important consideration in any analysis of the dispersion of funds aimed at improving policing services and enhancing social order in America.

Building on Frederickson's concern for social equity, Hero and his colleague Tolbert (1996) examined the effects of racial diversity and direct democracy electoral mechanisms in the analysis of California's illegal immigration initiative and analyzed the role that social heterogeneity brings to the policy sphere. Their findings revealed that support for this measure was particularly high in **bifurcated counties** where Latino populations were above average and white populations were dominant (Hero and Tolbert, 1996:816). Although this examination dealt specifically with patterns of voter participation, it is clear that there are theoretical implications that can be drawn with regard to the way policy is designed and implemented at the state and national level as well. A more thorough examination of this theory follows below.

THE HERO THEORY OF STATE POLITICS

One of the independent variables used in this research effort is the indicator of white ethnic diversity developed along the lines specified by Rodney Hero (HEROETH1). As noted in chapter three, this index is comprised of the total number of Greek, Hungarian, Irish, Italian, Polish, Portuguese, and Russian descendants who choose one of the above as their first ancestry in the 1990 Report of the Census. Hero (1998:3) contends that the "political and social status of ethnic/racial minorities groups in the United States may be characterized as *two-tiered pluralism*." The belief behind this line of thought is that even in the presence of what Hero calls procedural or formal democracy, a full manifestation of democracy has yet to be realized by many ethnic/racial minorities living in the United States. Hero argues that race and ethnicity continue to be pervasive influences in the political and social system, and that political coalitions and campaigns for public office are affected in noteworthy ways by the presence of ethnic/racial groups in a jurisdiction; the public policy consequences of these political factors, in turn, affect the character of public policies adopted in those jurisdictions.

As there is a difference in the degree of dispersion and concentration of ethnic and racial groups such as Blacks, Hispanics, and Asians across the nation which has been well noted by scholars, Hero contends that there are also pockets of "white ethnics" which serve to produce distinctive politics and political policy outcomes in local jurisdictions across the country as well (Hero, 1998:6). Although Hero discusses this phenomenon at the state level so that he can contrast his findings with those analyses of political culture developed by Daniel Elazar (1966) and Joel Lieske (1994), the presence of white ethnic diversity can be used for the purpose of this analysis in order to ascertain whether the presence of these white "subgroups" has any effect on the solicitation and subsequent granting of COPS Office funds.

Social diversity can be assessed at any level of population aggregation, but considering the presence of the above-noted ancestral groups in the jurisdictions represented in this study tests for the presence of social diversity effects on the application for and subsequent allocation of COPS Office funds. Hero classifies the state diversity patterns present in the United States, and analyzes their effect on public policy, as noted in Figure 4.1 below.

Figure 4.1: State types in Hero analysis [44]

Racial Ethnic Group	Homogenous	Heterogeneous	Bifurcated
White (Northern and Western European)	HIGH	MODERATE	HIGH
White Ethnic (Southern and Eastern European)	LOW	HIGH	LOW
Minority (Black/Latino/Asian)	LOW	MODERATE	HIGH

The analysis presented in this chapter features a social diversity variable which includes elements of all three categories of diversity defined by Hero. The measure **HEROETH1** represents the presence of "white ethnics" claiming a heritage different from Anglo-Saxon or Scandinavian. Interestingly, taken as a whole, this study is comprised of nearly 61 million people who reside in the 202 jurisdictions in this study. Of the 248,709,873 citizens served by local law enforcement agencies who were counted in the 1990 Census, 61 million (25%) are represented in this sample. Of this 61 million, 52% are Caucasian, 12% fall into Hero's white ethnic group classification, 19% are Black, 12% are Hispanic, and 5% are Asian. In order to build upon the Rodney Hero theory of political representation and assess the influence social diversity can have on public policy, in the overall aggregate this sample of cities falls into the **bifurcated** category specified in Figure 4.1 above. Of course, the true test of the value of the Hero analytical logic comes in seeing how it might enlighten patterns of application for and subsequent award of COPS Office funds for community policing officers and programs.

The results reported here indicate strongly that Hero's hypothesis developed at the level of state politics had direct applicability at the city level of aggregation with respect to community policing grant seeking and the awarding of funds. The multiple regression analysis presented here will indicate a significant effect on the policy making process attributable to the presence of both Hispanic subpopulations and white ethnic populations (non Anglo-Saxon and Scandinavian). Based on Hero's work on similar effects registered at the state level, I offer some speculation as to why these effects are present in the case of the extent of adoption of COP in the 197 grant-funded cities (5 cities received no federal funds under this program) studied here. In the next section, income inequality will be discussed as a means for assessing community wellness and how it relates to the incidence of crime and social disorder.

THE INDEX AND PUBLIC POLICY

The research hypothesis presented in this study also includes an examination of the levels of inequality present in the jurisdictions that received COP awards. Using a index of inequality aggregated at the household level (**HH**), one of the contentions originally put forth within the context of any federal subsidy-oriented program is that large-scale national redistributive public policies should be influenced by the **degree of need** present within a particular jurisdiction. Of course, social inequality has been a widely researched topic in the United States and elsewhere. Because law enforcement is the gatekeeper of the criminal justice system, it is particularly important to study large-scale crime control policies and document their relationship to socioeconomic factors. Inasmuch as COP advocates have set as a goal of public policy to "improve the quality of life" for citizens in American communities, the underlying premise for using inequality as an indicator of COP solicitation and funding is simply this: where there are disadvantaged, disenfranchised people who live in high crime areas, attention should be paid to improving their situation through initiatives that foster better police services and enhanced public safety.

I should make it clear that I do not believe that police can correct severe problems of socioeconomic disrepair. Moreover, it is the proactive and collaborative nature of COP that should motivate communities experiencing these types of problems to seek out viable approaches to crime control. Using inequality as a predictor is a forward thinking concept that may or may not have been a factor considered by local officials, but COPS Office grant reviewers were most certainly aware of and desirous of directing funds to communities in particular need of assistance. It was initially anticipated as a major predictor in the granting of federal funds for COP adoption and implementation. Although this factor was not statistically significant in the multivariate model discussed below, the bivariate correlation between household income inequality (based on a index calculation) and the measure of COP funding per household was marginally significant at the .069 level; hence, overall there was a weakly positive relationship between inequity and the receipt of COPS Office grant funds. This must be a comforting finding for the social equity advocates of the Clinton administration who argued strongly for need-based discretionary grant programs such as the school violence, domestic violence, problem-solving partnerships, and related innovative grants described in the previous chapter.

The   calculation has been used in various explorations of the relationship between crime and disorder and the lack of economic opportunity. For example, Johnson et al. (2000) have argued that income inequality is just one perspective that is used when examining the social status of African-American males in relation to their overall position in American society. Their empirical findings indicate that if American society is to contribute to the improvement of access to mainstream economic opportunities for black males, there must first be a redress or amendment to policies that contribute to their declining social and economic fortunes (Johnson et al., 2000). In a study of the relationship between socioeconomic status (SES) and criminal behavior, Thornberry and Farnworth (1982) found that the relationship between SES and criminal behavior in juveniles is only a weak one at best. Wright et al. (1999) also found weak correlations between the SES and self-reported delinquent behavior in a sample of youth using measures of parental SES. In an examination of the concentration of affluence in the United States, St. John (2002) examined the presence of affluent households in neighborhoods in metropolitan areas in 1990. He found that racial differences in the rate of concentrated affluence are influenced more by income differences between blacks and whites than by residential segregation. In addition, Massey (1996) noted that the presence of poverty within a specific geographic region contributes to the concentrations thought to be associated with poverty (e.g., high crime and high unemployment). With regard to the COP phenomenon, Choi, Turner and Volden (2002) found that household income was not a major influencing factor in the requesting or granting of COP funds. The findings in this study also reveal that levels of household income are not a significant factor in the grant solicitation and funding allocation process.

MEASUREMENT OF KEY INDICATORS

In order to examine the COPS Office grant distribution phenomenon, the **dependent variable** in the OLS regression analysis to follow will represent the level of award (in dollars per household) in each community (LNLEV7$) (natural log transformed variable). Division of the total COP award received by number of households reported in the 1990 Census was performed to arrive at the per household award amount for each jurisdiction. The per household standardization of this measure allows it to be used as a common measure of COPS Office support received across all levels of city size.

The **independent variables** used in the regression model were selected in order to control for local demographics, and to reveal how they may or may not affect the seeking after and granting of COPS Office funding. The total **crimes against persons** reported in the Uniform Crime Reports in 1993 (**PERS93**) is used to explore the presence of serious threats to public safety. This variable was calculated at the level of crimes against persons per 10,000 households. This variable is thought to be instrumental in the grant funding process as it portrays a picture of community safety, or lack thereof. Additionally, the level of **property crimes** per 10,000 households as reported in the 1993 UCR report (**PROP93**) is included as an additional indicator of the presence of crime. Again, this variable affects the perceptions of the condition of the social fabric within each community.

The third variable in this model deals with inequality issues (**HH**) discussed previously and indicates the degree of equity in the distribution of wealth within each jurisdiction. As noted earlier, coefficients have been used by a substantial number of scholars in a variety of disciplines (e.g., political economists, political theorists, policy analysts, and social science researchers) in an attempt to understand community dynamics, the effects of income dispersion on criminal justice issues (e. g., sentencing, discretionary arrest, and police patrol functions), and how economic inequities play out within the policy design, adoption, and implementation spheres. Further, with respect to policing, socioeconomic status effects upon how police choose to design and implement interventions aimed at improving public safety have not been well documented in the literature, aside from the examination of saturation patrol in relation to the policing of poor, disadvantaged neighborhoods (Bass, 2001).

The fourth variable in this model is the log of median household income, (**LNMEDHH**) representing a measure of relative wealth of the cities in the study. Again, the **per household** dollar amount was chosen so that the corresponding demographic and socioeconomic indicators would allow standardized comparisons to be made with regard to funding amounts and size of community.

In addition to socio-demographic issues, educational attainment can be seen as an important indicator of level of need within a given community. Because this is also an important concern for policy analysts, the fifth variable in the model is a measure of the percentage of the population over 25 who have not yet earned their high school diploma (**EDTOTALS**). The logic behind examining this variable stems from the literature suggesting that those who have not yet received their diploma by the time of the 25th year mark have a low likelihood of achieving economic security and contributing to the tax base of local government (Cameron and Heckman, 2001; Chuang, 1994; Lucas, 2001; Mayer, 2001). Because the lack of education has been documented as a predictor of criminal behavior in the criminology literature (Tanner, Davies and O'Grady, 1999), political economists have also examined this variable in connection with the economic stability of a given jurisdiction (Doyle, Ahmed and Horn, 1999). Because of the effects of poor educational attainment on the future achievements for those who have low levels of education (Fullerton, 2001), a measure of the level of educational attainment was included in the multivariate model reported below.

To widen the analysis of factors that may affect the granting of public funds in the case of COP, the number of total households in 1990 (**HH1990**) (serving as a measure of jurisdiction size), the percentage of Hispanics (**HISPOP**), and the percentage of Blacks (**BLACKPOP**) in the community are also important factors to consider in the examination of social equity. The model also includes variables related to the organizational strength of each agency as measured by the number of sworn officers per 10,000 households using the 1990 household count (**OFFHH93**) and the number of vacant positions as a percentage of the total authorized sworn officer force (**EMTPOS2**) (as a measure of the understaffing of police).

These independent variables are used to illuminate the grant funding process and assess its connection to social equity, diversity, and crime. These factors are important points of reference for understanding how COPS Office grant funds were distributed and what factors might have been examined during the grant application and funding allocation processes engaged in by municipalities and the COPS office staff. It is equally important to examine these issues when attempting to explore how public funds are distributed in areas where need is high and where additional resources might be used to make improvements in the delivery of local police services. Inasmuch as an important goal of the COPS Office grant program was to create connections in communities where the state of affairs are somewhat bleak for the ethnically diverse and impoverished sectors of the community, these variables are important points of analysis. In addition, the organizational variables will allow this analysis to explore whether the level of officer strength and/or extent of department vacancies affected the grant process. It should be noted, of course, that the vast majority of COPS Office grants provided for adding 100,000 officers "on the street" and local governments had to apply for federal funds on the condition they would continue to support those officer positions after grant funding was no longer available. The factors that influence both the decision to apply and the COPS Office decision to award a grant are both at play in this analysis of the factors affecting the distribution of COPS Office grant funds to local jurisdictions.

Some agencies may have applied for grants but not received them, and yet others may not have applied for any funding under the provisions of the 1994 Crime Bill. There are a variety of explanations that could be set forth here. One factor might be that local agencies with dwindling resources simply did not have the time or manpower to compose complex and exhaustive grant applications for the discretionary programs directed toward "need." Some jurisdictions located in close proximity to universities and colleges with criminal justice programs might have collaborated with educators to assist them with the grant application process, and still other agencies with sufficient resources to hire outside grant writers may have seen this as an opportunity to acquire supplemental funding for on-going operations. Another explanation might be purely financial in nature; jurisdictions with dwindling budgets could not set aside the required "matching funds" that were prerequisites for some funding opportunities.

Viewed from this perspective, the COP funding process sought to immediately enhance police operations through the provision of stipends to hire more officers, but the majority of these funding opportunities required city governments to find money to pay for these officers over the course of a two- to three-year time frame. It is highly probable that many agencies did not apply for as much funding as they could profitably use for police services enhancements due to any one of the above conditions of grant acceptance.

ESTIMATION METHOD

This study uses an Ordinary Least Squares (OLS) multiple regression model to examine the above hypothesis about the sources of influence on the amount of COPS Office funding (dollars per household) received. The use of this statistical model requires that a substantial amount of diagnostic work take place on the pattern of distribution present of both the dependent variable and the independent variables included in the statistical model. Data were analyzed using the OLS procedures contained in the SPSS 11.0.1 statistical software package.

PRELIMINARY ASSESSMENT OF THE INDICATORS

Prior to running a full regression analysis, I followed the lead of Lewis-Beck (1980) and assessed the underlying indicators to assure that they met basic regression model assumptions. The initial analysis of histograms and bivariate scatters against the dependent variable suggested that several transformations were necessary in order to meet linear modeling expectations. Since several of the primary indicators exhibited substantial positive skew (a long right tail in the distribution), I applied a natural log transformation to address the problem of non-normal distribution. Two indicators were transformed using a natural log (total COP award per household and median household income). Subsequent examination of histograms showed significant improvement in the univariate distribution on these indicators. I also reexamined the bivariate scatters, substituting in the log-transformed indicators, and the scatterplots were substantially more linear and exhibited equally distributed data throughout the full range of the independent variable. In the regression analysis (presented below), I produced an overall regression scatterplot and a plot of residuals. These illustrations show that the various components of the multivariate analysis are sufficiently normally distributed for the analytical model to be tested. Regression partial scatterplots further demonstrate that the independent variables used in this regression analysis exhibit approximated linear relationships to the dependent variable—the level of COP award dollars per household.

ANALYSIS OF THE REGRESSION RESULTS

Model 1 (Tables 4.1-4.3) introduces the primary variables studied in explorations of white ethnic diversity conducted by Hero (1998); effects of family income inequality in metropolitan counties studied by Levernier (1999); explorations of crime reported by Kelly (2000); and research conducted by Baumgartner and Leech (1998) that examines the importance of racial and ethnic groups and their interaction between observed conditions in the community and their relationship to the formation and implementation of public policies. The observed F-value for the first specification (5.802**) far exceeds the critical value of F at the .05 significance level and indicates that the model taken as a whole accounts for significant variation in COP award dollars. The adjusted R^2 (.239) provides further evidence of the overall goodness of fit of this model. One concern in regression models is that collinearity will undermine the estimation process. Model VIF scores for the coefficients in this model are all well below 10 (average VIF = 2.058) indicating that collinearity is not a problem in the analysis presented here (SPSS, 2001).

Table 4.1: Descriptive Statistics for 91% of entire sample with skewed variables logged

Variable Name	Mean	Std. Deviation	N
LNLEVEL7$	3.913400	.9447228	184
PERS93	125.023184	82.0392661	184
PROP93	749.937502	252.3609564	184
HH	.43558658	.045855576	184
LNMEDHH	10.24	.242	184
EDTOTALS	.154477	.0518356	184
EMTPOS93	.026787	.172710689	184
BLACKPOP	.19103040	.172710689	184
HEROETH1	.23331845	.116099712	184
HISPPOP	.11321977	.131781216	184
OFFHH93	57.632709	27.0712667	184
HH1990	99819.94	142422.814	184
ASIANPOP	.04713804	.072503866	184

Table 4.2: Model summary[b] with skewed variables logged

N=184 (94% of sample)

Model	R	R Square	Adjusted R Square	Std. Error of the Estimate	R Square Change	F Change	df1	df2	Sig. F Change
1	.538[a]	.289	.239	.8238667	.289	5.802	12	171	.000

a. Predictors: (Constant), ASIANPOP, OFFHH93, EMTPOS93, PROP93, HISPPOP, HH1990, HEROETH1, BLACKPOP, HH, EDTOTALS, PERS93, LNMEDHH

b. Dependent variable: LNLEV7$

Table 4.3: Coefficients[a] for model predicting funding awards

Model	Unstandardized Coefficients		Standardized Coefficients			Collinearity Statistics	
	B	SE	Beta	t	Sig.	Tolerance	VIF Scores
1 (Constant)	9.138	4.921		1.857	.065*		
PERS93	2.586	.001	.225	2.033	.044*	.341	2.935
PROP93	8.189	.000	.232	2.364	.019*	.440	2.273
HH	-2.626	1.764	-.127	-1.489	.138	.567	1.763
LNMEDHH	-.559	.447	-.143	-1.251	.213	.317	3.157
EDTOTALS	-1.654	1.984	-.091	-.834	.406	.351	2.851
EMTPOS93	2.004	1.226	.110	1.634	.104	.919	1.088
BLACKPOP	9.961	.557	.018	.179	.858	.401	2.495
HEROETH1	1.707	.728	.210	2.344	.020*	.519	1.928
HISPPOP	1.174	.668	.164	1.757	.081*	.478	2.090
OFFHH93	4.263	.003	.122	1.503	.135	.630	1.588
HH1990	7.052	.000	.106	1.533	.127	.864	1.158
ASIANPOP	.909	.982	.070	.925	.356	.732	1.367

a. Dependent Variable: LNLEV7$

* Significant at the .05 level

In addition to overall model results, an analysis of estimates on individual controls offers important insight into the primary demographic factors affecting COPS award dollar allocations. As noted above, the model presented introduces controls that are used in other analyses of policy implementation and reflects common assumptions made in this area of public policy research. The regression results presented here indicate that levels of crime against persons and property, the Rodney Hero white ethnic diversity index, and percentage of Hispanic population are factors closely associated with COP funding allocations. In addition, the police department's strength is a marginal predictor of crime funds, coming in at the .052 level of statistical significance. This set of findings provides evidence that all things considered, the above factors were the main determinants of grant application and subsequent funding in this sample of 197 municipal police agencies. Moreover, this model serves to provide insight into the grant application and funding process. Although this model does not present evidence that the officers who were provided under the provisions of the COPS funding were actually put to work in the area of COP, additional analyses will be presented below to assess whether the officers hired to enhance the COP function actually did so.

When considering the social equity context of this policy, it is very important to note that neither the median household income variable, nor the household   coefficient, nor the percentage of the population who are black, nor the percentage of the local population who are deficient in educational attainment (less than high school education) are empirically associated with the levels of COP funding per household in this set of cities. It can be assumed that the larger, well-staffed agencies might have made application for grants and received awards as a result of good grant seeking practices. It would be interesting to see whether these large agencies with high award levels actually have research units that compile and analyze local statistics; unfortunately, this particular information was not available in the 1993 LEMAS data.

In the case of the jurisdictions where the Hispanic population apparently had an effect on the grant solicitation and funding process, the implications of an upswing in political clout experienced by the Latino population may have affected the grant application process and influenced whether municipal police departments applied for and were subsequently approved for funding.

When considering crime rates, one might hypothesize that these variables prove to be significant predictors of funding allocations because they were brought forth in the dialogue between law enforcement officials and city government officials when discussing whether to apply for COP subsidies. Issues such as high crime rates, ethnic diversity, and agency staffing levels seem to have spurred municipal law enforcement agencies to urge their city governments to apply for COPS Office funds and to subsequently receive financial support to hire more officers (as the majority of the funding that was received by these agencies [92%] was used for the hiring of new police officers). The empirical results shown in the OLS multiple regression model reported below are also interesting because general assumptions can be made as to what factors may have precipitated the grant application process by municipal police agencies and city governments featured in this sample of major American municipalities. In addition, these same factors may have been included in the design and submission of the requests for funding, and may have been factors that were taken into consideration when the applications were scrutinized by the COPS Office staff—particularly with regard to the innovative grants (discretionary) described in considerable detail in the previous chapter.

In addition to the above, a scatterplot of the distribution of LNLEV7$ is presented in Figure 4.2 in order to illustrate the degree of normalcy associated with this model for both the regression adjusted predicted value and in Figure 4.3 to illustrate the regression standardized predicted value.

Figure 4.2: Scatterplot: DV: LNLEVEL7$: Model Normalcy

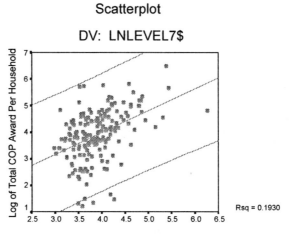

Scatterplot

DV: LNLEVEL7$

Rsq = 0.1930

Figure 4.3: Scatterplot: DV: LNLEVEL7$: Residual Plot

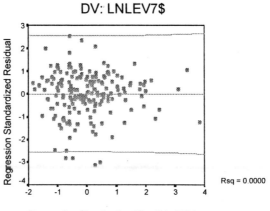

Scatterplot

DV: LNLEV7$

Rsq = 0.0000

DISCUSSION OF REGRESSION FINDINGS

When examining the results presented in the Model 1 (Table 4.2), it is clear that the social inequities associated with the LEAA funding program do not appear to be duplicated in the COPS Office program. In the case of the data analyzed in this research, both the factors that were and that were not predictive of COPS Office grants funds received by the jurisdictions in this sample are noteworthy. For example, both person and property crimes were statistically significant, giving rise to the observation that local problems at the local level were coming into play in the awarding of grant funds as was hoped by the advocates of the federal COP program. In addition, the Hero index of white social diversity was also a major factor achieving statistically significant status in this model. Rodney Hero (1998) might argue that because this sample of agencies is comprised of a bifurcated population, the application for and receipt of COP dollars is strongly related to the presence of these groups that have been shown to make a difference in the realm of decision making within the political arena. In sum, Hero's ethnic diversity argument suggests that there are different perspectives in relation to values and beliefs along the three dimensions noted in Figure 4.1. For example, in the heterogeneous jurisdictions, core values are not etched in stone and have a higher degree of variation because of the presence of different ethnicities that are associated with different values and belief systems. In contrast, in homogenous areas public policy issues that are thought to be neutral or universally ascribed to among those who identify with each other in relation to a set of core values and beliefs, people do not view the occasional differences that arise as being political in nature; they are viewed instead as reflecting honest differences of opinion on how to reach shared goals. Even further, in the bifurcated jurisdictions considerable agreement exists about a few basic, core values, at least among members of the white majority, which are grounded in beliefs concerning the need for public safety and the protection of private property and personal liberties. Rodney Hero's ethnic diversity-focused approach leads the researcher to ask profound questions about how group dynamics shape political debate and lead to the adoption of distinctive public policies in each type of ethnic diversity setting (Hero, 1998:18). Hero's arguments suggest that in the context of social order and social control within a given community, these ethnic and racial group factors are prime candidates for consideration when setting the stage for political and policy debates.

Because the percent of total population who are Hispanic was also a strong predictor of COP funding awards, it may just be that because Latinos in America have strengthened their position in the political arena (as noted by Hero, 1998) and also because Hispanics have finally become strong participants in community affairs as noted by Affigne (2001), the granting of COP funds has a strong relationship to level of Hispanics in the sample examined here. As a group, Hispanics have become more conservative in their political orientation over time, but they remain fiscally liberal with regard to the development of social policies that address community need. This profile of Hispanics might have been a strong factor in the level of support received by communities with high percentages of Hispanics (de la Garza and DeSipio, 1992; de la Garza and DeSipio, 1997).

In addition, the number of sworn officers per 10,000 households proves to be a significant predictor, as well as the size of the city as indicated by total number of households in the jurisdiction. These measures are both manifestations of police department influence in the policy process, and they provide evidence of enhanced political bargaining power for this group of public sector professionals at both the local and national levels. In addition, these findings suggest that some of the same strengths in the area of grant writing that plagued the LEAA funding program may again be factors somewhat at play in the granting of COP awards. Clearly, these effects are greatly modified by the obvious attempts to direct funds to those cities in need in the discretionary grant programs offered by the COPS office. It is important to note that Choi, Turner and Volden (2002) found that the distribution of COP grants was affected by high levels of crime and understaffed police agencies. Their research examined those agencies which did and did not request funding; the relationship between crime and staffing shortages are replicated in this study of 197 agencies that **did** receive awards. By examining the differences in the extent of COP orientation in relation to jurisdiction size and dollar award, this study will provide some insight into whether the COPS Office program was implemented in a way that is consistent with COP as a philosophy, or if the money was simply put to use to enhance the number of officers placed in patrol cars.

Some interesting observations also emerge from examining the factors that were **not** significant predictors of COP awards. For example, the inequality of income across households is not a strong predictor of COP awards, and the proportion of blacks in the population was not a significant predictor of COP funding solicitation and granting. Because the Hispanic population was a moderate factor in analyzing the distribution of grant awards, it might be the case that blacks continue to be marginalized in the policy realm. As noted above, the Hispanic population has become more politically mobilized (Affigne, 2000; Hero, 1998) and addressing their needs may be a higher priority for those in charge of deciding to seek COPS Office funds and those deciding how and where COPS Office funds were distributed when compared to African-American community members.

As the results of this analysis reveal, the COPS Office has prioritized crime abatement and the building of bridges in socially diverse communities; however, where the presence of substantial black populations is concerned, this factor does not appear to be a significant element in the pursuit of or the granting of federal COP dollars. For the most part, it would appear from the results of this exploration of the COP grant funding distribution pattern presented in the OLS regression analysis that the COPS Office (to a considerable extent) has avoided the pitfalls of the highly inequitable LEAA funding process, and that COPS Office staff were quite conscious of social equity factors associated with the stated goals and objectives of COP (e.g., bridging gaps between the police and their communities and solving local public safety problems). Rather than awarding COPS Office dollars to local law enforcement to develop armies of occupation equipped with helicopters, howitzer weaponry, and armored personnel vehicles, the COPS Office seems to have sought to promote social equity with their grant programs, particularly with respect to their discretionary innovative grants. While there is some evidence of advantages accruing to larger, well-staffed police agencies, there is no indication that the gross disparities associated with the LEAA program were repeated in the COPS program.

This analysis leads us to the exploration of how the COP dollars were put to use. For all jurisdictions, what were the differences noted in the 1999 LEMAS survey between highly funded and poorly funded agencies with respect to the adoption of COP programs? When the 197 jurisdictions receiving funding are segregated into large, mid-size, and small cities, what differences between highly funded and poorly funded agencies can be noted in this regard? The next section of this chapter sets forth T-Test findings for all 197 jurisdictions receiving COP funding, and analysis of variance (ANOVA) findings are also presented for large, medium and smaller jurisdictions in order to provide a more comprehensive understanding of the relationship between the receipt of COP funds and the how COP has been operationalized.

T-TEST ANALYSIS

The T-test analysis of difference in means will be used to explore at what level these funds have been operationalized in the agencies that received COP grants[45]. The measures used as COP indicators taken together can provide a picture of the level of COP orientation in different sized jurisdictions, and document the difference between those agencies which received high and low amounts of grant funds within these three groups. Initially, the entire sample will be compared using the size of the city as a control. The results of the One-way Analysis of Variance (ANOVA) are presented in Tables 4.4 and 4.5 and reveal that very little difference occurs with regard to adoption of COP practices when controlling for city size. The Independent-Samples T-Test procedure compares means for two groups of cases and will provide a basis for comparison of the extent of COP implementation along a range of dimensions thought to be associated with COP philosophy as distinguished by agency size, total award received, and breadth of COP oriented practices. Significant findings for the top third and bottom third of the grant recipients on these dimensions is presented below in Table 4.4. Because the directional hypothesis here posits that level of award should foster increased COP activity, the statistical significance is one-tailed in nature.

Of the 18 COP-related variables tested for differences of means between the top third and bottom third of award recipients, 13 produce statistically significant differences of means (at less than .05 likelihood of chance occurrence). Significance can be found with regard to the number of officers per household (more sworn officers in the agency workforce equals more COPS funds per household), and the absence of a complete complement of full time sworn officers; these are variables associated with agency lobbying resources and grounds for arguing "need for more cops;" these are resources with which police agencies

Table 4.4: Independent Samples T-Tests for top and bottom third of award recipients

	Top/Bot 1/3	N	Mean	SD	SE of Mean	t value
OFFHH99	Top	62	56.97	32.68	4.1505	
	Bottom	68	76.27	30.16	3.6578	-3.501*
EMTPOS2	Top	62	.022	.029	.0037	
	Bottom	68	.043	.079	.0096	-2.042*
TRNCIT99	Top	62	.69	.465	.059	
	Bottom	68	.87	.341	.041	-2.449*
ENSARA99	Top	62	.61	.491	.062	
	Bottom	68	.76	.427	.052	-1.884*
TOTVOLRA	Top	62	.8317	1.279	.1625	
	Bottom	68	2.499	6.79	.8242	-1.901*
CPPLAN99	Top	62	1.42	.641	.081	
	Bottom	68	1.69	.465	.056	-2.783*
FOOT99	Top	62	.63	.487	.062	
	Bottom	68	.90	.306	.037	-3.791*
BIKE99	Top	62	.87	.338	.043	
	Bottom	68	.96	.207	.025	-1.744*
RECSCP99	Top	62	2.53	.987	.125	
	Bottom	68	2.87	.571	.069	-2.397*
INSVCP99	Top	62	1.89	1.04	.132	
	Bottom	68	2.22	.990	.120	-1.871*
SRO99A	Top	62	.0206	.0208	.0026	
	Bottom	68	.0147	.0152	.0018	1.864*
OFF9399A	Top	62	.0576	.0911	.0115	
	Bottom	68	.1386	.1343	.0162	-3.981*
HHCOPPK	Top	62	3.356	2.866	.3640	
	Bottom	68	18.226	13.232	1.6047	-8.662*

*Significant at <.05

Table 4.5: One Way Analysis of Variance for small, medium and large cities

Variable	City Size	N	Mean	SD	SE of Mean	F	Sig.
LEVEL7$	Small	65	55.83	70.57	8.753		
	Medium	64	59.71	40.965	5.120	7.358	.001
	Large	68	98.96	92.937	11.270		
	Total	197	71.98	74.204	5.286		
OFFHH99	Small	65	62.46	32.824	4.07139		
	Medium	64	55.89	16.240	2.03003	8.290	.002
	Large	68	72.77	30.469	3.69500		
	Total	197	63.89	28.337	2.01876		
EMTPOS2	Small	65	.016920	.0261840	.00324		
	Medium	64	.027413	.0381269	.00476	3.265	.040
	Large	68	.040564	.0791542	.00959		
	Total	197	.028490	.0541130	.00385		
TRNCIT99	Small	65	.71	.458	.057		
	Medium	64	.81	.393	.049	6.551	.002
	Large	68	.94	.237	.029		
	Total	197	.82	.383	.027		
GEOPAT99	Small	65	.88	.331	.041		
	Medium	64	.98	.125	.016	3.585	.030
	Large	68	.96	.207	.025		
	Total	197	.94	.240	.017		
CPPLAN99	Small	65	1.45	.685	.085		
	Medium	64	1.64	.515	.064	4.127	.016
	Large	68	1.72	.452	.055		
	Total	197	1.60	.567	.040		
FOOT99	Small	65	.71	.458	.057		
	Medium	64	.70	.460	.058	3.994	.020
	Large	68	.88	.325	.039		
	Total	197	.77	.424	.030		

continued

Variable	City Size	N	Mean	SD	SE of Mean	F	Sig.
BIKE99	Small	65	.85	.364	.045		
	Medium	64	.91	.294	.037	4.227	.016
	Large	68	.99	.121	.015		
	Total	197	.91	.282	.020		
NUMSTA2	Small	65	1.377084	1.7322674	.2148613		
	Medium	64	1.131513	1.2179245	.1522406	5.771	.004
	Large	68	.632847	.7445447	.0902893		
	Total	197	1.040410	1.3206251	.0940906		
RECSCP99	Small	65	2.55	.919	.114		
	Medium	64	2.53	.975	.122	3.816	.024
	Large	68	2.88	.505	.061		
	Total	197	2.66	.834	.059		
SRO99A	Small	65	.0212	.017	.002		
	Medium	64	.0196	.020	.002	2.673	.072
	Large	68	.0146	.014	.002		
HHCOPPK	Small	65	7.994250	10.389254	1.2886284		
	Medium	64	9.345010	7.3476605	.9184576	8.686	.000
	Large	68	15.22615	13.2469507	1.6064287		
	Total	197	10.92936	11.0754673	.7890944		

can lobby their local government officials to urge application for COPS Office grant funds.

Of the variables connected to breadth of COP orientation in this comparison of large amount and small amount grant recipients across the entire sample, the findings are rather remarkable. For nearly all of these measures the expected outcome—i.e., more grant funds equals more COP activities—is NOT in evidence; rather, the **reverse** finding is documented. The training of citizens in COP, the use of the SARA model for public safety problem solving, ratio of volunteers per 10,000 households, use of routine foot patrol and bike patrol, training recruits in COP, providing in-service COP training to officers, level of change in full time sworn officers per the number of officers acquired with grant funds per 10 thousand households, change in number of officers from 1993-1999, and the number of COPS acquired with grant funds all prove to be significantly more likely to be present in LOW GRANT AWARD cities than in high grant award cities! Only in the two areas of the development of a formalized COP plan at various levels (formal plan, informal written plan or no COP plan) and the addition of School Resource Officers (SROs) do the high grant amount cities have higher levels of COP activity. This set of findings indicates that the high-amount grant recipients were disproportionately LOW OFFICER TO POPULATION SERVED RATIO agencies, and most of their COPS Office funds went to the hiring of new officers to enhance that ratio. These findings further indicate that many agencies which received relatively few grant funds NONETHELESS initiated and established COP activities such as bike patrols, foot patrols, SARA problem solving efforts, citizen volunteer recruitment, etc. It is entirely possible that agencies serving cities which could not afford the financial commitments associated with the Universal Hiring Program adopted those COP practices that **did not require the expenditure of large amounts of funds**.

The most interesting part of the analysis is presented above in Table 4.5. Using a One-Way Analysis of Variance (ANOVA), Table 4.5 describes the character of COP in small, medium, and large cities across the sample. As noted in the above tables, there is considerable difference in the way COP funds have been operationalized across this group of agencies. For instance, with regard to the level of departmental resources available for COP activities, there are significant differences in the mean of award dollars per household between small and large cities and medium and large cities, but very little difference between small and medium sized jurisdictions. Further, when examining the number of officers per household, the difference is significant between the three, with the major difference occurring between the means of the large (72.77) and the medium (55.89), and a much smaller difference observed between the means of the small (62.46) and large jurisdictions. The significance of the level of departmental resources is again a factor when looking at the number of empty positions across the continuum of these three categories. As noted in the ANOVA table, the large agencies experience higher rates of vacant positions in relation to number of full time sworn officers than do the medium or small agencies. This might be due to police work being more attractive in less populated areas for many reasons.

An example of the desire to work in a small, medium, or large jurisdiction is observed in the lack of response by students in my criminal justice classes when visited by recruiters from areas such as Los Angeles, Long Beach, and Sacramento. Very few of these college students express interest in making application for positions in these agencies. However, when smaller agencies such as the University of California Berkeley Campus Police, Vallejo, CA, and Mill Creek, CA come to class, students are decidedly more inquisitive with regard to job duties, salaries, and retirement benefits. Although such observations are entirely anecdotal in nature, this personal observation might just be a accurate reflection of general trends across the country and warrants some empirical investigation with regard to the higher rate of vacancies documented along the spectrum of jurisdiction size in the 1993 LEMAS survey. More interesting is the fact that the mean number of officers per 10,000 households acquired with grants funds in large jurisdictions is almost double that of the medium or small cities; large agencies continue to have more vacant positions on average than small or medium sized areas as reported in the 1999 LEMAS survey. It appears that more officers are being acquired with grant funds by large agencies, yet these larger areas are not experiencing much relief with regard to staffing concerns in comparison to their smaller, less populated counterparts.

When looking at the overall picture here, one can assume that small agencies are quite good at "making do with less"—something that has been preached by proponents of the reinventing government movement. When looking at the level of COP adoption in these three categories, large jurisdictions seem to be more apt to engage in the training of citizens, having a formal, written plan related to COP in their department, using foot and bicycle patrols on a routine basis, and training new recruits in COP.

It is clear from the analysis of the level of COP orientation across jurisdictions that larger agencies do more of some things than the smaller, less well-funded agencies, but those differences are only slight in magnitude. Taken as a whole, the analysis of COP across different sized jurisdictions that large agencies do attempt to initiate and carry out more COP activities, but they have received more subsidies in the form of street-level officers to do so. In addition, when looking at how COP is operationalized along this continuum of municipal police agencies, evidence reported here suggests that the large agencies which received more resources do more COP. In only one category do we find that the smaller agencies out-perform the larger, more complex organizations: the number of fixed neighborhood substations per 100 officers. With regard to comparisons between the medium and large agencies, medium agencies employ geographic patrol more routinely than is the case in large jurisdictions. With respect to comparisons between small and medium agencies, small agencies routinely use foot patrol as a strategy and train all new recruits in COP, but only by a slight margin. In addition, the number of SROs as a percentage of full time sworn officers is significantly higher in both the smaller and medium sized jurisdictions than in the larger ones. This might be attributable to the fact that larger areas are going to have more middle and high schools to man, and when taking the equity or fairness component into consideration, it would be unfair to some areas (as most likely taken as a snub) within the city to not have assigned SROs. This would not serve to "build bridges" in areas where they are in need of being built. Even further, the SRO grant process called for the creation of local partnerships, an activity that was scarcely in evidence at any of the three levels of jurisdiction size. Another factor might be that the SROs in the larger jurisdictions are simply spread more thinly than those in the less populated areas. Further analysis can help discern this difference in the adoption of the SRO program.

In short, the picture of COP presented here is one that allows for growth, development of community resources, and increasing the pool of full time sworn officers in the process. The presumption is that COP has taken root in many of these agencies, irrespective of the amount of money received to do so. In order to present a more vivid depiction of these differences, Figures 4.4—4.14 are presented to show how COP is administered across jurisdictions.

Figure 4.4: Mean of total award dollars per household

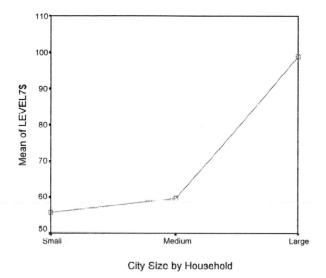

City Size by Household

Figure 4.5: Mean of number of officers per household in 1999

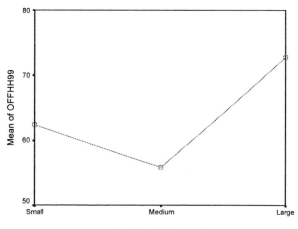

City Size by Household

Figure 4.6: Mean of vacant positions as percentage of sworn officers

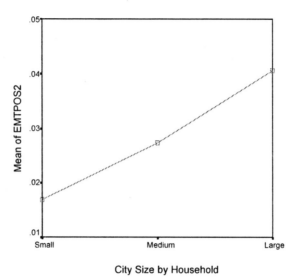

City Size by Household

Figure 4.7: Mean of citizens receiving COP training

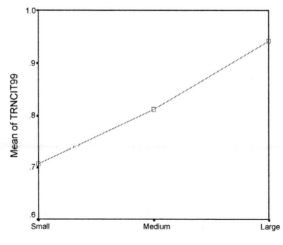

City Size by Household

Figure 4.8: Mean of use of geographic patrol

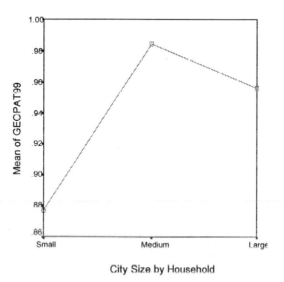

City Size by Household

Figure 4.9: Mean of routine foot patrol use

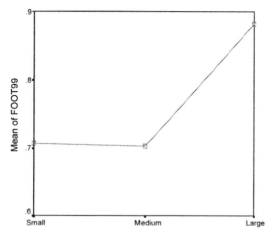

City Size by Household

Figure 4.10: Mean of routine use of bike patrol

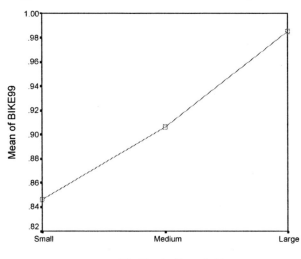

City Size by Household

**Figure 4.11: Mean of number of fixed neighborhood stations per
100 officers**

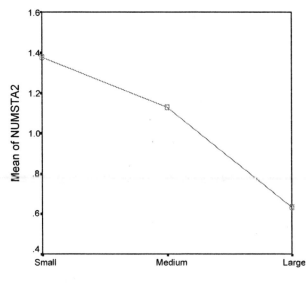

City Size by Household

Figure 4.12: Mean of amount of recruits trained in COP

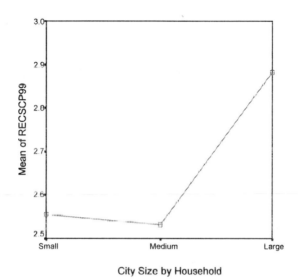

City Size by Household

Figure 4.13: Mean of SRO officers as ratio of full-time sworn officers

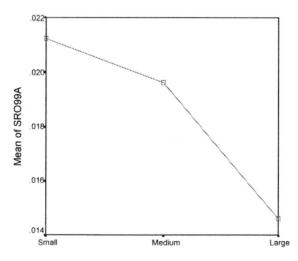

City Size by Household

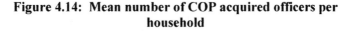

Figure 4.14: Mean number of COP acquired officers per household

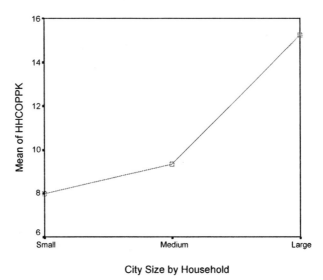

City Size by Household

SUMMARY OF FINDINGS

When examining the results of the OLS regression model, the findings reported here do not show a replication of the LEAA problems noted in the earlier chapters. In particular, these findings suggest that COP grants were applied for and granted in a way that attempts to promote equity in areas where there are high degrees of diversity and in areas where there are high levels of crime. It was argued earlier that it might be the case that **good grant writing** might be the driving force behind the COP funding phenomenon rather than local need as in the LEAA experience. The findings presented in the OLS regression model do provide evidence that some limited amount of this "grantmanship effect" is likely present in the pattern of distribution of COPS Office funds.

Taking the OLS multiple regression findings and the results of the T-tests that explore the differences between the high and low award groups in this study together, it appears that COPS Office funding is **not** the driving force behind the growth of COP in American policing.

On the contrary, it just may be that COP is experiencing growth so agencies can make better use of their resources—in particular, the newly acquired officers that were hired to work in areas that are COP-oriented such as foot patrol and bike patrol. Evidence reported here suggests that they are being oriented to COP strategies upon reporting to the department. Those with small awards are also looking more toward using volunteers to assist them with crime abatement, but the evidence reported here does not indicate that volunteers are being used as genuine partners in solving local problems very often. Although not statistically significant, the bottom third of the award recipients are also providing more in-service training to officers with regards to COP-related activities, have a higher ratio of COP officers to full-time sworn officers, have more written, formalized COP plans, had a higher degree of change in manpower acquisition most likely due to the higher acquisition of officers per 10,000 households in the low funded jurisdictions.

COP appears to be in good standing across all three categories of jurisdictional size, and is exceeding expectations in areas where funds were not as available as in others. Whether or not the agencies received federal funds does not appear to affect the implementation of COP. COP seems to be thriving irrespective of the level of federal funding received. Given this fact, it appears that COP is approaching the level of philosophy in the agencies examined here. Although it must be stressed that all these agencies applied for and were granted funding under this large-scale public policy, the COP phenomenon is directed toward the practice of decentralization and enhanced problem solving; the evidence reported here indicates that organizational structural change is occurring much more slowly than the adoption of COP operational practices and training.

The primary goal of the COP program was simply to put 100,000 new officers on the street by the year 2000 in an attempt to make the public feel safer and more secure in their communities. During the development of the COPS Program agenda, a collaboration between academics and the federal government was established to look toward alternative mechanisms of ensuring public order. As noted earlier, COP funds were not disproportionately allocated to areas that did not have problems with crime, rather the dollars were allocated to those areas that were experiencing social disorder. In addition, in areas where there were high concentrations of Latinos and white ethnics, the level of

COPS Office awards was also significantly enhanced. Because these two groups are considered to be socially conservative (Hero, 1998), they may have had the political wherewithal to join in the debate for city governments to make financial commitments for improving the rank and file officer count.

As level of award might not be the best measure to make some of these assumptions, it does provide interesting information that warrants future investigation. What this research does provide is a solid framework for future analysis. We know that award distribution is affected by crime and ethnic variation within the community. We have also observed significant differences along the size of the jurisdiction with regard to COP, and we have seen that the level of funding does not seem to affect COP in the way one might imagine. What we have is an inverse relationship between award level and breadth of COP at some levels. Agencies with smaller allocations are outperforming agencies with large COP allocations in areas that do not require the expenditure of significant budgetary assets to do so. This allows us to view the architecture of community policing as being one that is not built solely on an economic gain base. In the final chapter, I will discuss some areas of research that will allow us to more thoroughly examine (and eventually determine) if the architecture of community policing is flawed or exists in good condition for future use. The foundation of COP seems to be stable even in areas where funding is relatively low. Constructing the next levels of progress toward humane and democratic policing practices can be enhanced by engaging some of the forthcoming recommendations for future analysis presented in Chapter Five.

Enhancing Knowledge in the Study of Contemporary Policing

EXPLORING THE IMPLICATIONS OF THIS RESEARCH

As noted throughout this study, community policing differs substantially across the levels of city size and by looking at the level of award received to implement community oriented policing within a given jurisdiction. However, the strong presence of COP in contemporary American policing is undeniable. According to Eck and Rosenbaum (1994:3):

> Community policing has become a new orthodoxy for cops. Simultaneously ambitious and ambiguous, community policing promises to change radically the relationship between the police and the public, address underlying community problems, and improve the living conditions of neighborhoods. One reason for its popularity is that community policing is a plastic concept, meaning different things to different people. There are many perspectives on community policing, and each of them is built on assumptions that are only partially supported by empirical evidence.

Using this working definition of COP, it would seem that given this potential of COP to affect change within communities across the country it is important for explorations of the adoption of COP practices and the allocation of federal funds to speed this adoption to include race, ethnicity and economic distributional dimensions in their analyses. This is particularly the case given the rather unfortunate record vis-à-vis social equity concerns of the previous attempt to change American policing through federal subsidization of "police professionalism" in the LEAA program. Part of the potential for success at the community level with regard to COP can be found in the relationship a law enforcement agency has with its own community. In areas where societal diversity and wide gaps in the distribution of wealth exist, police may be seen as agents of occupation rather than partners in developing solutions to crime and disorder by disadvantaged citizens, who themselves are disproportionately represented among the victims of crimes (Barak, Flavin and Leighton, 2001; Bass, 2001). One fundamental question underlying the type of analysis presented here is whether funding levels were appropriately higher in areas where crime is high, social diversity is present, and the gap between the rich and poor is wide and deep. As police agencies across the nation continue to grapple with the task of making communities safer via the adoption of community policing ideas, practices and programs, this research reveals that ethnic diversity and high levels of crime were priority concerns in the application for and in the granting of COPS Office grant funds. It is also very important to note an interesting finding which emerges when looking at highly and poorly funded agencies within categories of small, medium, and large jurisdictions within the study population: having more money or having more officers does **not** necessarily translate into the development of COP practices in municipal law enforcement agencies which have at least 100 sworn, full-time positions authorized by their municipal authorities.

The preponderance of available research on COP stems from either nation-wide cross-sectional studies like this one, or case studies of innovative police agencies. Data of these types are valuable to our knowledge, yet they provide only limited evidence to guide the policy formation process. According to Greenwood and Hinings (1996:1022), "the complexity of political, regulatory, and technological changes confronting most organizations has made organizational change and adaptation a central research issue of the 1990s." It is this dimension of organizational change attributable to COP that has received only scant attention to date, and consequently serves as a focus of this research endeavor. Upon release of the forthcoming LEMAS survey data for 2001, it will be possible to assess at what level COP has progressed since the 1997 and 1999 LEMAS reports were published. I believe important answers to questions concerning the levels of organizational commitment to COP, the extent to which COP is practiced as a philosophy rather than a strategy or tactic, and if the organization has moved toward decentralization by engaging communities through the use of surveys, focus groups, and community meetings will emerge as a result of analysis. The combination of the new LEMAS data and the release of the 2000 census for communities (scheduled for late September or early October of 2002) will provide the basis for updating the analyses presented here and extending that analysis to the several research questions noted below. The present study should most appropriately be viewed as **foundational**; that is, it represents a strong foundation upon which to build for further study. The fact that the COPS Office was scheduled to "sunset" in 2001, and the agency continues in only a wind down capacity for the next two years, means that no new major funding initiatives for subsidizing the implementation of COP are likely to emerge in the foreseeable future. The tract record of COPS Office grants captured in the dataset for this study constitutes, therefore, the complete record of the attempt to recast American law enforcement through a federal funding initiative. It is important, then, that continued monitoring and follow-up studies be conducted using this dataset as a base.

The main benefit of **this** particular study is its potential to explain the distributional equities (or inequities) associated with COPS Office grants documented in this sample of 197[16] agencies receiving COP funding allocations, and assessing the connection between the receipt of COPS Office funds and the implementation of COP practices and programs. As argued in Chapter One, when considering the evolution of policing practices in the United States in an historical perspective, the political alliance between the police and local political authorities, the technological developments experienced in relation to the development of the patrol car and a centralized command center, the perceived insensitivity to minorities and the underclass exhibited by "professionalized" law enforcement, and the paramilitary organizational structure that have served to structure the practice of contemporary policing taken in combination have stifled the development of mutually supporting partnerships between police and the local residents they are intended to serve. The clear reflection of democratic principles and the promotion of a strong sense of community have become secondary concerns to the overriding law enforcement goal of catching the crook and developing evermore advanced technology for the surveillance of suspicious conduct and the investigation of criminal activities. Although the COPS Office grant awards made to law enforcement agencies included in this sample appear to have been allocated in a way that reflects sensitivity to community need in relation to diversity and the extent of the local crime problem, vast areas of productive research remain that have yet to be explored with regard to the COP phenomenon in American policing.

This research investigated how demographic characteristics (ethnic diversity, socioeconomic conditions, and aggregate level of educational attainment), the percentage of departmental resources set aside to do community policing, size of jurisdiction, and the range of community-based programs affect the potential for successful implementation of community policing. This effort offers information that can assist both local government policy makers and law enforcement agencies in making choices that are appropriate for the jurisdiction in question. It should be noted that pressures by citizens and local government to make progress toward solving vexing problems (e.g., poverty, neighborhood deterioration, youth crime, substance abuse, and now the terrorism threat) and substantial financial inducements for experimentation in these areas from the federal government were thought to be primary factors responsible for the application for and receipt of COP funds. To further our understanding of the complex problems present in communities across the nation, an exploration of the community characteristics that are present prior to application for and receipt of funding to implement COP provided some insight into the creation of local initiatives directed towards alleviating these vexing social problems. For example, when we look at the differences between large, medium and small agencies analyzed in this study, we find that the top ten award recipients in large jurisdictions are below the norm with regard to COP type programs in relation to the number of dollars that were invested in these areas. In addition, the medium and small jurisdictions seem to have held their own with regard to making changes directed toward COP adoption irrespective of the level of award they received.

RESEARCH REMAINING TO BE DONE: REGIONAL EFFECTS

While previous research suggests the presence of regional effects with respect to particular factors associated with change in police practices in the United States—e.g., the percentage black population in the South has a strong effect on the presence of women in policing but no such effect in the West (Warner et al., 1989)—little is known about such regional effects in the area of COP program and practice adoption. In terms of the practical importance of such information, it can be asked whether the presence or absence of regional training in COP might be a factor in the COP adoption story. As noted above, the research presented here implies that many of the agencies that received small monetary enhancements to operationalize COP in their communities have adopted COP policies and practices in spite of the lack of financial resources available to them. This prompts further inquiry and examination of police agencies at the regional level to explore whether region affects the adoption of COP in relation to the level of award and whether training at the regional level was provided by the Regional Community Policing Institutes (RCPIs). At some future data the records of the COPS Office can be reviewed to document the amount of training provided by the RCPIs in the 28 regions covered by these COPS Office-funded programs.

As noted by scholar Daniel Kemmis (1990), individual regions may well feature considerable attitudinal and value differences that might affect the solicitation of funds and affect how these funds are used once they are received. Kemmis (1990) suggests that shared historical development experiences influence the "sense of place" people in a region develop, and that these concepts of civic life in turn influence the ability of citizens to engage in collective action (including the co-production of public safety). Other scholars argue that historical patterns of migration have created distinctive, long-lasting political cultures throughout the many regions that make up the United States (Elazar, 1984). Both of these factors likely play an important role in the relative effectiveness of public organizations, and directly affect their ability to work together and adapt to changing conditions in their respective areas. It will be interesting indeed to examine these region-focused issues in future studies making use of the database assembled for this study. It will be possible to merge regional data, political culture data derived from the work of Elazar (1994), Lieske (1993), and Hero (1998), subsequent LEMAS information on COP practices and programs operating within the municipal police organizations included in this study, and to code all changes in demographics occurring over the course of the past decade in order to enhance the present vision of the state of COP implementation presented in this research. It is the case, for example, that a good deal of demographic change occurred in some regions over the course of the 1990s. The Hispanic population grew rapidly in many Midwestern communities, for instance. Is it the case that COP was adopted disproportionately in such communities within the Midwest? Similarly, in areas where "de-population" occurred was COP adopted as a means of compensating for lost tax base—particularly in rural areas? Questions such as these beg for our attention, and they can be addressed quite readily by building upon the foundation of the dataset compiled for this research.

RESEARCH REMAINING TO BE DONE: PROBLEM SOLVING AND COP

As early as 1968, research on comprehensive alternatives to traditional methods of law enforcement aroused the interest of a number of prominent scholars of policing (Wilson, 1968; Reiss, 1971; Skolnick and Bayley, 1986; Wilson and Kelling, 1982; Trojanowicz and Bucqueroux, 1990). Of all these explorations, few efforts have had more impact than the widely read work of Herman Goldstein (1979; 1987; 1990). As noted earlier, Herman Goldstein's work on problem solving policing provides many interesting insights into the way police agencies can become **learning organizations**. The results of the research reported here reveal that many of the agencies included in this study continue to lack skills for the systematic development of problem solving partnerships, as evidenced by their lack of focus upon these activities in their COP policies and practices. In keeping with the ideas and concepts that are thought to be COP-oriented, Greene (2000:302) indicates that:

> The promises of community policing are many. They include strengthening the capacity of communities to resist and prevent crime and social disorder; creating a more harmonious relationship between the police and the public, including some power sharing with respect to police policymaking and tactical priorities; restructuring police service delivery by linking it with other municipal services; reforming the police organization model; and creating larger and more complex roles for individual police officers. This new style of policing

is said to produce more committed, empowered, and analytic police officers; flatten police hierarchies; and open the process of locally administered justice to those who are often the object of justice decision-making. This shift also makes crime prevention, not crime suppression, the ascendant goal of policing.

By studying the problem solving partnership efforts undertaken in the agencies present in this examination of COP at benchmark year 1999 in an in-depth way, it would be possible to inform police scholars of both the problems and potentialities of this type of effort considered by many of scholars of community policing as a core element of COP. In order to accomplish this analysis, it will be necessary to examine these agencies using a **qualitative** approach to police research, one that brings researchers in close touch with those who are charged with forming and sustaining problem solving partnerships. The process of collaboration that develops during the course of problem solving efforts can take a number of different forms and lead to a variety of outcomes; a systematic assessment of these forms and outcomes would constitute valuable information for criminal justice planners, policy designers, and program evaluators.

It should be noted that while the work of Goldstein is widely read and broadly considered to represent first-rate scholarship in policing studies, there has been relatively little follow-up work done in this area in the Criminal Justice literature. The observations made by Goldstein have yet to undergo systematic replication by policing scholars. The in-depth studies of local agencies (e.g. Spokane, WA; Ann Arbor, MI; Newport News, VA; Houston, TX; New York, NY; Portland, OR; Flint, MI; Madison, WI; Kansas City, KS; Hayward, CA; Savannah, GA; Las Vegas, NV; Santa Barbara, CA; Philadelphia, PA; Edmonton, Alberta in Canada; Louisville, KY; and San Diego, CA) by scholars supported with COPS Office funds come the closest in this regard. However, given the sponsorship of this research the utility of these projects remains somewhat limited. Because so many of these agencies are included in the dataset compiled for this study, it would be possible to conduct a qualitative follow-up assessment of several of these agencies to determine two important facts: 1) were the COPS Office assessments fair and objective, or were they efforts to put the "best face" on the problem solving activities of these advanced COP agencies; and 2) does a longitudinal follow-up assessment reveal a sustained COP implementation or does it document backsliding after federal funds are no longer underwriting this activity?

RESEARCH REMAINING TO BE DONE: PUBLIC BUY-IN AND COP

Because of the continuing process of societal diversification in America with regard to race, ethnicity, and country of origin, American police agencies are very well-advised to be in close touch with a variety of issues that surface when seeking out support for COP from both internal and external constituents (Angell, 1971; Goldstein, 1979 and 1990; Kelling and Moore, 1988). Along the same line, Trojanowicz and Bucqueroux (1990:339) hypothesize that "community policing will likely find its warmest reception in police departments where the administration has demonstrated its openness to new ideas and the importance of keeping pace with changing times." Further, with respect to the achievement of lasting change in police organizations Rosenbaum and Lurigio (1994:303) argue that "the longevity of these (COP) reforms will depend on their ability to become institutionalized and to change the status quo in police agencies." An interesting research undertaking aimed at addressing this area of concern for transitory versus lasting COP effects is one that features an analysis of the organizational dynamics attendant to the implementation of COP programs and practices in the top ten agencies at each level of jurisdictional size (large, medium and small). The dataset assembled for this jurisdiction could be augmented with follow-up survey information collected from each of these thirty agencies as to which of the COP programs and practices listed in the 1999 LEMAS survey were still being maintained. Telephone interviews could then be arranged with the Chief and/or principal deputy chief to answer questions about each of the COP programs and practices being maintained and each program and practice which had been abandoned. Although research on community policing at the local level indicates there is a significant amount of citizen support for this initiative as a way to make communities safer and reduce fear of crime within Washington state[47], it has yet to be determined if communities across the United States experience these same high levels of public support for COP.

In contrast to these high public levels of support for COP are the low levels of COP implementation reported in some studies. For example, Moore et al. (2000) examined 10 agencies widely considered to be advanced in the area of their COP orientation. Moore and his colleagues found that the degree of institutionalization ranged from high (5), to medium high (1), to medium (2), to medium-low (1), and to low (1). Inasmuch as 8 of 10 of these law enforcement agencies are included as cases in this study, I thought it would be informative to see if these agencies are significantly more advanced in regard to the breadth of COP programs explored in Chapter Four than the average agency. The resulting crosstabulation analysis revealed some interesting information, indeed. This brief analysis revealed that there is no indication that these agencies (thought to be forerunners in the COP adoption process) are any different than the other agencies in this sample with regard to the level of COP orientation constructed for this research as per 1999 LEMAS reporting.[48] It is possible, of course, that the measures chosen by the U.S. Department of Justice as indicators of COP adoption in the LEMAS survey are not particularly good measures. Perhaps only a balanced combination of aggregate quantitative analyses and qualitative follow-up studies permit an accurate assessment of the extent of adoption of COP in an American law enforcement agency.

When looking further into the capacity for COP to take hold in agencies across the country, evaluation research shows that the inability to rally broad citizen support is among the main reasons for much of the failure experienced in COP implementation in many of the police agencies studied (Sadd and Grinc, 1994). Research on the dynamics of organizational change associated with the development of community policing tends to be limited to reports on national trends taken from samples of large departments. For example, in a study of municipal police departments in jurisdictions with populations over twenty-five thousand, Solomon Zhao (1996) examined the change versus continuity perspective of police executives with regard to the implementation of community policing in 228 American police agencies. Using variables that measure what types of organizational practices take place in these agencies vis-à-vis employee empowerment and organizational decentralization for neighborhood-level patrol focus, his results revealed that a combination of internal and external pressures for change in policing practices have yet to force a shift in organizational change among police chiefs. Zhao's findings suggest that relatively little organizational change has occurred to match the substantial programmatic efforts made to promote COP, and further that much of this change has been externally driven by insistent mayors, council members, or activist community-based groups rather than internally generated by police officials and rank-and-file officers. The findings reported here lend considerable support to Zhao's conclusions in this area of COP movement effects upon American policing. In the long term, continuing pressure from elected officials and citizens (and critical university-based scholars and their questioning graduate students) is more likely to bring on serious change efforts than internal inclination to change at this point in time.

In yet another nation-wide study conducted in 1994 using police agencies with patrol areas with populations over 30,000, Pingitore describes 126 programs identified as innovative by the mayors of the cities included in the survey sample. Program categories include comprehensive community policing programs, crime and drug enforcement programs, crime and drug task forces, diversion programs, domestic violence units, drug abuse education, environmental improvement programs, and gang prevention and elimination programs. The breadth of these innovations indicated to Pingitore that police agencies are moving in a different direction than **either** further professionalization, or team policing, or the proliferation of mini-stations—but rather are moving rapidly towards a multi-functional complex of specialized services contained under an inclusive umbrella of law enforcement broadly understood (Pingitore, 1994). We see the same type of results found by Pingitore in this sample of municipal police agencies. There is clear evidence that SRO programs, Domestic Violence Units, Crime Prevention Through Environmental Design operations, DARE instruction, Block Watch programs, etc, have become commonplace in contemporary police agencies, and that these COP-reflecting activities are only loosely coupled within the police agency setting.

In still another nation-wide study of police agencies, McEwen (1995) found that more than 8 out of 10 police chiefs who participated in a survey on COP adoption indicated that they were either presently engaged in a transition toward COP or intended to undertake such a transition in the near future. Presently, COP seems to be the standing order in many law enforcement agencies, whether or not they currently have many COP related programs or practices in place.

RESEARCH REMAINING TO BE DONE: COP AND CROSS-REGIONAL DIFFERENCES

An important question that remains unanswered at this point is that of the degree to which community policing is experienced as a REGIONAL phenomenon. In particular, are there patterns of adoption and correlates of change that are common to Pacific Northwest law enforcement agencies which would give impetus to effective regional training and applied research efforts that are DIFFERENT for the South or the Border States or the Eastern Seaboard? The regions of the United States have experienced different rates of change with respect to population gain and loss, with regard to the extent of racial and ethnic diversity, with respect to economic growth or decline, etc. Is it the case that the regional context within which a city finds itself has a good deal to do with its level of interest in and implementation of COP programs and practices in its police department? The data collected for this study would permit such an analysis to be undertaken.

It is also possible that the rising and falling fortunes of the political parties in the various regions of the country has a good deal more to do with the adoption and retention of COP innovations than any other factor(s). Since COP and "100,000 cops on the street" were widely regarded as synonymous with the Clinton Administration, could it be that declining regional fortunes for Democrats are associated with loss of interest in and continued support of COP programs and practices in many law enforcement agencies? The addition of regional partisan electoral outcomes for the cities included in the study dataset would make this type of analysis possible.

RESEARCH REMAINING TO BE DONE: ORGANIZATIONAL CHANGE AND COP

One way of looking at how far police agencies have gone with regard to the implementation of a community policing philosophy is to define what type of organizational model is typically used by law enforcement agencies. Noel Tichy, in his book *Managing Strategic Change: Technical, Political, and Cultural Dynamics*, describes some of the formal organizational models used for carrying planned organizational change in public and private sector agencies. In the case of law enforcement organizations, it is widely accepted that the hierarchical control model predominates. Tichy (1983) refers to this as the classical/mechanical model. Within the framework of this model you find the acclaimed aspects of a classical/mechanistic organizational structure—namely, an inviolate chain of command and a narrow span of control—both of which are believed to be essential for a strong accountability structure.

In contrast, the COP approach to policing requires that law enforcement organizations move away from the command and control management philosophy and toward a participatory/distributive model of operation (Stamper, 1992). Examination of the agencies in this sample with regard to their level of commitment to **community connectivity** (the commissioning of surveys, the organization of public forums, and the use of focus group discussions) and employee empowerment is another interesting undertaking for future research exploration. Such an examination would allow scholars to examine the level of decentralization that has occurred by analyzing which agencies consistently examine their service base by soliciting various types of input from local residents. It appears from the results presented in Chapter Four that police agencies continue to stress manpower and patrol enhancement issues over the development of a comprehensive COP philosophy.

When looking at why police organizations change, there is a significant amount of scholarship that describes the change process and the factors associated with both successful and unsuccessful efforts (Tichy, 1983; Behr, 1985; Hout and Carter, 1995; and Zhao et al., 1996). Although police agencies are a ubiquitous public service organization operating at the federal, state, tribal, and local levels, relatively few policy analysts, evaluation researchers, or social scientists have conducted systematic research on organizational change in police agencies. The addition of the next LEMAS survey data to the dataset compiled for this study will permit such systematic analyses to be undertaken in the context of a national COP program advocating organizational change in police organizations and providing "seed money" for agencies to undertake such change. The data reported in the series of LEMAS surveys reported on here reveal that, at the bottom line, police agencies have at long last begun to accept the view that making communities safe is a job they can not accomplish by their own efforts alone. Partnerships, active collaboration with community groups and other public agencies, and innovation in programs and street-level practices have all become important concepts for police agencies to adopt in their agency operations. To this end, it is important for police departments to look at what the public wants from the police, while at the same time assessing the internal effects that organizational change efforts bring to the fore as new paradigms of policing emerge. Once again, the research reported here suggests that relatively few municipal police agencies identified "problem solving partnerships" as an area that they seek to develop as part of their approach to crime abatement. What remains to be determined is what are these relatively few agencies like? What is the partisan political setting for these agencies? What is the background of the chief of police (e.g., internal promotion or external hire)? What is their situation with respect to level of crime—high, mid-range, or low? What degree of societal diversity and economic inequality characterizes the local jurisdictions involved?

During the past decade, police agencies across the country have started to look toward program and organizational innovation as promising methods for controlling crime. The Clinton administration (through the COPS Office initially headed up by Joe Brann, former Chief of Police of the innovative Santa Anna [California] police department) fought long and hard to establish public safety programs that seek out the underlying issues that perpetuate crime in order to embody a new spirit of community. As noted earlier, Amitai Etzioni (1993) is a strong proponent of community building and the adoption of a communitarian outlook for public policy. Some of the values and societal arrangements espoused by Etzioni and his communitarian followers are principles inherent in the COP philosophy. Neighborhood organization and the ability to have a voice in local concerns are at the very core of communitarian thought, and it is possible that the connection between Etzioni and Vice President Gore found its way to the public debate regarding the funding of COPS programs (Etzioni, 1993). As the OLS regression model presented in Chapter Four reveals, ethnic variation within a community is a strong predictor of COP funding. Budget allocations for hiring more police officers and funding COP programs that address community wellness was an important goal for the Clinton administration. Former President Clinton had pledged political support, and he also allocated the resources required to study community oriented policing programs across the country. In his inaugural address, President Clinton declared to the nation that "our greatest responsibility is to embrace a new spirit of community for a new century."[49]

Which agencies can be said to be truly making significant strides toward this end? Further, can this new organizational paradigm experience success in departments already strapped by dwindling budgets, increased calls for service, and well-established and habitualized hierarchical decision making patterns? What are some of the challenges that block the full implementation of a department-wide COP philosophy? How many departments are currently using the COP programs (e.g., foot patrol, bike patrol, neighborhood watch, ministations, and citizen volunteers) as indicators that community policing is alive and well within their respective jurisdiction? In order to facilitate policy design for public safety and to provide those faced with making these important decisions with sound information, many of the above questions have yet to be addressed through the analysis of empirical data.

Presently, community oriented policing is, and needs to be, many different things to many different police departments. Although the concept of COP is a rather difficult idea to define, many law enforcement agencies remain enthusiastic about its ultimate promise (Thurman and McGarrell, 1997). The innovative strategies that arise in one jurisdiction can provide similar jurisdictions with valuable information for their own efforts. In addition, examining the findings of this research can also contribute to the exploration of the types of agencies which choose to implement COP early on and the types that became "late adopters." As the results of the research conducted with the study dataset reveal, it is more often the small or middle size agency that finds COP a more attractive alternative to traditional policing because, unlike the larger police organization, smaller and moderate sized agencies must be more responsive to their constituency and cannot divorce themselves from their clients as their more bureaucratic brethren are able to do.

This study of what has taken place in law enforcement agencies with relation to COPS Office funding, manpower enhancement, the effects of local community demographics, and the range of COP program and practice adoption can help provide structure for future research efforts on the COP phenomenon in American policing. This examination of a significant pool of grantees (receiving 24% of the total COPS Office budget) can be used to measure the effects of change over time in law enforcement agencies that choose to enhance police services delivery through COP initiatives. Some of the most interesting questions to be addressed will require examining the change in demographics taking place over time in these communities upon the release of the 2000 Report of the Census for communities. Given this course for future research, it might be possible to assess if COP continues to develop at the current pace (small agencies in relatively homogenous areas outperforming large agencies in ethnically diverse regions of the country) or if COP succumbs to the new world order and the 'home security" agenda presently touted by conservative politicians. Surely, some lessons may be derived from this form of ongoing research on the level of community policing programs and if community connectivity can survive in an era of potential militaristic occupation.

The ensuing time series analysis made possible by the supplementation of the current study dataset with more recent LEMAS and 2000 census data can be enhanced by using a qualitative case study approach to help pinpoint any trends that may develop over the course of COP in the absence of federal funding. As noted earlier, the resulting findings can be useful for citizens, practitioners, and policy makers alike as they decide how best to address crime and ameliorate community disarray.

SOME FINAL THOUGHTS

As noted in the introduction, attempting to discern the optimal indicators of the presence of COP for systematic analysis is rather like designing a house without a blueprint, or surfing without a surfboard, or boxing without gloves and without the boundaries of a boxing ring. If one had the time and resources to analyze the history of policing in relation to levels of inequality, racial and ethnic diversity, and organizational change, any truly comprehensive analysis would likely take years to be performed. The rhetoric, philosophy, strategy, and tactics associated with COP are indeed important aspects of the COP story. COP is the largest scale federal law enforcement subsidy in the history of organized policing in the United States; consequently, it is very important for political scientists and students of public policy and public administration to examine how the core concepts of such a major public policy have been operationalized and what consequences for public safety have resulted from this operationalization. Since COP is an ongoing phenomenon, it is important that a strong base for future follow-up work be built, and that such follow-up research indeed be conducted to determine what mixture of philosophical acceptance, rhetorical posturing, strategic application, and tactical use of COP have occurred across the landscape of American policing. Much work remains to be done in this regard, and much of it will have to take the form of a combination of quantitative and qualitative analysis of strategically selected cases.

The recent effort at welfare reform also enacted during the Clinton Administration is being examined in this way (Hout, 1997; Peterson, 2000; Martinson and Holcomb, 2002), and the levels of educational funding associated with income inequality have been investigated as well (Joyner, 1997) in this same general way. Social equity has been explored in these areas with the same fundamental desire to uncover the extent to which planned change has taken the concrete form of changed philosophical beliefs or merely the recitation of rhetorical concern with little actual change in belief or behavior taking place. Similarly, reform in welfare and in school finance can either take the form of strategic action to address deep inequities, or tactical fixes that address the need of seeming to be concerned until public attention turns to other matters. The findings of studies in both of these areas suggest that planned changed to enhance social equity is difficult work indeed, and that a mixture of philosophical conversion, rhetorical compliance, strategic action and tactical maneuvering to avoid change are all to be expected. Such seems to also be the case for COP, at least at this relatively early juncture in its history.

The events of 9/11 have made it likely that new partnerships between the military and federal law enforcement agencies and local law enforcement will be a major aspect of 'homeland defense' in the years ahead. Attorney General Ashcroft is fond of characterizing local law enforcement as "the frontline troops in the war against terrorism." The homeland security initiative represents a potentially new, large scale recasting of the role of law enforcement in American society that should indeed attract the scrutiny of social scientists given its impact on the federal budget and how it will affect the relationship between law enforcement and the general public. How much of the community outreach and civic engagement activities of police agencies associated with COP will survive in the new era of homeland security promotion? Will there be only limited abandonment or wholesale retreat from the COP paradigm in the years immediately ahead? Is the advent of homeland security a turning point for COP? Will local law enforcement build upon COP in the homeland security work, or will they use this new aspect of their official mission to jettison COP programs that take time and agency resources and redirect those resources to a paramilitary purpose of preparing for attack by an unknown adversary?

The data analyzed in this study set the stage for the ongoing exploration of the relationship between inequality, crime, and ethnic diversity in communities, and federal funding awards that affect social justice. The war on terrorism is going to pour vast resources into the US economy toward the goal of protecting the homeland; community connectivity between local law enforcement and the citizenry is certainly one important way to ensure that American citizens are made to feel safe in times of uncertainty. A major consideration for policy makers and law enforcement managers in law enforcement agencies is to ensure that the positive bonds existing between police and citizens are not broken in the rush to detect and apprehend people from various "suspicious" ethnic groups. The promotion of the TIPS program (Turning in Suspicious Persons) by the Bush administration is symptomatic of the political fight brewing over what type of approach is best needed to enhance homeland security—one reflecting a focus on "suspicion" or one reflecting belief in the value of more trusting connections among neighbors and between neighborhoods and their police.

When reading an article in *Footnotes* by Joyce Iutcovich, it became apparent that research as presented here makes an important contribution to the role of social science in policy debates. According to Iutcovich (2002), in our quest for research and data that can inform legislative policy-making concerns, it is critically important to clarify the types of questions we ask as researchers. Even further, those who choose to study social problems and the subsequent policies that emerge in an attempt to alleviate them should examine the measurement tools we have in our arsenal that can provide answers to these questions. This research project attempts to reach into that arsenal and examine evidence and generate statistics that are available to all researchers and policy analysts alike when attempting to explain the difference between empirical relationships that exist in the policy making process and "political relationships" which are purely plausible but serve important political advocacy goals.

One of the key goals of the COPS Office grant program was for rank-and-file law enforcement officers to make lasting connections with their communities in order to enhance public safety and improve the quality of life for all citizens, rich and poor alike. With regard to the distribution of COPS Office grant awards, this analysis reported here reveals that important social equity concerns were used to make decisions about the level of need in the communities present in the 197 communities explored here. The social equity problems associated with the previous large-scale federal law enforcement subsidy program known as the LEAA were largely avoided by the COPS Office. In the case of the 1994 Crime Bill, it seems that a relatively even balance was found with regard to the conservative approach (or get tough on crime view) through the federal funding of more prisons and harsher sentencing and the pursuit of a more equitable form of policing (COP).

The ensuing debate over the continued funding of programs that further the aims of COP and community building could result in the wholesale abandonment of the work done over the past 7 years to proliferate the idea of proactive and community-engaging policing with estranged racial and ethnic communities. As noted by Thayer and Reynolds (1997), the widening gap between police and communities was a major factor in the seeking of alternatives to public safety such as the COP program. "The citizens and the police in partnerships should identify potential problem areas and work to ensure that these problems do not disrupt the community" (Thayer and Reynolds, 1997:103). From this standpoint, it will be interesting to see the research and statistical weaponry pulled from the arsenal of liberal and conservative political camps as they attempt to discern whether the continuation of these types of proactive programs will be abandoned for the more conservative approach that attempts to once again militarize law enforcement operations.

A prime example of this coming political debate over the proper character of American policing is the move by conservative politicians to reverse the *Posse Comitatus Act* (18USC1385)[50] of 1873. During the Post Civil War reconstruction period, the U.S. Army exercised police functions in much of the South. This type of intervention left a sour taste in the mouth of many citizens and led to the enactment of the *Posse Comitatus Act* that prohibits the Army (and with the advancement of technology, the Air Force) from being used to enforce the law on home soil. Although Congress has sanctioned the use of the military during the drug interdiction programs established in the 1980s, these operations were clandestine in nature and were endorsed by the majority of citizens concerned with a growing drug problem. Having the military in our communities is akin to the establishment of martial law, a world away from the concepts of community building associated with the basic precepts of the community policing movement. It is only since the terrible tragedy that was September 11, 2001 that this idea of using the military to enforce local laws and apprehend those suspected of suspicious behaviors emerges as a policy question in relation to the way our communities are and will be policed in the future. This is an issue that will surely come to the forefront of the policy debate regarding the role of the federal government in law enforcement policy at the state and local level. Police functions are supposed to be state and local, and a militia always held only a role as a backup. Again, these restrictions might be ignored, particularly in time of stress and confusion, but it would seem that the Constitutional protections that call for a separation of powers at the state and federal levels of authority should be adopted in any planning effort that attempts to affect change in criminal justice practices generally, and more specifically at the level of local law enforcement.

In this vein, it should be noted that the architecture of community policing may indeed be in place, but that architecture will be severely tested in the years ahead. The advent of the homeland security issue will either bring about a systematic remodeling and enhancement of COP or lead to its dismantling as federal funds to sustain experimentation and policy learning are redirected to homeland security. The results presented herein indicate that agencies with sufficient municipal resources opted to hire more officers rather than engage in innovation and outreach, but that agencies lacking such resources tended to adopt many of the COP programs and practices that did not require substantial municipal resources. With this study as a base, it will be possible to monitor the reactions of these agencies to the political arguments to come over how best to achieve homeland security, and what role in that effort is to be played by COP. The challenges facing American law enforcement will be great indeed in the years ahead, and research such as reported here will hopefully help enlighten the public policy choices facing us all.

Endnotes

1. Distributional equity is defined as the distribution of policy funds and services to communities in need. For the purpose of this analysis, need for each jurisdiction in this study will be defined in terms of ethnic diversity, levels of income inequality, deficits in educational attainment for those over 25 years of age, and areas where crime is a concern. Although this definition is general in nature, need can be defined further in terms of community connectivity by examining the 202 cities in this preliminary analysis and through the exploration of how each department elicits and uses feedback from the community regarding their experiences with crime, police services delivery, and community cohesion.

2. The COPS Office has developed a wide variety of training materials for departmental use in the implementation of COP. See the Department of Justice, Office of Community Policing Services website at http://www.usdoj.gov/cops/cp_resources/pubs_prod/ s29.htm

3. The organizational anthropology view posits that organizational development can be traced to antecedent conditions that are associated with social change that are basic to the concerns of both organizational and political theorists (see Bate, 1997).

4. A description of the three lines of defense to crime can be found in LaGrange (1998). COP philosophy espouses a move up from the second line through the development of partnerships and collaboration.

5. COP as a rhetoric can be linked to the policy process and how interest groups promote the tenets of COP as a federally subsidized policy. The philosophical approach to COP is grounded in certain beliefs about the role of police in modern society and how pluralism affects the adoption of COP in diverse communities across the nation. Strategy deals with the changing of the organizational structure, and tactics are designed within the constraints of the organization to address specific needs by using interventions such as problem oriented policing and community collaboration.

6. From the COPS Office website (http://www.usdoj.gov/cops/news_ info/legislate/leg_history.htm).

7. Hero's white ethnic diversity category is comprised of persons of Greek, Hungarian, Irish, Italian, Polish, Portuguese, and Russian heritage.

8. See the U.S. Department of Justice, Office of Community Oriented Policing Services (2001). "Making Officer Redeployment Effective (MORE): Using Technology to Keep America's Communities Safe," COPS Fact Sheet. Washington DC.

9. See U.S. Department of Justice, Office of Community Oriented Policing Services (2002). "Universal Hiring Program: Adding Patrol Officers to the Street." COPS Fact Sheet. Washington, DC.

10. See U.S. Department of Justice, Office of Community Oriented Policing Services (2002). "COPS in Schools." COPS Fact Sheet. Washington, DC.

11. Information on this program was taken from the COPS Office Website at the following internet address: http://www.usdoj.gov/ cops/pa/grant_prog/ troop_cops/sc/default.htm.

12. See U.S. Department of Justice, Office of Community Oriented Policing Services (2002). "Distressed Neighborhoods: Helping Communities Help Themselves," COPS Fact Sheet. Washington, DC.

13. Information on this program was taken from the COPS Office Website at the following internet address: http://www.usdoj.gov/cops/gpa/grant_prog/ ahead/default.htm.

14. Information on this program was taken from the COPS Office Website at the following internet address: http://www.usdoj.gov/cops/gpa/grant_prog/ fast/default.htm.

15. Four agencies received funding under this program. Coral Gables, FL received $300,000 and 4 officers. Beverly Hills, CA received $225,000 and 3 officers. Fort Meyers, FL received $225,000 and 3 officers. Kalamazoo, MI received $75,000 and 1 officer. These cities were omitted from Appendix Table 6 in the interest of space.

16. Information on this program was taken from the COPS Office Website at the following internet address: http://www.usdoj.gov/cops/gpa/grant_prog/ phase1/default.htm.

17. Information on this program was taken from the COPS Office Website at the following internet address: http://www.usdoj.gov/cops/gpa/grant_prog/ acp/default.htm.

18. Information on this program was taken from the COPS Office Website at the following internet address: http://www.usdoj.gov/cops/gpa/grant_prog/ anti_gang/default.htm.

19. Again, for the purpose of space management, 12 agencies were omitted from Appendix Tables 6 and 7. Chicago, IL, Phoenix, AZ, Dallas, TX, and Detroit, MI all received awards for $1 million. Austin, TX and Boston, MA received stipends of $750,000. Miami, FL and Kansas City, MO

received $500,000. Jersey City, NJ, Salt Lake City, UT and Oakland, CA were allocated over $499,000 and St. Louis, MO received $488,854. The total for these departments is $8,488,854.

20. Information on this program was taken from the COPS Office Website at the following internet address: http://www.usdoj.gov/cops/gpa/grant_prog/ com violence/ default.htm.

21. Information on this program was taken from the COPS Office Website at the following internet address: http://www.usdoj.gov/cops/gpa/grant_prog/ ccp/default.htm.

22. Information on this program was taken from the COPS Office Website at the following internet address: http://www.usdoj.gov/cops/gpa/grant_prog/ demo/default.htm.

23. See U.S. Department of Justice, Office of Community Oriented Policing Services (2001). "COPS Methamphetamine Initiatives," COPS Fact Sheet. Washington, DC.

24. See U.S. Department of Justice, Office of Community Oriented Policing Services (1997). "Problem-Solving Partnerships," COPS Facts. Washington, DC.

25. See U.S. Department of Justice, Office of Community Oriented Policing Services (2001). "Regional Community Policing Institutes," COPS Fact Sheet. Washington, DC.

26. Each RCPI has a specialty and draws upon the resources of local scholars to assist with specific problem areas law enforcement may encounter. For example, in San Diego, CA the RCPI provides assistance with community policing problem solving. In Spokane, WA the Western Regional Institute for Community Oriented Public Safety (WRICOPS) has worked to develop organizational and community assessments to assist with COP implementation in a five-state region. The Kansas RCPI at Wichita State University specializes in technology as a COP resource. In Sacramento, CA the RCPI assists with neighborhood revitalization efforts. The Michigan RCPI focuses on training and organizational change to enhance COP efforts.

27. For more information see U.S. Department of Justice, Office of Community Oriented Policing Services (1998). "COPS School Based Partnerships Grant Assessment Solicitation." Washington, DC.

28. See U.S. Department of Justice, Office of Community Oriented Policing Services (1999). "Troops to COPS '99 Grant Owners Manual," in COPS Manual. Washington, DC.

29. Information on this program was taken from the COPS Office Website at the following internet address: http://www.usdoj.gov/cops/gpa/grant_prog/ youth_fire/default.htm.

30. See U.S. Department of Justice, Office of Community Oriented Policing Services (2001). "Value Based Initiatives: Innovative Promising Practices," COPS Fact Sheet. Washington, DC.

31. See U.S. Department of Justice, Office of Community Oriented Policing Services (2001). "311 for Non Emergencies: Helping Communities One Call at a Time," COPS Fact Sheet. Washington, DC

32. See U.S. Department of Justice, Office of Community Oriented Policing Services (2001). "Justice Based After School Program: COPS Supports Local Law Enforcement," COPS Fact Sheet. Washington, DC.

33. See U.S. Department of Justice, Office of Community Oriented Policing Services (1997). "Problem Solving Partnerships," COPS Facts. Washington, DC

34. Best practices have been used in the field of education to encourage the use of tested pedagogical theories in the classroom to improve student learning. In this vein, best practices for law enforcement has yet to be explained in terms of theory, but there is a great deal of documentation that explores the effects of various crime control interventions that have used Scanning, Assessment, Response, and Analysis (SARA) to engage in community problem solving exercises.

35. Lt. Joe Valenzuela of the Sacramento Police Department generously supplied information on PSPM. Lt. Valenzuela attended the conference noted above and provided information about the discussions in the workshops and the types of interventions that have been proposed to enhance police-community collaborations.

36. Information on this program was taken from the COPS Office Website at the following internet address: http://www.usdoj.gov/cops/gpa/grant_prog/ca/ca_recruit.htm.

37. Information on the Integrity program was gained from conversations with COPS office staff.

38. Information on the CICP program was gained from quantitative interviews with Major Zamora with the Santa Fe Police Department.

39. Information on the PSP program was gained while employed as a research associate at the Western Regional Institute for Community Oriented Public Safety (WRICOPS).

40. See the U.S. Department of Justice, Office of Community Oriented Policing Services (2000). "Training and Technical Assistance," COPS Fact Sheet. Washington, DC.

41. The totals presented here DO NOT include the $8,487,848 for GANGS and $90,000 for SCGP that are not reported in the Appendix.

42. Because many jurisdictions do not report arson, it has been excluded from the analysis. It should also be noted that some agencies (36 total) did not have a full compliment of crime reporting data.

43. In order to properly identify the effects of COP and award levels, the agencies (5) which did not receive funding will be excluded from the analysis of the level of COP implementation

44. Taken from Hero (1998).

45. The factors that are considered to be appropriate outcome measures for gauging COP activity in 1999 are: level of commitment to COP in each agency (COPRAT99), number of officers per household (OFFHH99), percentage of vacancies in relation to the number of full-time authorized personnel in 1999 (EMTPOS2), whether citizens are trained in COP (TRNCIT99), whether geographic patrol is used routinely (GEOPAT99), presence of encouragement for use of the SARA model of assessing and solving local problems (ENSARA99), whether the agency is actively engaged in forming problem-solving partnerships (FPSP99), ratio of total volunteers to 10,000 households (TOTVOLRA), degree to which a community policing plan is in effect (CPPLAN99), routine use of foot patrol (FOOT99) and bicycle patrol (BIKE99), number of fixed neighborhood stations per 100 officers (NUMSTA2), extent of training in the principles of COP for recruits (RECSCP99) and other sworn personnel through the provision of in-service training (INSVCP99), ratio COP officers to full-time sworn officers in 1999 (COP99A), ratio of school resource officers to full-time sworn officers (SRO99A), change in the number of full-time sworn officers per 10, 000 households in 1999 (OFF9399A), the number of grant-acquired officers per 10,000 households (HHCOPPK).

46. As noted earlier, the original sample included 202 agencies. The analysis was performed using only those agencies receiving funding under the COPS program.

47. See McGarrell and Thurman, 1995; Thurman and Reisig, 1996; and Gutierrez, Benitez and Thurman, 1996.

48. Using the same variables that were present in the examination of the top and bottom ten award recipients in Chapter Four, an Independent samples T-test was performed on these agencies revealing only a difference in one area: encouraging the use of the SARA model (sig. at .003). No other differences were found between these eight agencies and the rest of the sample.

49. 1997 Presidential Inaugural Address.

50. Army Appropriations Act, Ch. 263, § 15, 20 Stat. 145, 152 (1878) (codified as amended at 18 U.S.C. § 1385 [1994]).

References

Affigne, T. (2000). "Latino Politics in the United States: An Introduction." *Political Science and Politics.* 33:523-527.

Alex-Assensoh, Y. (1995). "Myths About Race and the Underclass: Concentrated Poverty and 'Underclass' Behaviors," *Urban Affairs Review.* 31:3-19.

Alpert, G. and Moore, M. (1993). "Measuring Police Performance in the New Paradigm of Policing," in *Performance Measures for the Criminal Justice System.* Washington, DC: U.S. Department of Justice, Office of Justice Programs, Bureau of Justice Statistics, pp. 109-140.

Alpert, G. and Smith, W. (1996). "Developing Police Policy: An Evaluation of the Control Principle," in G. W. Cordner and D. J. Kenney (Eds.), *Managing Police Organizations.* Cincinnati, OH: Anderson Publishing, pp. 111-126.

Anderson, D. (1997). "The Mystery of the Falling Crime Rate," *American Prospect.* 32:49-55.

Andranovich, G. and Lovrich, N. (1996). "Editors Introduction: Community-Oriented Research," *American Behavioral Scientist.* 39:525-535.

Angell, J. (1971). "Alternative to Police Organization," *Criminology.* 9:186-206.

Bailey, W. (1984). "Poverty, Inequality, and City Homicide Rates," *Criminology.* 22:531-550.

Barak, G., Flavin, J., and Leighton, P. (2001). *Class, Race, Gender, and Crime: Social Realities of Justice in America.* Los Angeles, CA: Roxbury Publishing Company.

Bass, S. (2001). "Policing Space, Policing Race: Social Control Imperatives and Police Discretionary Decisions," *Social Justice.* 28:156-176.

Bate, S. (1997). "Whatever Happened to Organizational Anthropology? A Review of the Field of Organizational Ethnography and Anthropological Studies," *Human Relations.* 50:1147-1175.

Baumgartner, F. and Leech, B. (1998). *Basic Interests: The Importance of Groups in Politics and in Political Science*. Princeton, NJ: Princeton University Press.

Bayley, D. (1994). *Police for the Future*. New York, NY: Oxford University Press.

_____ (1988). "Community Policing: A Report from the Devil's Advocate," in J. Greene and S. Mastrofski (Eds.), *Community Policing: Rhetoric or Reality*. New York: Praeger, pp.225-237.

Beckett, K. and Sasson, T. (2000). *The Politics of Injustice: Crime and Punishment in America*. Thousand Oaks, CA: Pine Forge Press.

Behr, R. (1995). "Creating an Innovative Organization: Ten Hints for Involving Front Line Workers," *State and Local Government Review*. 27:221-234.

Bell, D. (1993). *Communitarianism and Its Critics*. Oxford, England: Clarendon Press.

Berry, J. (1997). *The Interest Group Society* (3rd Edition). New York, NY: Longman.

Bittner, E. (1970). *The Functions of Police in Modern Society*. Chevy Chase, MD: National Institute of Mental Health.

Blau, J. and Blau, P. (1982). "The Cost of Inequality: Metropolitan Structure and Violent Crime," *American Sociological Review*. 47:114-129.

Bonger, W. (1916). *Criminality and Economic Conditions*. Boston, MA: Little and Brown.

Braithwaite, J. (1979). *Inequality, Crime, and Public Policy*. London: Routledge and Keegan Paul.

Brann, J. (1995). Statement Before the Subcommittee on the Judiciary, U.S. House of Representations Concerning Oversight of the Office of Community Oriented Policing Services. Washington, DC: U.S. House of Representatives.

Breci, M. and Erickson, T. (1998). "Community Policing: The Process of Transitional Change," *FBI Law Enforcement Bulletin*. 67:16-22.

Brooks, L. (1997). "Police Discretionary Behavior: A Study of Style," in R. Dunham and G. Alpert (Eds.), *Critical Issues in Policing: Contemporary Readings* (3rd Edition). Prospect Heights, IL: Waveland Press, pp. 149-166.

Brown, L. (1989). *Perspectives on Policing—Community Policing: A Practical Guide for Police Officials*. Washington, DC: U.S. Department of Justice, National Institute of Justice, Program in Criminal Justice Policy and Management.

Buerger, M. (1993). "The Challenge of Reinventing Police and Community," in D. Weisburd and C. Uchida (Eds.), *Police Innovation and Control of the Police: Problems of Law, Order, and Community*. New York, NY: Springer Verlag, pp. 104-124.

_____ (1994). "The Limits of Community Policing," in D. Rosenbaum (Ed.), *The Challenge of Community Policing: Testing the Promises*. Thousand Oaks, CA: Sage Publications, pp. 270-273.

Bureau of Justice Assistance (1994). *Neighborhood-Oriented Policing in Rural Communities: A Program Planning Guide*. Washington, DC: U.S. Department of Justice.

Caldwell, D. and Dorling, E. (1995). "Networking Between Practitioners and Academics in Law Enforcement," *Public Administration Review*. 55:107-110.

Cameron, S. and Heckman, J. (2001). "The Dynamics of Educational Attainment for Black, Hispanic, and White Males," *Journal of Political Economy*. 109:455-499.

Center for Research on Criminal Justice (1975). *The Iron Fist and the Velvet Glove: An Analysis of the U.S. Police*. Berkeley, CA: The Center for Research on Criminal Justice.

Choi, C., Turner, C. and Volden, C. (2002). "Means, Motive, and Opportunity: Politics, Community Needs, and Community Oriented Policing Services Grants," *American Politics Research*. 30:423-455.

Chuang, H. (1994). "An Empirical Study of Reenrollment for Male High School Dropouts," *Applied Economics*. 26:1071-1081.

Cohen, M., March, J. and Olsen, J. (1972). "A Garbage Can Model of Organizational Choice," *Administrative Science Quarterly*. 17:1-25.

Cordner, G. (1997). "Community Policing: Elements and Effects," in R. Dunham and G. Alpert (Eds.), *Critical Issues in Policing: Contemporary Readings* (3rd Edition). Prospect Heights, IL: Waveland Press, pp. 451-468.

Correia, M. (2000). *Citizen Involvement: How Community Factors Affect Progressive Policing*. Washington, D.C.: Police Executive Research Forum.

Crank, J. and Langworthy, R. (1996). "Fragmented Centralization and the Organization of the Police," *Policing and Society*. 6:213-229.

Dahl, R. (1961). *Who Governs?* New Haven, CT: Yale University Press.

_____ (1982). *Dilemmas of Pluralist Democracy: Autonomy vs. Control*. New Haven, CT: Yale University Press.

Davis, G., Mulhausen, D., Ingram, D., and Rector, R. (2000). *The Facts About COPS: A Performance Review of Community Oriented Policing Services Programs*. Washington, DC: Heritage Foundation.

DeFronzo, J. and Hannon, L. (1998). "Welfare Assistance and Homicide Rates," *Homicide Studies*. 2:31-45.

de la Garza, R. and DeSipio, L. (1992). *From Rhetoric to Reality: Latinos and the 1988 Election*. Boulder, CO: Westview Press.

_____ (1997). "The Best of Times, The Worst of Times: Latinos and the 1996 Elections," *The Harvard Journal of Hispanic Policy*. 10:3-26.

Donahue, J. (1999). *Hazardous Crosscurrents: Confronting Inequality in an Era of Devolution*. New York, NY: The Century Foundation Press.

Duffy, B. (1992). "Days of Rage," *United States News and World Report*. Vol.112, No.18, pp. 20-26.

Eck, J. and Maguire, E. (2000). "Have Changes in Policing Reduced Violent Crime? An Assessment of the Evidence," in A. Blumstein and J. Wallman (Eds.), *The Crime Drop in America*. New York, NY: Cambridge, pp. 207-265.

Eck, J. and Rosenbaum, D. (1994). "The New Police Order: Effectiveness, Equity, and Efficiency in Community Policing," in D. Rosenbaum (Ed.), *The Challenge of Community Policing: Testing the Promise*. Thousand Oaks, CA: Sage Publications, pp. 3-23.

Eck, J. and Spelman, W. (1987). *Solving Problems: Problem-Oriented Policing in Newport News*. Washington, DC: Police Executive Research Forum.

Elazar, D. (1966): *American Federalism: A View From the States* (3rd Edition). New York, NY: Harper and Row.

_____ (1984). *American Federalism*, (3rd Edition). New York, NY: Harper and Row.

_____ (1994). *The American Mosaic: The Impact of Space, Time, and Culture on American Politics*. Boulder, CO: Westview Press.

Etzioni, A. (1993). *The Spirit of Community: Rights, Responsibilities, and the Communitarian Agenda*. New York, NY: Crown Publishers.

_____ (1961). *A Comparative Analysis of Complex Organizations*. New York, NY: Free Press.

_____ (1968). *The Active Society: A Theory of Societal and Political Processes*. New York, NY: Free Press.

_____ (1975). *A Comparative Analysis of Complex Organizations: On Power, Involvement, and Their Correlates*. New York, NY: Free Press.

_____ (1984). *Capital Corruption: The New Attack on American Democracy*. San Diego, CA: Harcourt Brace Jovanovich.

Feins, J. (1983). *Partnerships for Neighborhood Crime Prevention.* Washington, DC: National Institute of Justice, U.S. Department of Justice.

Feeley, M. and Sarat, A. (1980). *The Policy Dilemma: Federal Crime Policy and the Law Enforcement Assistance Administration.* Minneapolis, MN: University of Minnesota Press.

Ford, J., Boles, J., Plamondon, K., and White, J. (1999). "Transformational Leadership and Community Policing: A Roadmap for Change," *Police Chief.* 66:12, 14, 16, 18-22.

Ford, K. and Morash, M. (2002). "Transforming Police Organizations," in M. Morash and J. Ford (Eds.), *The Move to Community Policing: Making Change Happen.* Thousand Oaks, CA: Sage Publications, pp. 1-11.

Frederickson, H. (1990). "Public Administration and Social Equity," *Public Administration Review.* 50:228-237

_____ (1980). *New Public Administration.* University, AL: The University of Alabama Press.

_____ (1990). "Public Administration and Social Equity," *Public Administration Review.* 50:228-237.

_____ (1993). "Ethics and Public Administration: Some Assertions," in H. George Frederickson (Ed.), *Bureaucracies, Public Administration, and Public Policy: Ethics and Public Administration* New York, NY: M. E. Sharpe, pp. 243-262.

Fullerton, T. (2001). "Educational Attainment and Border Income Performances," *Economic and Financial Review.* 3:2-10.

Gaffigan, S., Roth, J. and Buerger, M. (2000). "Origins and Objectives of the COPS Program," in *National Evaluation of the COPS Program—Title I of the 1994 Crime Act.* Washington, DC: National Institute of Justice/Urban Institute, 25-62.

Gaines, L., Kappeler, V. and Vaughn, J. (1999). *Policing in America,* (3rd Edition). Cincinnati, OH: Anderson Publishing.

George, D. and Mallory, P. (2001). *SPSS for Windows Step by Step: A Simple Guide and Reference, 10.0 Update.* Boston, MA: Allyn and Bacon.

Giankis, G. and Davis, J. (1998). "Reinventing or Repackaging Public Services: The Case of Community-Oriented Policing," *Public Administration Review.* 58:485-511.

Giorgi, L and Pohoryles, R. (1999). "Income Analysis and Social Inclusion Policies," *Innovation.* 12:549-566.

Glasser, J. (2000) "The Case of the Missing Cops: The Plan for 100,000 Patrolmen is Flat-Footed," *U.S. News and World Report.* 17 July, 2000, pp.22-23.

Glensor, R. and Peak, K. (1996). "Implementing Change: Community-Oriented Policing and Problem Solving," *The FBI Law Enforcement Journal.* 65:8.

Goldstein, H. (1977). *Policing a Free Society.* Cambridge, MA: Ballinger Press.

_____ (1979). "Improving Policing: A Problem-Oriented Approach," *Crime and Delinquency.* 22:236-258.

_____ (1987). "Toward Community-Oriented Policing: Potential, Basic Requirements, and Threshold Questions," *Crime and Delinquency.* 35:6-30.

_____ (1990). *Problem-Oriented Policing.* New York, NY: McGraw-Hill.

_____ (1990). *SARA Problem Oriented Policing.* Philadelphia, PA: Temple University Press.

Golembiewski, R. (1985). *Humanizing Public Organizations.* Mt. Airy, MD: Lomond Publications, Inc.

Gordon, D. (1971). "Class and the Economics of Crime," *Review of Radical Political Economy.* 3:51-72.

Green, J. and Mastrofski, S. (1988). *Community Policing: Rhetoric or Reality.* New York, NY: Praeger.

Greene, J. (2000). "Community Policing in America: Changing the Nature, Structure, and Function of the Police." In *Criminal Justice 2000: Policies, Processes and Decisions of the Criminal Justice System.* Washington, D.C.: U.S. Department of Justice, Office of Justice Programs, pp. 299-370.

_____ (1982). "Implementing Police Programs: Some Environmental Impediments," in M Morash (Ed.), *Implementing Criminal Justice Policies.* Beverly Hills, CA: Sage Publications, pp. 71-88.

Greenwood, R. and Hinings, C. R. (1996). "Understanding Radical Organizational Change: Bringing Together the Old and the New Institutionalism," *Academy of Management Review.* 21:1022-1054.

Gutierrez, R., Benitez, S. and Thurman, Q. (1996). "Findings from the 1996 Pasco Police Department Community Survey: Final Results." Spokane, WA: Washington State Institute for Community Oriented Policing.

Hart, D. and Hart, D. (1992). "George C. Marshall and J. Edgar Hoover: Noblesse Oblige and Self-Serving Power," in T. Cooper and N. Dale Wright (Eds.), *Exemplary Public Administrators: Character and Leadership in Government.* San Francisco, CA: Jossey-Bass, pp. 80-107.

Hero, R. (1998). *Faces of Inequality: Social Diversity in American Politics.* New York, NY: Oxford University Press.

Hirshi, T. (1969). *Causes of Delinquency.* Berkeley, CA: University of California Press.

Hout, M. (1997). "Inequality at the Margins: The Effects of Welfare, the Minimum Wage, and Tax Credits on Low-Wage Labor," *Politics and Society.* 25:513-524.

Iutcovich, J. (2002). "Congressional Fellow Report: The Role of Science in Policy Debates," *Footnotes.* 30:2.

Johnson, D. (1981). *American Law Enforcement: A History.* St. Louis, MO: Forum Press.

Johnson, J., Farkas, S., Bers, A., Connolly, C. and Maldonado, Z. (1999). "Americans' Views on Crime and Law Enforcement: A Look at Recent Survey Findings," in R. Langworthy (Ed.), *Measuring What Matters: Proceedings From the Police Institute Meetings.* Washington, DC: National Institute of Justice and Office of Community Oriented Policing Services, pp. 133-140.

Johnson, J., Farrell, W. and Stoloff, J. (2000). "An Empirical Assessment of the Four Perspectives on the Declining Fortunes of the African-American Male," *Urban Affairs Review.* 35:695-716.

Joyner, C. (1997). *School Finance: State Efforts to Reduce Funding Gaps Between Poor and Wealthy Districts.* Washington, D.C.: United States General Accounting Office, Report to Congressional Requesters.

Kane, R. (2000). "Permanent Beat Assignments in Association with Community Policing: The Impact on Police Officers' Field Activity," *Justice Quarterly.* 17:259-280.

Kelling, G. (1987). "Acquiring a Taste for Order: The Community and the Police," *Crime and Delinquency.* 35:90-102.

_____ (1999). *"Broken Windows" and Police Discretion.* Washington, DC: National Institute of Justice, U.S. Department of Justice.

Kelling, G. and Bratton, W. (1993). "Implementing Community Policing: The Administrative Problem," *(United States Department of Justice) Perspectives on Policing,* No.17, pp. 1-11.

Kelling, G. and Moore, M. (1988). "From Political to Reform to Community: The Evolving Strategy of Police," in J. R. Greene and S. D. Mastrofski (Eds.), *Community Policing: Rhetoric or Reality?* New York, NY: Praeger, pp. 3-26.

Kelling, G., Pate, T., Dieckman, D. and Brown, C. (1974). *The Kansas City Preventive Patrol Experiment: A Summary Report.* Washington, DC: The Police Foundation.

Kelly, M. (2000). "Inequality and Crime," *Review of Economics and Statistics.* 82-14:530-539.

Kelman, S. (1987). *Making Public Policy: A Hopeful View of American Government.* New York, NY: Basic Books.

Kemmis, D. (1990). *Community and the Politics of Place*. Norman, OK: University of Oklahoma Press.

Kingdon, J.W. (1995). *Agendas, Alternatives, and Public Policies* (2nd Edition). New York, NY: HarperCollins.

Klockars, C. (1991). "The Rhetoric of Community Policing," in J. Greene and S. Mastrofski (Eds.), *Community Policing: Rhetoric or Reality?* New York, NY: Praeger, pp.239-258.

Kovandzic, T., Vieraitis, L., and Yeisley, M. (1998). "The Structural Covariates of Homicide: Reassessing the Impact of Income Inequality and Poverty in the Post-Reagan Era," *Criminology*. 36:569-600.

Kuznets, S. (1955). "Economic Growth and Income Inequality," *American Economic Review*. 45:1-28.

LaFree, G. (1999). "Declining Violent Crime Rates in the 1990s: Predicting Crime Booms and Busts," *Annual Review of Sociology*. 225:145-168.

LaGrange, R. (1998). *Policing in America* (2nd Edition). Chicago, IL: Nelson-Hall Publishers.

Langworthy, R., Hughes, T. and Sanders, B. (1995). *Law Enforcement Recruitment, Selection and Training: A Survey of Major Police Departments in the U.S.* Highland Heights, KY: Academy of Criminal Justice Sciences—Police Section.

Levernier, W. (1999). "An Analysis of Family Income Inequality in Metropolitan Counties," *Social Science Quarterly*. 80:154-165.

Lewis-Beck, M. (1980). *Applied Regression: An Introduction*. Beverly Hills, CA: Sage Publications.

Lieske, J. (1993). "Regional Subcultures of the United States," *The Journal of Politics*. 55:888-913

Lowi, T. (1979). *The End of Liberalism: The Second Republic of the United States* (2nd Edition). New York, NY: W.W. Norton.

Lucas, S. (2001). "Effectively Maintaining Inequality: Education Transitions, Track Mobility, and Social Background Effects," *The American Journal of Sociology*. 106:1642-1690.

Lurigio, A. and Skogan, W. (1994). "Winning the Hearts and Minds of Police Officers: An Assessment of Staff Perceptions of Community Policing in Chicago," *Crime and Delinquency*. 40:315-330.

Madden, J. (2000). *Changes in Income Inequality within U.S. Metropolitan Areas*. Kalamazoo, MI: W. E. Upjohn Institute for Employment Research.

Maddox, G., Clark, D. and Steinhauser, K. (1994). "Dynamics to Functional Impairment in Late Adulthood," *Social Science & Medicine*. 38:925-936.

Maguire, E. (1997). "Structural Change in Large Municipal Police Organizations During the Community Policing Era," *Justice Quarterly*. 14:547-576.

Maguire, E., Kuhns, J., Uchida, C. and Cox, S. (1997) "Patterns of Community Policing in Nonurban America," *Journal of Research in Crime and Delinquency*. 34:368-395.

Maltz, M. (1999). "Bridging Gaps in Police Crime Data: A Discussion Paper from the BJS Fellows Program." Washington, DC: U.S. Department of Justice, Office of Justice Programs, Bureau of Justice Statistics.

Martinson, K and Holcomb, P. (2002). *Reforming Welfare: Institutional Change and Challenges: Occasional Paper Number 60, Assessing the New Federalism*. Washington, D.C.: The Urban Institute.

Mastrofski, S. (1991). "Community Policing as Reform: A Cautionary Tale," in J. Greene and S. Mastrofski (Eds.), *Community Policing: Rhetoric or Reality*. New York, NY: Praeger, pp. 47-67.

Mastrofski, S. and Uchida, C. (1993). "Transforming the Police," *Journal of Research in Crime and Delinquency*. 30:330-350.

Mastrofski, S., Worden, R. and Snipes, J. (1995). "Law Enforcement in a Time of Community Policing," *Criminology*. 33:539-563.

Mayer, S. (2001). "How Did the Increase in Economic Inequality Between 1960 and 1990 Affect Children's Educational Attainment," *American Journal of Sociology*. 107:1-33.

McCabe, K. and Fajardo, R. (2001). "Law Enforcement Accreditation: A National Comparison of Accredited vs. Nonaccredited Agencies," *Journal of Criminal Justice*. 29:127-131.

McEwen, T. (1995). "National Assessment Program: 1994 Survey Results," in National Institute of Justice, *Research in Brief*. Washington, D.C.: U.S. Department of Justice.

McGarrell, E., London, R., and Benitez, S. (1997). "Getting to Know Your Employees Better," in Q. C. Thurman and E. F. McGarrell (Eds.), *Community Policing in Rural America*. Cincinnati, OH: Anderson Publishing, pp. 65-73.

McGarrell, E. and Thurman, Q. (1996). "Findings From the 1995 Spokane Police Department Citizen Survey: Final Report." Spokane, WA: Washington State Institute for Community Oriented Policing.

Merton, R. (1938). *Social Theory and Social Structure*. New York, NY: Free Press.

Messner, S. (1982). "Poverty, Inequality, and the Urban Homicide Rate," *Criminology*. 20:103-114.

Messner, S. and Tardiff, K. (1986). "Income Inequality and Levels of Homicide: An Analysis of Urban Neighborhoods," *Criminology*. 24:297-313.

Miller, W. (1977). *Cops and Bobbies: Police Authority in New York and Long Island, 1830-1870*. Chicago, IL: University of Chicago Press.

Moe, R. (1987). "Exploring the Limits of Privatization," *Public Administration Review*. 47:453-460.

Monkkonen, E. (1992). "History of Urban Police," in M. Tonry and N. Morris (Eds.), *Modern Policing*. Chicago, IL: University of Chicago Press, pp. 547-580.

Moore, M., Thacher, D., Coles, C., Sheingold, P. and Hartmann, F. (2000). "COPS Grants, Leadership and Transitions to Community Policing." *National Evaluation of the COPS Program—Title I of the 1994 Crime Act*. Washington, DC: National Institute of Justice/Urban Institute, pp.247-274.

O'Connor, A. (2001). "Understanding Inequality in the Late Twentieth Century Metropolis: New Perspectives on the Enduring Racial Divide," in A. O'Connor, C. Tilly and L. Bobo (Eds.), *Urban Inequality: Evidence from Four Cities*. New York, NY: Russell Sage Foundation, pp. 1-33.

Office of Community Oriented Policing Services (2001). *Attorney General Report to Congress: Office of Community Oriented Policing Services*. Washington, DC: United States Department of Justice.

Office of Community Oriented Policing Services. (2002). http://www.usdoj.gov/cops/gpa/grant_prog/default.htm.

Office of Community Oriented Policing Services. (2002). http://www.usdoj.gov/cops/home.htm

Oliver, J. (2001). *Democracy in Suburbia*. Princeton, NJ: Princeton University Press.

Olsen, M. (1965). *The Logic of Collective Action*. Chicago, IL: University of Chicago Press.

Olson, M., Jr. (1965). *The Logic of Collective Action*. Chicago, IL: University of Chicago Press.

Paoline, E., III, Myers, S., and Worden, R. (2000). "Police Culture, Individualism, and Community Policing: Evidence from Two Police Departments," *Justice Quarterly*. 17:575-605.

Parker, R. (1989). "Poverty, Subculture of Violence, and Type of Homicide, *Social Forces*. 67:983-1007.

Parks, R., Mastrofski, S., DeJong, C., and Gray, M. (1999). "How Officers Spend Their Time with the Community," *Justice Quarterly*. 16:483-518.

Parsons, T. (1960). *Structure and Process in Modern Societies*. New York, NY: Free Press.

Peterson, J. (2000). "Welfare Reform and Inequality: The TANF and UI Programs," *Journal of Economic Issues*. 34:517-526

Pingitore, M. (1994). *On the Front Lines: A Directory of Community Policing Programs in America's Cities*. Washington, D.C.: U.S. Conference of Mayors' Criminal Justice Clearinghouse.

Pound, R. (1922). *Criminal Justice in the American City—A Summary*. Cleveland, OH: Cleveland Foundation.

Putman, R. (1995a). "Tuning in, Tuning Out: The Strange Disappearance of Social Capital in America," *Political Science and Politics*. 28:664-683.

Putnam, R. (1995b). "Bowling Alone: America's Declining Social Capital," *Journal of Democracy*. 6:65-79.

Reaves, B. (1997). Law Enforcement Management and Administrative Statistics, 1997: Data for Individual State and Local Agencies with 100 or More Officers. Washington, DC: U.S. Department of Justice.

_____ (1999). Law Enforcement Management and Administrative Statistics, 1999: Data for Individual State and Local Agencies with 100 or More Officers. Washington, DC: U.S. Department of Justice.

Reaves, B. and Smith, P. Z. (1993). *Law Enforcement Management and Administrative Statistics, 1993: Data for Individual State and Local Agencies with 100 or More Officers*. Washington, DC: U.S. Department of Justice.

Reiman, J. (2000). *The Rich Get Richer and the Poor Get Prison: Ideology, Class and Criminal Justice* (6th Edition). Needham Heights, MD: Allyn and Bacon.

Reiss, A. J., Jr. (1971). *The Police and the Public*. New Haven, CT: Yale University Press.

Rennison, C. (2000). "Criminal Victimization 1999," *National Crime Victimization Survey*. Washington, DC: Bureau of Justice Statistics.

Roehl, J., Johnson, C., Buerger, M., Gaffigan, S., Langston, E. and Roth, J. (2000). "Cops and the Nature of Policing." *National Evaluation of the COPS Program—Title I of the 1994 Crime Act*. Washington, DC: National Institute of Justice and the Urban Institute, pp.179-245.

Rohe, W., Adams, R. and Arcury, T. (2001). "Community Policing and Planning," *American Planning Association Journal*. 67:78-90.

Rosenbaum, D. (1994). *The Challenge of Community Policing: Testing the Promise*. Thousand Oaks, CA: Sage Publications.

Rosenbaum, D. P. and Lurigio, A. J. (1994). "An Inside Look at Community Policing Reform: Definitions, Organizational Changes, and Evaluation Findings," *Crime and Delinquency*. 40-3:299-314.

Roth, J., Johnson, C., Maenner, G., and Herrschaft, D. (2000). The Flow of COP Funds. *National Evaluation of the COPS Program—Title I of the 1994 Crime Act*. Washington, DC: National Institute of Justice/Urban Institute, pp.63-100.

Roth, J., Koper, C., White, R. and Langston, E. (2000). "Using COPS Resources." *National Evaluation of the COPS Program—Title I of the 1994 Crime Act*. Washington, DC: National Institute of Justice and the Urban Institute, pp.101-148.

Roth, J. and Ryan, J. (2000). "Overview," *National Evaluation of the COPS Program—Title I of the 1994 Crime Act*. Washington, DC: National Institute of Justice/Urban Institute, pp. 1-24.

Roth, J., Ryan, J., Gaffigan, S., Koper, C., Moore, M., Roehl, J., Johnson, C., Moore, G., White, R., Buerger, M., Langston, E. and Thacher, D. (2000). *National Evaluation of the COPS Program—Title I of the 1994 Crime Act*. Washington, DC: National Institute of Justice and the Urban Institute.

Rudovsky, D. (1992). "Police Abuse: Can the Violence Be Contained?" *Harvard Civil Rights-Civil Liberties Law Review*. 27:467-501.

Ryscavage, P. (1999). *Income Inequality in America: An Analysis of Trends*. Armonk, NY: M. E. Sharpe, Inc.

Sadd, S. and Grinc, R. (1994). "Innovative Neighborhood Oriented Policing: An Evaluation of Community Policing in Eight Cities," in D. Rosenbaum (Ed.), *The Challenge of Community Policing: Testing the Promises*. Thousand Oaks, CA: Sage Publications, pp. 27-52.

Schattschneider, E. (1960). *The Semi-Sovereign People: A Realist's View of Democracy in America*. New York: Holt, Rinehart and Winston.

Schein, E. (1985). *Organizational Culture and Leadership*. San Francisco, CA: Jossey-Bass, Inc., pp. 128-135.

Seidman, H. and Gilmour, R. (1986). *Politics, Position, and Power: From the Positive to the Regulatory State* (4th Edition). New York, NY: Oxford University Press.

Shaw, C. and McKay, H. (1942). *Juvenile Delinquency and Urban Areas*. Chicago, IL: University of Chicago Press.

Sherman, L. (1997). "Policing for Crime Prevention." In *Preventing Crime: What Works, What Doesn't, What's Promising*. Washington, DC: Office of Justice Programs, pp. 8-58.

Skogan, W. (1988). "Community Organizations and Crime," in M. Tonry and N. Morris (Eds.), *Crime and Justice: A Review of Research Vol.10*. Chicago: University of Chicago Press, pp. 39-78.

_____ (1990). *Disorder and Decline*. Berkeley, CA: University of California Press.

Skogan, W. and Atunes, G. (1979). "Information, Apprehension and Deterrence: Exploring the Limits of Police Productivity," *Journal of Criminal Justice*. 7-3:217-241.

Skogan W. and Hartnett, S. (1997). *Community Policing Chicago Style*. New York, NY: Oxford University Press.

Skolnick, J. and Bayley, D. (1986). *The New Blue Line: Police Innovation in Six American Cities*. New York, NY: Free Press.

Skolnick, J. and Fyfe, J. (1993). *Above the Law: Police and the Excessive Use of Force*. New York, NY: Free Press.

Stamper, N. (1992). *Removing Managerial Barriers to Effective Police Leadership: A Study of Executive Leadership and Executive Management in Big-City Police Departments*. Washington, D.C.: Police Executive Research Forum.

St. John, C. (2002). "The Concentration of Affluence in the United States, 1990," *Urban Affairs Review*. 37:500-520.

Steffensmeier, D. and Harer, M. D. (1999). "Making Sense of Recent U.S. Crime Trends, 1980 to 1996/1998: Age Composition Effects and Other Explanations," *Journal of Research in Crime and Delinquency*. 36:235-274.

Steinberg, A. (1989). *The Transformation of Criminal Justice: Philadelphia, 1800-1880*. Chapel Hill, NC: University of North Carolina Press.

Stojkovic, S., Kalinich, D. and Klofas, J. (1998). *Criminal Justice Organizations: Administration and Management* (2nd Edition). Belmont, CA: Wadsworth Publishing Company.

Stone, D. (1997). *Policy Paradox: The Art of Political Decision Making*. New York, NY: W.W. Norton.

Tanninen, H. (1998). "Income Inequality, Government Expenditures and Growth," *Applied Economics*. 31:1-13.

Thacher, D. (2001). "Equity and Community Policing: A New View of Community Partnerships," *Criminal Justice Ethics*. 20:3-16.

Thayer, R. and Reynolds, M. (1997). "Community Oriented Policing," *Journal of Planning Literature*. 12:93-105

Thompson, J. (1967). *Organizations in Action*. New York, NY: McGraw-Hill.

Thornberry, T. and Farnworth, M. (1982). "Social Correlates of Criminal Involvement: Further Evidence of the Relationship Between Social Status and Criminal Behavior," *American Sociological Review*. 47:505-518.

Thurman, Q. (1995). "The Police as a Community-Based Resource," in P. Adams and K. Nelson (Eds.), *Reinventing Human Services: Community and Family-Centered Practice*. New York, NY: Adeline de Gruyter, pp. 175-187.

Thurman, Q. and Reisig, M. (1996). "Community-Oriented Research in an Era of Community-Oriented Policing," *American Behavioral Scientist.* 39:570-587.

Thurman, Q. and McGarrell, E. (1997). "Community Policing in a Rural Setting: Innovations and Organizational Change," in Q. C. Thurman and E. F. McGarrell (Eds.), *Community Policing in a Rural Setting.* Cincinnati, OH: Anderson Publishing, pp 1-7.

Thurman, Q., Zhao, J. and Giacomazzi, A. (2001). *Community Policing in a Community Era.* Los Angeles, CA: Roxbury Publishing Company.

Tichy, N. (1983). Managing Strategic Change: Technical, Political, and Cultural Dynamics. New York, NY: John Wiley & Sons.

Toch, H. and Grant, J. (1991). *Police as Problem Solvers.* New York, NY: Plenum Press.

Tolbert, C. and Hero, R. "Dealing With Diversity: Racial/Ethnic Context and Social Policy Change," *Political Research Quarterly.* 54:571-604

Toqueville, Alexis de (1966). *Democracy in America,* [translated and edited by J. P. Mayer and Max Lerner]. New York, NY: Harper and Row.

Tosi, H. (1975). *Theories of Organization.* Chicago, IL: St. Clair Press.

Trojanowicz, R. (1982). *An Evaluation of the Neighborhood Foot Patrol Program in Flint, Michigan.* East Lansing, MI: Michigan State University Press.

_____ (1994). *Community Policing: A Survey of Police Departments in the United States.* East Lansing, MI: National Center for Community Policing, Michigan State University.

Trojanowicz, R. and Bucqueroux, B. (2001). *Community Policing: How to Get Started* (2nd Edition). Cincinnati, OH: Anderson Publishing Company.

_____ (1990). *Community Policing: A Contemporary Perspective.* Cincinnati, OH: Anderson Publishing.

Trojanowicz, R., Kappeler, V., Gaines, L. and Bucqueroux, B. (1998). *Community Policing: A Contemporary Perspective* (2nd Edition). Cincinnati, OH: Anderson Publishing.

Truman, D. (1951). *The Governmental Process: Political Interests and Public Opinion.* New York, NY: Alfred A. Knopf.

Uchida, C. (1997). "The Development of the American Police," in R. Dunham and G. Alpert (Eds.), *Critical Issues in Policing: Contemporary Readings.* Prospect Heights, IL: Waveland Press, Inc.

U.S. Department of Justice, Bureau of Justice Statistics Bulletin (1994). *Criminal Victimization.* Washington, DC: U.S. Government Printing Office.

U.S. Department of Justice, Office of Community Oriented Policing Services COPS Fact Sheet (2000). *Training and Technical Assistance*. Washington, DC: U.S. Government Printing Office.

Walker, S. (1992). *The Police in America: An Introduction* (2nd Edition). New York, NY: McGraw-Hill, Inc.

Warner, R., Steele, B., and Lovrich, N. (1989). "Conditions Associated with the Advent of Representative Bureaucracy: The Case of Women in Policing." *Social Science Quarterly*. 70:562-578.

Weingast, B. and Moran, M. (1983). "Bureaucracy: Discretional Congressional Control? Regulatory Policy Making by the Federal Trade Commission," *Journal of Political Economy*. 91:756-800.

Weisel, D. and Eck, J. (1994). "Toward a Practical Approach to Organizational Change: Community Policing Initiatives in Six Cities," in D. Rosenbaum (Ed.), *The Challenge of Community Policing: Testing the Promises*. Thousand Oaks, CA: Sage Publications, pp. 53-72.

Weitzer, R. and Tuch, S. (1999). "Race, Class and Perceptions of Discrimination by the Police," *Crime and Delinquency*. 45:494-507.

Wilson, F. and Hammer, R. B. (2001). "Ethnic Residential Segregation and Its Consequences," in A. O'Connor, C. Tilly and L. Bobo (Eds.), *Urban Inequality: Evidence from Four Cities*. New York, NY: Russell Sage Foundation, pp. 272-303.

Wilson, J. (1968). *Varieties of Police Behavior*. New York, NY: Atheneum.

_____ (1989). "Making Neighborhoods Safe," *Atlantic Monthly*. 236:46-52.

Wilson, J. and Kelling, G. (1982). "Broken Widows: The Police and Neighborhood Safety," *The Atlantic Monthly*. March, pp. 29-38.

Wilson, W. (1987). *The Truly Disadvantaged: The Inner City, the Underclass, and Public Policy*. Chicago, IL: The University of Chicago Press.

Wilson, W. and Vaughn, M. (1996). "Support and Confidence: Public Attitudes Toward the Police," in T. Flanagan and D. Longmire (Eds.), *Americans View Crime and Justice: A National Public Opinion Survey*. Thousand Oaks, CA: Sage Publications, pp. 31-45.

Wolpert, C. (1999). "Considering Race and Crime: Distilling Non-Partisan Policy From Opposing Theories," *American Criminal Law Review*. 36:265-289.

Wood, B. and Waterman, R. (1991). "The Dynamics of Political Control Over the Bureaucracy," *American Political Science Review*. 85:801-828.

Worrall, J. (2001) *Civil Lawsuits, Citizen Complaints, and Policing Innovations*. New York: LFB Scholarly Publishing LLC.

Wright, B., Caspi, A., Moffitt, T., Miech, R. and Silva, P. (1999). "Reconsidering the Relationship Between SES and Delinquency: Causation but not Correlation," *Criminology*. 37:175-194.

Wycoff, M. and Skogan, W. (1994). "Community Policing in Madison: An Analysis of Implementation and Impact," in D. Rosenbaum (Ed.), *The Challenge of Community Policing: Testing the Promises*. Thousand Oaks, CA: Sage Publications, pp 75-91.

Yates, D. and Pillai, V. (1996). "Attitudes Toward Community Policing: A Causal Analysis," *The Social Science Journal*. 33:193-207.

Zhao, J. (1996). *Why Police Organizations Change: A Study of Community Oriented Policing*. Washington, DC: Police Executive Research Forum.

Zhao, J. and Thurman, Q. (1997). "Community Policing: Where Are We Now?" *Crime and Delinquency*. 43:345-357.

_____. (2001). *A National Evaluation of the Effect of COP Grants on Crime from 1994 to 1999*. Washington, DC: U.S. Department of Justice, Office of Community Oriented Policing Services.

Zhao, J., Thurman, Q., and Lovrich, N. (1995). "Community-Oriented Policing Across the U.S.: Facilitators and Impediments to Implementation," *The American Journal of Police*. 14:11-28.

Appendix

Table 1: Award data for each department

CITY	ST	TOTAL AWARD	INNOVATIVE AWARDS	HIRING AWARDS	PERCENT INNOVATION	PERCENT HIRING	OFFICERS ACQUIRED UNDER GRANT	HIRING DOLLAR PER NEW OFFICER	HIRING DOLLAR PER CITIZEN	HIRING DOLLAR PER HOUSEHOLD	HIRING DOLLAR PER FAMILY
Birmingham	AL	$5,849,644	$1,885,341	$3,964,303	32%	63%	41.20	$96,221	$14.91	$37.76	$58.70
Mesa	AZ	$8,783,978	$205,530	$8,578,448	2%	93%	122.40	$70,085	$29.78	$79.64	$114.98
Phoenix	AZ	$55,617,867	$2,410,805	$53,207,062	4%	96%	751.30	$70,820	$54.11	$143.76	$213.92
Tempe	AZ	$5,369,865	$741,081	$4,628,784	14%	86%	65.70	$70,453	$22.63	$83.12	$142.89
Anaheim	CA	$1,102,026	$5,000	$1,097,026	0%	100%	25.90	$42,356	$4.12	$12.58	$17.15
Berkeley	CA	$1,712,634	$260,886	$1,451,748	15%	85%	31.00	$46,831	$14.13	$33.34	$75.90
Beverly Hills	CA	$600,000	$0	$600,000	0%	100%	6.00	$100,000	$18.77	$41.33	$75.42
Burbank	CA	$800,000	$0	$800,000	0%	100%	10.00	$80,000	$8.54	$20.35	$33.88
Concord	CA	$1,929,583	$665,653	$1,263,930	34%	66%	20.80	$60,766	$11.35	$30.03	$43.07
Costa Mesa	CA	$250,000	$0	$250,000	0%	100%	1.00	$250,000	$2.59	$6.64	$11.41
Daly City	CA	$355,222	$0	$355,222	0%	100%	2.40	$148,009	$3.85	$12.19	$16.31
Fremont	CA	$1,624,356	$250,000	$1,374,356	15%	85%	20.40	$67,370	$7.93	$22.85	$30.12
Fresno	CA	$26,529,610	$1,695,855	$24,829,755	6%	94%	314.00	$79,076	$70.10	$203.33	$292.85
Garden Grove	CA	$2,444,308	$0	$2,444,308	0%	100%	74.00	$33,031	$17.09	$54.60	$71.02
Glendale	CA	$1,954,494	$229,494	$1,725,000	12%	88%	23.00	$75,000	$9.58	$25.11	$38.11
Hayward	CA	$2,174,306	$387,616	$1,786,690	18%	82%	49.70	$35,950	$16.02	$44.39	$63.76
Inglewood	CA	$2,986,981	$1,536,981	$1,450,000	51%	49%	30.00	$48,333	$13.23	$39.81	$58.22
Long Beach	CA	$18,644,619	$981,000	$17,663,619	5%	95%	313.90	$56,271	$41.13	$110.93	$186.12
Los Angeles	CA	$298,404,156	$2,266,756	$296,137,400	1%	99%	3730.80	$79,376	$84.97	$242.78	$385.06
Oakland	CA	$26,227,459	$879,436	$25,348,023	3%	97%	335.70	$75,508	$68.10	$175.10	$298.17
Ontario	CA	$1,341,058	$91,534	$1,249,524	7%	95%	15.00	$83,302	$9.38	$30.87	$39.41
Orange	CA	$1,926,090	$5,000	$1,921,090	0%	100%	53.00	$36,247	$17.36	$53.73	$70.41

171

continued

Table 1, cont.

City	St	Total Award	Innovative Awards	Hiring Awards	Percent Innovation	Percent Hiring	Officers Acquired Under Grant	Hiring Dollar Per New Officer	Hiring Dollar Per Citizen	Hiring Dollar Per Household	Hiring Dollar Per Family
Pasadena	CA	$3,510,246	$3,060,246	$450,000	87%	13%	6.00	$75,000	$3.42	$8.93	$14.78
Pomona	CA	$122,966	$122,966	$0	100%	0%	.00	$0	$0.00	$0.00	$0.00
Redondo Beach	CA	$311,508	$56,508	$255,000	18%	82%	8.40	$30,357	$4.24	$9.51	$17.78
Richmond	CA	$3,192,471	$349,981	$2,842,490	11%	89%	38.90	$73,072	$32.51	$86.67	$129.75
Riverside	CA	$3,026,659	$663,685	$2,362,974	22%	78%	50.40	$46,884	$10.43	$31.19	$43.16
Sacramento	CA	$47,044,921	$3,654,337	$43,390,584	8%	92%	468.00	$92,715	$117.47	$299.95	$491.67
Salinas	CA	$3,229,916	$1,188,348	$2,041,568	37%	63%	48.00	$42,533	$18.77	$60.91	$80.58
San Bernardino	CA	$7,907,143	$125,000	$7,782,143	2%	98%	59.20	$131,455	$21.07	$142.42	$198.95
San Diego	CA	$35,628,313	$5,275,081	$30,353,232	15%	85%	1013.80	$29,940	$27.33	$74.70	$120.33
San Francisco	CA	$19,893,639	$200,000	$19,693,639	1%	99%	675.70	$29,146	$27.20	$64.36	$136.93
San Jose	CA	$11,859,118	$602,916	$11,256,202	5%	95%	260.90	$43,144	$14.39	$44.84	$60.47
San Mateo	CA	$709,939	$0	$709,939	0%	100%	18.40	$38,584	$8.30	$20.00	$32.71
Santa Ana	CA	$6,934,261	$1,667,455	$5,266,806	24%	76%	115.30	$45,679	$17.93	$73.29	$95.61
Santa Barbara	CA	$314,410	$164,410	$150,000	52%	48%	2.00	$75,000	$1.75	$4.35	$8.03
Santa Clara	CA	$125,000	$0	$125,000	0%	100%	1.00	$125,000	$1.34	$3.42	$5.58
Stockton	CA	$8,273,739	$0	$8,273,739	0%	100%	179.10	$46,196	$39.22	$120.04	$167.63
Sunnyvale	CA	$0	$0	$0	0%	.	.00	$0	$0.00	$0.00	$0.00
Torrance	CA	$0	$0	$0	0%	.	.00	$0	$0.00	$0.00	$0.00
Vallejo	CA	$1,865,730	$138,097	$1,727,633	7%	93%	35.00	$49,361	$15.82	$46.17	$63.01
West Covina	CA	$770,151	$452,370	$317,781	59%	41%	3.40	$93,465	$3.31	$10.56	$13.10
Aurora	CO	$4,367,490	$153,497	$4,213,993	4%	96%	76.40	$55,157	$18.97	$47.12	$71.85

City	St	Total Award	Innovative Awards	Hiring Awards	Percent Innovation	Percent Hiring	Officers Acquired Under Grant	Hiring Dollar Per New Officer	Hiring Dollar Per Citizen	Hiring Dollar Per Household	Hiring Dollar Per Family
Colorado Springs	CO	$8,264,186	$2,831,164	$5,433,022	34%	66%	115.60	$46,998	$19.32	$48.95	$72.37
Denver	CO	$8,455,982	$398,800	$8,057,182	5%	95%	222.00	$36,294	$17.23	$38.16	$72.97
Fort Collins	CO	$409,410	$0	$409,410	0%	100%	9.00	$45,490	$4.67	$12.11	$20.69
Bridgeport	CT	$5,874,052	$1,440,477	$4,433,575	25%	75%	61.30	$72,325	$31.29	$84.40	$127.33
Bristol	CT	$1,592,704	$156,593	$1,436,111	10%	90%	33.40	$42,997	$23.68	$60.08	$85.74
Hartford	CT	$7,977,492	$599,056	$7,373,436	8%	92%	139.80	$52,779	$146.25	$143.03	$234.12
New Britain	CT	$500,000	$0	$500,000	0%	100%	14.30	$34,965	$6.62	$16.61	$26.21
West Hartford	CT	$352,500	$0	$352,500	0%	100%	8.10	$43,519	$5.86	$14.77	$21.72
Washington	DC	$28,899,795	$2,042,361	$26,357,434	7%	92%	761.30	$35,273	$44.25	$107.85	$217.33
Coral Gables	FL	$2,073,250	$0	$2,073,250	0%	100%	64.90	$31,945	$51.71	$31.22	$211.77
Fort Lauderdale	FL	$4,270,366	$744,393	$3,525,973	17%	83%	88.70	$39,752	$23.60	$226.68	$101.43
Fort Meyers	FL	$3,492,096	$288,846	$3,206,250	8%	92%	92.00	$34,851	$70.93	$176.81	$297.62
Gainesville	FL	$3,565,055	$2,118,071	$1,446,984	59%	41%	18.10	$79,944	$17.07	$45.28	$82.57
Hollywood	FL	$2,286,107	$347,476	$1,938,631	15%	85%	47.40	$40,899	$15.93	$36.61	$59.78
Jacksonville	FL	$13,698,108	$755,858	$12,947,250	5%	95%	221.90	$58,347	$20.38	$53.75	$77.03
Lakeland	FL	$4,658,615	$182,847	$4,475,758	4%	96%	66.70	$67,103	$63.42	$150.24	$230.54
Miami	FL	$85,552,066	$2,134,885	$83,417,131	2%	98%	1183.50	$70,483	$232.65	$640.44	$981.26
Orlando	FL	$9,253,018	$0	$9,253,018	0%	100%	144.10	$54,212	$55.18	$140.98	$249.33
Pensacola	FL	$970,963	$147,373	$823,590	15%	85%	10.00	$82,359	$14.16	$34.24	$53.07
St. Petersburg	FL	$4,636,522	$786,522	$3,850,000	17%	83%	89.20	$43,161	$15.13	$36.35	$61.75
Tallahassee	FL	$1,650,000	$750,000	$900,000	45%	55%	12.00	$75,000	$7.21	$17.87	$34.12
West Palm Beach	FL	$3,549,020	$21,562	$3,527,458	1%	99%	102.40	$34,448	$52.15	$122.59	$219.59
Atlanta	GA	$14,833,357	$239,172	$14,594,185	2%	98%	286.20	$50,993	$37.04	$93.62	$165.89

continued

Table 1, cont.

City	St	Total Award	Innovative Awards	Hiring Awards	Percent Innova-tion	Percent Hiring	Officers Acquired Under Grant	Hiring Dollar Per New Officer	Hiring Dollar Per Citizen	Hiring Dollar Per Household	Hiring Dollar Per Family
Augusta	GA	$0	$0	$0	0%	0%	.00	$0	$0.00	$0.00	$0.00
Columbus	GA	$694,955	$94,597	$600,358	14%	86%	9.00	$66,706	$3.36	$9.14	$12.63
Macon	GA	$748,350	$748,350	$0	100%	0%	.00	$0	$0.00	$0.00	$0.00
Marietta	GA	$2,005,083	$0	$2,005,083	0%	100%	46.30	$43,306	$45.44	$101.35	$192.72
Honolulu	HI	$12,522,500	$200,000	$12,322,500	2%	98%	413.50	$29,800	$33.74	$91.43	$140.07
Chicago	IL	$125,463,675	$2,124,476	$123,339,199	2%	98%	1593.10	$77,421	$44.31	$120.81	$193.80
Elgin	IL	$1,788,690	$0	$1,788,690	0%	100%	23.90	$74,841	$23.23	$67.09	$94.51
Oak Park Village	IL	$373,532	$0	$373,532	0%	100%	8.10	$46,115	$6.96	$16.49	$28.01
Peoria	IL	$2,821,154	$155,504	$2,665,650	6%	94%	48.60	$54,849	$23.49	$59.39	$93.68
Rockford	IL	$1,180,469	$0	$1,180,469	0%	100%	16.00	$73,779	$8.47	$21.53	$32.12
Skokie Village	IL	$444,700	$0	$444,700	0%	100%	7.80	$57,013	$7.48	$19.55	$25.71
Springfield	IL	$2,931,205	$303,163	$2,628,042	10%	90%	34.00	$77,295	$24.97	$58.56	$98.05
Anderson	IN	$700,724	$115,984	$584,740	17%	83%	15.80	$37,009	$9.84	$24.03	$36.47
Gary	IN	$4,980,186	$0	$4,980,186	0%	100%	101.50	$49,066	$42.69	$122.21	$170.39
Hammond	IN	$1,077,247	$99,328	$977,919	9%	91%	14.00	$69,851	$11.61	$30.39	$43.84
Kokomo	IN	$380,000	$5,000	$375,000	1%	99%	5.00	$75,000	$8.34	$20.11	$30.40
Muncie	IN	$246,350	$125,000	$121,350	51%	49%	4.90	$24,765	$1.71	$4.47	$7.55
South Bend	IN	$2,549,750	$700,000	$1,849,750	27%	73%	72.70	$25,444	$17.53	$44.04	$68.75
Davenport	IA	$779,850	$4,850	$775,000	1%	99%	13.00	$59,615	$8.13	$20.91	$31.44
Des Moines	IA	$3,368,238	$463,426	$2,904,812	14%	86%	50.70	$57,294	$15.04	$36.96	$58.83
Sioux City	IA	$9,188,639	$8,049,139	$1,139,500	88%	12%	14.20	$80,246	$14.15	$37.38	$54.23

City	St	Total Award	Innovative Awards	Hiring Awards	Percent Innovation	Percent Hiring	Officers Acquired Under Grant	Hiring Dollar Per New Officer	Hiring Dollar Per Citizen	Hiring Dollar Per Household	Hiring Dollar Per Family
Waterloo	IA	$1,055,011	$80,011	$975,000	8%	92%	13.00	$75,000	$14.67	$35.87	$53.65
Overland Park	KS	$2,120,000	$520,000	$1,500,000	25%	75%	20.00	$80,000	$14.31	$35.57	$51.50
Wichita	KS	$13,529,355	$2,515,700	$11,013,655	19%	81%	143.00	$77,019	$36.23	$89.05	$136.17
Lexington-Fayette	KY	$6,682,642	$3,258,400	$3,424,242	49%	51%	48.10	$71,190	$15.19	$38.24	$60.21
Louisville	KY	$7,232,564	$1,393,064	$5,839,500	19%	81%	138.60	$42,132	$21.70	$51.76	$86.06
Bossier City	LA	$252,713	$0	$252,713	0%	00%	4.00	$63,173	$4.42	$13.17	$17.54
Lafayette	LA	$1,310,391	$130,532	$1,179,859	10%	90%	20.00	$58,993	$12.49	$32.48	$50.04
Shreveport	LA	$3,051,806	$308,500	$2,743,306	10%	90%	79.00	$34,725	$13.82	$36.40	$53.02
Baltimore	MD	$58,360,289	$3,288,870	$55,071,419	6%	94%	599.80	$91,816	$74.82	$199.55	$314.64
Boston	MA	$13,402,703	$4,501,553	$8,901,150	34%	66%	148.10	$60,102	$15.50	$39.05	$75.65
Newton	MA	$335,000	$200,000	$135,000	60%	40%	6.30	$21,429	$1.63	$4.60	$6.77
Quincy	MA	$1,275,000	$0	$1,275,000	0%	100%	17.00	$75,000	$15.00	$35.65	$60.96
Worcester	MA	$5,074,064	$223,205	$4,850,859	4%	96%	70.90	$68,418	$23.57	$76.29	$119.97
Ann Arbor	MI	$1,728,181	$534,381	$1,193,800	31%	69%	17.70	$67,446	$10.89	$28.50	$55.97
Battle Creek	MI	$788,824	$114,177	$674,647	14%	86%	3.00	$84,331	$12.60	$31.59	$47.91
Dearborn	MI	$351,561	$0	$351,561	0%	100%	14.10	$24,933	$3.94	$9.96	$14.55
Detroit	MI	$31,616,640	$178,409	$31,438,231	1%	99%	550.60	$57,098	$30.58	$84.09	$127.03
Flint	MI	$4,458,252	$73,616	$4,384,636	2%	98%	49.00	$89,482	$33.15	$81.37	$122.77
Grand Rapids	MI	$2,399,340	$299,340	$2,100,000	12%	88%	50.00	$42,000	$11.10	$30.24	$45.68
Kalamazoo	MI	$878,261	$249,315	$628,946	28%	72%	15.20	$41,378	$7.84	$21.30	$37.90
Pontiac	MI	$1,661,104	$0	$1,661,104	0%	100%	27.30	$60,846	$23.34	$66.86	$97.90
Saginaw	MI	$975,000	$0	$975,000	0%	100%	13.00	$75,000	$14.03	$37.22	$54.55
Warren	MI	$1,095,983	$145,983	$950,000	13%	87%	10.00	$95,000	$6.56	$17.37	$23.56

continued

Table 1, cont.

City	St	Total Award	Innovative Awards	Hiring Awards	Percent Innovation	Percent Hiring	Officers Acquired Under Grant	Hiring Dollar Per New Officer	Hiring Dollar Per Citizen	Hiring Dollar Per Household	Hiring Dollar Per Family
Duluth	MN	$1,607,854	$462,479	$1,145,375	29%	71%	16.10	$71,141	$13.40	$33.06	$54.21
Minneapolis	MN	$9,455,473	$1,160,272	$8,295,201	12%	88%	153.70	$53,970	$22.52	$51.67	$105.72
St. Paul	MN	$5,738,623	$2,161,721	$3,576,902	38%	62%	88.10	$40,600	$13.14	$32.34	$56.54
Kansas City	MO	$13,390,417	$1,397,478	$11,992,939	10%	90%	194.20	$61,756	$27.56	$67.70	$108.82
Springfield	MO	$2,243,459	$250,000	$1,993,459	11%	89%	26.80	$74,383	$14.19	$34.75	$21.73
St. Louis	MO	$10,701,766	$862,702	$9,839,064	8%	92%	246.70	$39,883	$24.80	$59.85	$282.67
Omaha	NE	$15,655,557	$3,832,033	$11,823,524	24%	76%	200.20	$59,059	$35.21	$88.31	$138.68
Las Vegas	NV	$5,811,239	$3,420,600	$2,390,639	59%	41%	34.00	$70,313	$9.26	$23.92	$36.29
North Las Vegas	NV	$24,221	$0	$24,221	0%	100%	1.00	$24,221	$0.51	$1.68	$2.16
Reno	NV	$2,735,787	$559,093	$2,176,694	20%	80%	56.40	$38,594	$16.26	$37.98	$67.46
Manchester	NH	$2,029,344	$15,402	$2,013,942	1%	99%	38.50	$52,310	$20.23	$49.85	$79.45
Bayonne	NJ	$7,918,203	$0	$7,918,203	0%	100%	106.60	$74,280	$128.87	$312.74	$471.71
Clifton	NJ	$900,000	$0	$900,000	0%	100%	12.00	$75,000	$12.54	$30.91	$44.85
Edison	NJ	$2,350,561	$0	$2,350,561	0%	100%	39.90	$58,911	$26.51	$73.97	$97.85
Elizabeth	NJ	$3,277,815	$0	$3,277,815	0%	100%	46.00	$71,257	$29.80	$83.89	$119.97
Irvington	NJ	$7,157,728	$199,560	$6,958,168	3%	97%	65.00	$107,049	$116.41	$323.00	$478.75
Jersey City	NJ	$13,580,983	$2,811,411	$10,769,572	21%	79%	198.30	$54,309	$47.12	$130.85	$198.97
Linden	NJ	$973,046	$0	$973,046	0%	100%	18.70	$52,035	$26.51	$67.22	$95.66
Newark	NJ	$25,711,375	$509,717	$25,201,658	2%	98%	380.50	$66,233	$91.57	$277.31	$398.03
Paterson	NJ	$6,558,265	$0	$6,558,265	0%	100%	92.90	$70,595	$46.55	$149.52	$198.10
Woodbridge	NJ	$773,762	$149,974	$623,788	19%	81%	11.60	$53,775	$35.78	$88.80	$128.56

City	St	Total Award	Innovative Awards	Hiring Awards	Percent Innovation	Percent Hiring	Officers Acquired Under Grant	Hiring Dollar Per New Officer	Hiring Dollar Per Citizen	Hiring Dollar Per Household	Hiring Dollar Per Family
Albuquerque	NM	$11,827,941	$208,219	$11,519,722	2%	98%	127.00	$91,494	$30.20	$75.56	$116.00
Santa Fe	NM	$1,120,264	$375,000	$745,264	33%	67%	8.00	$93,158	$13.31	$32.71	$53.24
Albany	NY	$3,939,488	$262,553	$3,676,935	7%	93%	62.90	$58,457	$36.38	$87.48	$179.35
Rochester	NY	$5,691,000	$583,900	$5,107,100	10%	90%	53.00	$96,360	$22.05	$54.61	$96.94
Syracuse	NY	$4,297,012	$353,884	$3,943,128	8%	92%	57.70	$68,338	$24.06	$60.62	$111.98
Yonkers	NY	$4,002,756	$75,000	$3,927,756	2%	98%	67.10	$58,535	$20.88	$54.33	$79.00
Charlotte	NC	$31,361,074	$3,364,441	$27,996,633	11%	89%	734.60	$38,111	$73.70	$176.14	$270.65
Durham	NC	$1,853,470	$0	$1,853,470	0%	100%	20.00	$92,674	$13.57	$33.07	$55.87
Greensboro	NC	$1,628,267	$15,000	$1,613,267	1%	99%	42.60	$37,870	$8.79	$21.60	$34.88
High Point	NC	$630,644	$0	$630,644	0%	100%	9.00	$70,072	$9.09	$22.92	$33.24
Raleigh	NC	$6,351,158	$20,000	$6,331,158	0%	100%	102.00	$62,070	$33.45	$73.78	$129.76
Wilmington	NC	$2,161,137	$0	$2,161,137	0%	100%	32.20	$67,116	$33.92	$92.42	$156.21
Akron	OH	$3,955,112	$533,565	$3,421,547	13%	87%	57.00	$60,027	$15.34	$37.97	$59.71
Cincinnati	OH	$5,638,312	$13,312	$5,625,000	0%	100%	75.00	$75,000	$15.45	$36.47	$67.45
Cleveland	OH	$29,419,641	$936,996	$28,482,645	3%	97%	258.50	$110,184	$56.33	$142.69	$229.37
Columbus	OH	$4,448,030	$5,000	$4,443,030	0%	100%	83.70	$53,083	$7.02	$17.26	$29.25
Dayton	OH	$934,621	$0	$934,621	0%	100%	15.70	$59,530	$5.13	$12.89	$21.22
Springfield	OH	$725,000	$0	$725,000	0%	100%	7.00	$103,571	$10.29	$26.53	$39.90
Toledo	OH	$5,486,678	$297,080	$5,189,598	5%	95%	123.10	$42,158	$15.59	$39.68	$61.05
Lawton	OK	$379,839	$86,940	$292,899	23%	77%	4.00	$73,225	$3.64	$10.25	$13.09
Norman	OK	$862,572	$0	$862,572	0%	100%	12.00	$71,381	$10.77	$26.92	$44.56
Oklahoma City	OK	$750,000	$750,000	$0	100%	0%	.00	$0	$0.00	$0.00	$0.00
Tulsa	OK	$1,993,503	$57,816	$1,535,687	3%	97%	26.00	$74,450	$5.27	$12.45	$19.80

continued

Table 1, cont.

City	St	Total Award	Innovative Awards	Hiring Awards	Percent Innovation	Percent Hiring	Officers Acquired Under Grant	Hiring Dollar Per New Officer	Hiring Dollar Per Citizen	Hiring Dollar Per Household	Hiring Dollar Per Family
Eugene	OR	$721,597	$382,159	$339,438	53%	47%	6.00	$56,573	$3.01	$7.32	$12.79
Portland	OR	$18,258,829	$1,383,901	$16,874,928	8%	92%	258.20	$65,356	$38.58	$90.11	$160.73
Salem	OR	$1,155,418	$0	$1,155,418	0%	100%	40.90	$28,250	$10.72	$27.44	$45.26
Erie	PA	$116,988	$0	$116,988	0%	100%	9.60	$12,186	$1.08	$0.19	$4.34
Philadelphia	PA	$59,242,772	$93,592	$59,149,180	0%	100%	853.80	$69,278	$37.30	$385.07	$155.11
Pittsburgh	PA	$4,518,322	$200,000	$4,318,322	4%	96%	196.00	$22,032	$11.67	$137.97	$49.05
Reading	PA	$1,250,000	$0	$1,250,000	0%	100%	16.00	$78,125	$15.95	$21.36	$64.52
Providence	RI	$6,195,469	$398,184	$5,797,285	6%	94%	175.50	$33,033	$36.07	$171.61	$163.92
Columbia	SC	$2,102,768	$999,000	$1,103,768	48%	52%	13.00	$84,905	$11.26	$27.65	$57.82
Sioux Falls	SD	$925,000	$0	$925,000	0%	100%	9.00	$102,778	$9.18	$13.22	$35.52
Knoxville	TN	$11,656,340	$5,646,815	$6,009,525	48%	52%	194.90	$30,834	$36.18	$26.16	$145.76
Memphis	TN	$11,885,884	$317,634	$11,568,250	3%	97%	184.50	$62,701	$18.95	$58.24	$74.69
Nashville-Davidson	TN	$21,626,453	$1,054,725	$20,571,728	5%	95%	387.40	$53,102	$42.11	$537.15	$163.74
Abilene	TX	$1,839,610	$755,000	$1,084,610	41%	59%	16.00	$67,788	$10.17	$17.66	$39.70
Amarillo	TX	$2,431,762	$0	$2,431,762	0%	100%	52.70	$46,143	$15.43	$24.06	$56.90
Arlington	TX	$7,146,370	$696,370	$6,450,000	10%	90%	84.00	$76,786	$24.64	$33.57	$93.17
Austin	TX	$23,445,589	$2,449,341	$20,996,248	10%	90%	317.90	$66,047	$45.10	$483.64	$199.18
Beaumont	TX	$1,815,893	$0	$1,815,893	0%	100%	44.60	$40,715	$15.88	$20.33	$60.83
Corpus Christi	TX	$3,247,534	$77,284	$3,170,250	2%	98%	86.80	$36,524	$12.31	$7.86	$48.03
Dallas	TX	$6,018,306	$1,236,306	$4,782,000	21%	79%	71.40	$66,975	$4.75	$29.78	$20.03
El Paso	TX	$26,319,378	$193,480	$26,125,898	1%	99%	317.30	$82,338	$50.70	$1,080.48	$204.65

City	St	Total Award	Innovative Awards	Hiring Awards	Percent Innova- tion	Percent Hiring	Officers Acquired Under Grant	Hiring Dollar Per New Officer	Hiring Dollar Per Citizen	Hiring Dollar Per Household	Hiring Dollar Per Family
Galveston	TX	$300,000	$0	$300,000	0%	100%	4.00	$75,000	$5.08	$4.72	$20.57
Garland	TX	$525,000	$0	$525,000	0%	100%	7.00	$75,000	$2.91	$0.85	$10.61
Houston	TX	$45,963,911	$817,464	$45,146,447	2%	98%	889.00	$50,783	$27.69	$714.37	$115.22
Irving	TX	$150,592	$0	$150,592	0%	100%	6.10	$24,687	$0.97	$5.53	$3.84
Longview	TX	$592,854	$0	$592,854	0%	100%	18.00	$32,936	$3.43	$8.58	$31.01
Lubbock	TX	$787,147	$10,000	$777,147	1%	99%	11.90	$65,306	$4.17	$23.68	$16.96
Odessa	TX	$0	$0	$0	0%	0%	.00	$0	$0.00	$0.00	$0.00
Tyler	TX	$1,145,023	$0	$1,145,023	0%	100%	18.90	$60,583	$15.18	$29.06	$58.39
Waco	TX	$1,521,770	$330,660	$1,191,110	22%	78%	20.00	$59,556	$11.50	$33.51	$49.25
Wichita Falls	TX	$403,065	$0	$403,065	0%	100%	8.10	$49,761	$4.19	$6.05	$16.20
Salt Lake City	UT	$9,089,897	$2,780,918	$6,308,979	31%	69%	142.60	$44,242	$39.45	$118.48	$167.62
Alexandria	VA	$1,691,220	$197,582	$1,493,638	12%	88%	18.40	$81,176	$13.43	$18.97	$61.12
Arlington	VA	$3,803,898	$0	$3,803,898	0%	100%	71.70	$53,055	$22.25	$90.33	$100.57
Chesapeake	VA	$6,519,419	$212,670	$6,306,749	3%	97%	106.50	$62,754	$41.50	$120.62	$150.05
Hampton	VA	$3,084,790	$200,000	$2,884,790	6%	94%	45.40	$63,542	$21.56	$58.05	$81.67
Lynchburg	VA	$725,194	$77,267	$647,927	11%	89%	11.50	$56,341	$9.81	$26.00	$39.99
Newport News	VA	$5,602,200	$149,700	$5,452,500	3%	97%	117.90	$46,247	$32.07	$85.28	$118.76
Norfolk	VA	$7,291,213	$1,149,307	$6,141,906	16%	84%	113.90	$53,924	$23.51	$68.67	$105.45
Richmond	VA	$10,864,971	$1,064,515	$9,800,456	10%	90%	217.20	$45,122	$48.26	$114.94	$207.10
Roanoke	VA	$111,429	$111,429	$0	100%	0%	.00	$0	$0.00	$0.00	$0.00
Virginia Beach	VA	$10,192,835	$45,533	$10,147,302	0%	100%	144.40	$70,272	$25.82	$74.76	$98.55
Everett	WA	$1,200,000	$0	$1,200,000	0%	100%	14.00	$85,714	$17.15	$41.94	$67.96
Seattle	WA	$9,951,443	$6,649,053	$3,302,390	67%	33%	59.00	$55,972	$6.40	$13.94	$29.00

continued

Table 1, cont.

City	St	Total Award	Innovative Awards	Hiring Awards	Percent Innovation	Percent Hiring	Officers Acquired Under Grant	Hiring Dollar Per New Officer	Hiring Dollar Per Citizen	Hiring Dollar Per Household	Hiring Dollar Per Family
Spokane	WA	$7,464,296	$1,599,997	$5,864,299	21%	79%	91.10	$64,372	$33.09	$77.93	$130.39
Yakima	WA	$460,459	$10,459	$450,000	2%	98%	6.00	$75,000	$8.21	$20.81	$32.51
Kenosha	WI	$1,000,000	$0	$1,000,000	0%	100%	8.00	$125,000	$12.44	$33.32	$47.69
Madison	WI	$6,180,203	$2,228,478	$3,951,725	36%	64%	54.00	$73,180	$20.66	$51.54	$98.19
TOTALS		**$1,793,006,630**	**$138,808,165**	**$1,654,198,465**			**26,983.2**				

180

Table 2: Community Demographics

City	St	Population	% Caucasian	% Northern European	% Black	% Asian	% Hispanic	1990 Households	1990 Families	HH GINI	Fam GINI
Birmingham	AL	265852	0.3573	0.3640	0.6337	0.0030	0.0044	104991	67534	0.4655	0.4363
Mesa	AZ	288091	0.9039	0.1557	0.0182	0.0114	0.1060	107717	74606	0.3814	0.3490
Phoenix	AZ	983403	0.8175	0.1608	0.0521	0.0147	0.1974	370119	248721	0.4290	0.4073
Tempe	AZ	141865	0.8687	0.1808	0.0322	0.0398	0.1057	55691	32395	0.4186	0.3736
Anaheim	CA	266406	0.7165	0.1294	0.0250	0.0926	0.3095	87224	63983	0.3827	0.4151
Berkeley	CA	102724	0.6230	0.1555	0.1880	0.1473	0.0778	43549	19127	0.5057	0.4729
Beverly Hills	CA	31971	0.9140	0.2984	0.0143	0.0531	0.0525	14518	7955	0.8635	0.9085
Burbank	CA	93643	0.8280	0.1916	0.0161	0.0671	0.2207	39215	23610	0.4123	0.3872
Concord	CA	111348	0.8393	0.2144	0.0213	0.0833	0.1147	42095	29346	0.3498	0.3205
Costa Mesa	CA	96357	0.8445	0.1606	0.0122	0.0610	0.1993	37653	21910	0.3815	0.3708
Daly City	CA	92315	0.3983	0.1059	0.0770	0.4245	0.2192	29148	21778	0.3539	0.3266
Fremont	CA	173339	0.7075	0.1832	0.0379	0.1880	0.1290	60138	45632	0.3351	0.3137
Fresno	CA	354202	0.5935	0.1030	0.0827	0.1240	0.2906	122113	84788	0.4486	0.4376
Garden Grove	CA	143050	0.6731	0.1174	0.0153	0.2015	0.2275	44771	34415	0.3542	0.3376
Glendale	CA	180038	0.7429	0.1072	0.0113	0.1404	0.2012	68694	45260	0.4676	0.4650
Hayward	CA	111498	0.6181	0.1564	0.0984	0.1402	0.2341	40246	28023	0.3698	0.3528
Inglewood	CA	109602	0.1747	0.0177	0.5195	0.0214	0.3791	36419	24907	0.3965	0.3866
Long Beach	CA	429433	0.5845	0.1150	0.1370	0.1259	0.2326	159234	94905	0.4419	0.4354
Los Angeles	CA	3485395	0.5294	0.1101	0.1394	0.0961	0.3952	1219770	769078	0.5046	0.5006
Oakland	CA	372242	0.3247	0.0832	0.4393	0.1451	0.1324	144766	85011	0.3599	0.4567
Ontario	CA	133179	0.6465	0.1049	0.0735	0.0319	0.4148	40482	31705	0.4689	0.3429

continued

Table 2, cont.

City	St	Population	% Caucasian	% Northern European	% Black	% Asian	% Hispanic	1990 House-holds	1990 Families	HH GINI	Fam GINI
Orange	CA	110658	0.8318	0.1450	0.0145	0.0762	0.2240	35756	27283	0.3532	0.3677
Pasadena	CA	131591	0.5713	0.0943	0.1899	0.0807	0.2690	50409	30443	0.4975	0.4926
Pomona	CA	131723	0.5724	0.0551	0.1440	0.0645	0.5055	36566	27755	0.3953	0.3818
Redondo Beach	CA	60167	0.8716	0.2091	0.0139	0.0612	0.1166	26804	14342	0.3658	0.3407
Richmond	CA	87425	0.3622	0.0772	0.4377	0.1139	0.1385	32798	21907	0.4163	0.3908
Riverside	CA	226505	0.7092	0.1234	0.0744	0.0473	0.2549	75763	54745	0.4082	0.3808
Sacramento	CA	369365	0.6016	0.1321	0.1528	0.1429	0.1590	144661	88251	0.4253	0.4043
Salinas	CA	108777	0.5473	0.0925	0.0298	0.0752	0.5004	33518	25336	0.3778	0.3711
San Bernardino	CA	369365	0.6016	0.1321	0.1528	0.1429	0.1590	54644	39117	0.4251	0.4089
San Diego	CA	1110549	0.6721	0.1454	0.0933	0.2246	0.2014	406316	252260	0.4312	0.4131
San Francisco	CA	723959	0.5364	0.1627	0.1090	0.2873	0.1335	305984	143818	0.4679	0.4572
San Jose	CA	782225	0.6299	0.1497	0.0465	0.1907	0.2608	251050	186149	0.3604	0.3418
San Mateo	CA	85486	0.7866	0.2236	0.0339	0.1230	0.1529	35496	21705	0.4057	0.3765
Santa Ana	CA	293742	0.6813	0.0475	0.0259	0.0941	0.6467	71860	55086	0.3596	0.3605
Santa Barbara	CA	85571	0.7761	0.1447	0.0254	0.0220	0.3097	34466	18683	0.4579	0.4398
Santa Clara	CA	93613	0.7406	0.1990	0.0247	0.1822	0.1452	36548	22418	0.3548	0.3205
Stockton	CA	210943	0.5753	0.1133	0.0968	0.2252	0.2388	68923	49356	0.4268	0.4103
Sunnyvale	CA	117229	0.7165	0.1590	0.0337	0.1878	0.1282	48592	29828	0.3564	0.3334
Torrance	CA	133107	0.7328	0.1610	0.0127	0.2162	0.0990	52831	35696	0.3820	0.3450
Vallejo	CA	109199	0.5038	0.1174	0.2127	0.2196	0.1026	37422	27417	0.3641	0.3297
West Covina	CA	96086	0.6005	0.1000	0.0850	0.1710	0.3421	30105	24255	0.3697	0.3491

City	St	Population	% Caucasian	% Northern European	% Black	% Asian	% Hispanic	1990 Households	1990 Families	HH GINI	Fam GINI
Aurora	CO	222110	0.8239	0.1600	0.1158	0.0360	0.0646	89432	58649	0.3553	0.3249
Colorado Springs	CO	281140	0.8512	0.1518	0.0598	0.0219	0.0890	111002	75069	0.4061	0.3796
Denver	CO	467610	0.7220	0.1386	0.1290	0.0222	0.2279	211137	110414	0.4725	0.4521
Fort Collins	CO	87758	0.9312	0.1478	0.0103	0.0241	0.0696	33810	19791	0.4335	0.3839
Bridgeport	CT	141686	0.5867	0.2719	0.2665	0.0207	0.2530	52531	34819	0.4203	0.3909
Bristol	CT	60640	0.9527	0.3730	0.0174	0.0080	0.0255	23903	16750	0.3537	0.3024
Hartford	CT	50452	0.8684	0.3634	0.0846	0.0203	0.0538	51587	31515	0.4653	0.4576
New Britain	CT	75491	0.8185	0.4234	0.0741	0.0171	0.1600	30099	19074	0.3948	0.3636
West Hartford	CT	60110	0.9425	0.4232	0.0184	0.0293	0.0323	23361	16229	0.4764	0.4422
Washington	DC	606900	0.2961	0.0843	0.6587	0.0182	0.0517	249034	123580	0.4981	0.4998
Coral Gables	FL	40091	0.9329	0.1736	0.0336	0.0150	0.4149	66412	9790	0.5380	0.5689
Fort Lauderdale	FL	149377	0.6963	0.1951	0.2811	0.0070	0.0708	15555	34763	0.5880	0.5513
Fort Meyers	FL	45206	0.6422	0.1233	0.3190	0.0092	0.0726	18134	10773	0.4777	0.4844
Gainesville	FL	84770	0.7334	0.1508	0.2148	0.0338	0.0445	34955	17524	0.4850	0.4325
Hollywood	FL	121697	0.8845	0.2975	0.0838	0.0131	0.1170	52956	32427	0.4718	0.4427
Jacksonville	FL	635230	0.7384	0.1394	0.2525	0.0182	0.0245	240875	168078	0.4222	0.3934
Lakeland	FL	70576	0.7811	0.1353	0.2031	0.0073	0.0308	23791	19414	0.4533	0.4355
Miami	FL	358548	0.6583	0.0321	0.2728	0.0058	0.6232	150250	85010	0.5298	0.5032
Orlando	FL	164693	0.6857	0.1447	0.2692	0.0146	0.0857	65635	37111	0.4193	0.4091
Pensacola	FL	58165	0.6578	0.1285	0.3182	0.0161	0.0171	24055	15519	0.4880	0.4678
St. Petersburg	FL	238629	0.7787	0.1816	0.1954	0.0177	0.0239	105907	62350	0.4463	0.4091
Tallahassee	FL	124773	0.6822	0.1320	0.2907	0.0174	0.0311	50575	26374	0.4752	0.4161
West Palm Beach	FL	67643	0.6325	0.1555	0.3260	0.0113	0.1360	25774	16064	0.4842	0.4849

183

continued

Table 2, cont.

City	St	Population	% Caucasian	% Northern European	% Black	% Asian	% Hispanic	1990 House-holds	1990 Families	HH GINI	Fam GINI
Atlanta	GA	394017	0.3106	0.0545	0.6706	0.0083	0.0194	155894	87976	0.6025	0.6474
Augusta	GA	44639	0.4253	0.0717	0.5604	0.0066	0.0105	18795	10584	0.5530	0.5350
Columbus	GA	178701	0.5887	0.1016	0.3807	0.0126	0.0293	65715	47531	0.4564	0.4318
Macon	GA	106640	0.4715	0.0747	0.5221	0.0036	0.0038	41227	27487	0.4946	0.4714
Marietta	GA	44129	0.7638	0.1468	0.2046	0.0177	0.0321	19784	10404	0.4355	0.4260
Honolulu	HI	365272	0.2673	0.0709	0.0122	0.6048	0.0423	134768	87974	0.4459	0.4113
Chicago	IL	2783726	0.4548	0.1919	0.3903	0.0370	0.1923	1020911	636423	0.3608	0.4441
Elgin	IL	77010	0.7796	0.1622	0.0726	0.0338	0.1844	26662	18925	0.4658	0.3212
Oak Park Village	IL	53648	0.7688	0.3033	0.1854	0.0333	0.0303	22651	13336	0.4060	0.3650
Peoria	IL	113504	0.7653	0.1333	0.2101	0.0152	0.0160	44883	28454	0.4703	0.4390
Rockford	IL	139426	0.8106	0.1833	0.1484	0.0172	0.0374	54839	36756	0.4387	0.4081
Skokie Village	IL	59432	0.8137	0.3423	0.0215	0.1550	0.0417	22747	17297	0.4010	0.3639
Springfield	IL	105227	0.8567	0.1854	0.1313	0.0081	0.0076	44879	26803	0.4160	0.3773
Anderson	IN	59449	0.8487	0.1072	0.1432	0.0031	0.0041	24335	16034	0.4324	0.3992
Gary	IN	116646	0.1628	0.0440	0.8060	0.0012	0.0539	40752	29229	0.3920	0.4394
Hammond	IN	84236	0.8494	0.2805	0.0904	0.0030	0.1169	32177	22308	0.4654	0.3535
Kokomo	IN	44962	0.8934	0.1115	0.0878	0.0079	0.0169	18651	12335	0.4122	0.3755
Muncie	IN	71035	0.8914	0.1164	0.0923	0.0072	0.0102	27167	16072	0.4642	0.4179
South Bend	IN	105536	0.7626	0.2661	0.2099	0.0070	0.0327	42000	26904	0.4146	0.3796
Davenport	IA	95333	0.8912	0.1386	0.0782	0.0092	0.0352	37069	24654	0.4214	0.3843
Des Moines	IA	193187	0.8925	0.1545	0.0707	0.0227	0.0236	78587	49374	0.4275	0.3942

184

City	St	Population	% Caucasian	% Northern European	% Black	% Asian	% Hispanic	1990 Households	1990 Families	HH GINI	Fam GINI
Sioux City	IA	80505	0.9251	0.1382	0.0248	0.0140	0.0301	30486	21012	0.4504	0.4335
Waterloo	IA	66467	0.8683	0.0980	0.1215	0.0057	0.0076	27185	18173	0.4412	0.4092
Overland Park	KS	111790	0.9562	0.1822	0.0162	0.0186	0.0208	44983	31066	0.3835	0.3465
Wichita	KS	304011	0.8242	0.1100	0.1124	0.0245	0.0471	122682	80879	0.4225	0.3882
Lexington-Fayette	KY	225366	0.8466	0.1434	0.1339	0.0147	0.0105	89542	56873	0.4552	0.4185
Louisville	KY	269157	0.6916	0.1242	0.2968	0.0073	0.0055	112815	67853	0.4765	0.4480
Bossier City	LA	57218	0.7308	0.1353	0.1644	0.0124	0.0290	19188	14409	0.3982	0.3652
Lafayette	LA	94460	0.7067	0.0687	0.2715	0.0449	0.0176	36328	23577	0.5061	0.4781
Shreveport	LA	198528	0.5431	0.1060	0.4481	0.0041	0.0104	75365	51741	0.4960	0.4697
Baltimore	MD	736014	0.3912	0.1245	0.5919	0.0136	0.0095	275977	175032	0.4625	0.4367
Boston	MA	574283	0.6295	0.3277	0.2554	0.0526	0.1039	227953	117656	0.4638	0.4352
Newton	MA	82585	0.9296	0.4396	0.0203	0.0459	0.0195	29366	19952	0.4778	0.4629
Quincy	MA	84985	0.9193	0.5250	0.0100	0.0641	0.0131	35765	20916	0.3921	0.3348
Worcester	MA	169759	0.8728	0.3533	0.0451	0.0257	0.0935	63588	40433	0.4254	0.3856
Ann Arbor	MI	109592	0.8230	0.1955	0.0893	0.3775	0.0240	41885	21331	0.4606	0.4044
Battle Creek	MI	53540	0.8089	0.1300	0.1617	0.0124	0.0171	21355	14081	0.4461	0.4168
Dearborn	MI	89286	0.9761	0.3296	0.0048	0.0094	0.0257	35298	24160	0.4138	0.3732
Detroit	MI	1027974	0.2159	0.0790	0.7573	0.0080	0.0264	373857	247480	0.4798	0.4571
Flint	MI	140761	0.4957	0.0925	0.4795	0.0054	0.0265	53882	35713	0.4640	0.4463
Grand Rapids	MI	189126	0.7675	0.1676	0.1858	0.0100	0.0447	69452	45972	0.4094	0.3831
Kalamazoo	MI	80227	0.7720	0.1503	0.1883	0.0208	0.0258	29534	15595	0.4868	0.4735
Pontiac	MI	71166	0.5148	0.0851	0.4218	0.0114	0.0771	24844	15967	0.4366	0.4155
Saginaw	MI	69512	0.5220	0.0046	0.4038	0.0042	0.1004	26197	17874	0.4624	0.4372

continued

185

Table 2, cont.

City	St	Population	% Caucasian	% Northern European	% Black	% Asian	% Hispanic	1990 Households	1990 Families	HH GINI	Fam GINI
Warren	MI	144864	0.9741	0.4050	0.0066	0.0129	0.0071	54688	40322	0.3642	0.3264
Duluth	MN	85493	0.9569	0.1611	0.0099	0.0096	0.0057	34646	21127	0.4433	0.3946
Minneapolis	MN	368383	0.6407	0.1331	0.1304	0.0405	0.0198	160531	78461	0.4498	0.4244
St. Paul	MN	272235	0.8239	0.1652	0.0747	0.0697	0.0379	110608	63260	0.4262	0.3969
Kansas City	MO	435141	0.6685	0.1368	0.2961	0.0107	0.0387	177157	110206	0.4362	0.4035
Springfield	MO	140494	0.9558	0.1427	0.0240	0.0093	0.0088	57365	91747	0.4600	0.4261
St. Louis	MO	396685	0.5099	0.1280	0.4739	0.0088	0.0122	164404	34808	0.4634	0.4261
Omaha	NE	335795	0.8391	0.2042	0.1305	0.0072	0.0289	133888	85255	0.4391	0.4033
Las Vegas	NV	258295	0.7844	0.1886	0.1141	0.0332	0.1210	99944	65878	0.4187	0.3903
North Las Vegas	NV	47707	0.4512	0.0851	0.3738	0.0217	0.2170	14450	11226	0.3954	0.3823
Reno	NV	133850	0.8593	0.2018	0.0286	0.0446	0.1080	57318	32267	0.4370	0.4051
Manchester	NH	99567	0.9673	0.2630	0.0093	0.0117	0.0215	40398	25348	0.3921	0.3468
Bayonne	NJ	61444	0.9071	0.5783	0.0474	0.0183	0.0945	25319	16786	0.4161	0.3586
Clifton	NJ	71742	0.9296	0.4921	0.0144	0.0322	0.0646	29114	20065	0.3904	0.3334
Edison	NJ	88680	0.7975	0.4342	0.0542	0.1365	0.0402	31777	24021	0.3506	0.3203
Elizabeth	NJ	110002	0.6558	0.2748	0.1993	0.0269	0.3893	39072	27321	0.4101	0.3860
Irvington	NJ	59774	0.2262	0.0972	0.6992	0.0237	0.0953	21542	14534	0.3958	0.3659
Jersey City	NJ	228537	0.4842	0.2107	0.2978	0.1132	0.2373	82306	54127	0.4383	0.4105
Linden	NJ	36701	0.7634	0.4406	0.1993	0.0137	0.0726	14476	10172	0.3751	0.3278
Newark	NJ	275221	0.2859	0.1331	0.5853	0.0117	0.2514	90878	63316	0.4588	0.4274
Paterson	NJ	140891	0.4120	0.1301	0.3606	0.0102	0.4049	43862	33106	0.4283	0.4003

City	St	Population	% Caucasian	% Northern European	% Black	% Asian	% Hispanic	1990 Households	1990 Families	HH GINI	Fam GINI
Woodbridge	NJ	17434	0.8712	0.4937	0.0544	0.0576	0.0571	7025	4852	0.3746	0.3314
Albuquerque	NM	384736	0.7348	0.1197	0.0297	0.1680	0.3417	152781	100170	0.4288	0.3976
Santa Fe	NM	55993	0.9782	0.1032	0.0038	0.0045	0.4751	22783	13999	0.4636	0.4560
Albany	NY	101082	0.7550	0.3622	0.2070	0.0225	0.0319	42034	20501	0.4369	0.3994
Rochester	NY	231636	0.6128	0.2295	0.3156	0.0162	0.0817	93521	52681	0.4366	0.4198
Syracuse	NY	163860	0.7490	0.3155	0.2024	0.0225	0.0255	65046	35214	0.4461	0.4079
Yonkers	NY	188082	0.7650	0.4503	0.1407	0.0292	0.1627	72291	49718	0.4368	0.4051
Charlotte	NC	396003	0.6558	0.1100	0.3185	0.0157	0.0133	158946	103442	0.4342	0.4110
Durham	NC	136594	0.5162	0.0921	0.4568	0.0195	0.0125	56049	33174	0.4409	0.4066
Greensboro	NC	183521	0.6394	0.0993	0.3398	0.0138	0.0076	74690	45246	0.4430	0.4150
High Point	NC	69394	0.6818	0.0929	0.3036	0.0053	0.0064	27517	18972	0.4609	0.4234
Raleigh	NC	207951	0.6934	0.1077	0.2752	0.0246	0.0118	85813	43793	0.4192	0.3788
Wilmington	NC	55530	0.6506	0.1163	0.3383	0.0050	0.0070	23384	13835	0.4856	0.4569
Akron	OH	223019	0.7393	0.1801	0.2439	0.0113	0.0067	90119	57304	0.4550	0.4245
Cincinnati	OH	364040	0.6049	0.1191	0.3794	0.0114	0.0064	154243	83399	0.4966	0.4787
Cleveland	OH	505616	0.4959	0.1824	0.4649	0.0096	0.0442	199617	124176	0.4574	0.4256
Columbus	OH	632958	0.7454	0.1580	0.2253	0.0226	0.0090	257376	151877	0.4096	0.3787
Dayton	OH	182044	0.5827	0.0999	0.4051	0.0058	0.0066	72513	44048	0.4328	0.4083
Springfield	OH	70487	0.8165	0.1296	0.1747	0.0045	0.0049	27226	18170	0.4351	0.4021
Toledo	OH	332943	0.7705	0.2068	0.1972	0.0106	0.0359	130774	85010	0.4310	0.3916
Lawton	OK	80561	0.7083	0.1220	0.1937	0.0286	0.0610	28580	22380	0.3795	0.3628
Norman	OK	80071	0.8782	0.1477	0.0352	0.0447	0.0241	32641	19356	0.4601	0.3935
Oklahoma City	OK	444730	0.7490	0.1287	0.1594	0.0221	0.0476	178885	117629	0.4416	0.4124

continued

187

Table 2, cont.

City	St	Population	% Caucasian	% Northern European	% Black	% Asian	% Hispanic	1990 House-holds	1990 Families	HH GINI	Fam GINI
Tulsa	OK	367193	0.7932	0.1348	0.1353	0.0126	0.0254	155433	97771	0.4860	0.4600
Eugene	OR	112669	0.9331	0.1460	0.0121	0.0318	0.0285	46385	26534	0.4639	0.4112
Portland	OR	437398	0.8485	0.1501	0.0757	0.0495	0.0300	187262	104992	0.4460	0.4106
Salem	OR	107786	0.9124	0.1211	0.0139	0.0222	0.0576	42113	25526	0.4197	0.3894
Erie	PA	108718	0.8619	0.3536	0.1221	0.0038	0.0216	160595	26969	0.4181	0.3811
Philadelphia	PA	1585577	0.5354	0.2866	0.3989	0.0257	0.0531	600740	381339	0.4489	0.4120
Pittsburgh	PA	369879	0.7209	0.3017	0.2586	0.0140	0.0092	153607	88044	0.5018	0.4658
Reading	PA	78380	0.7880	0.1914	0.0976	0.0119	0.1803	31299	19373	0.4245	0.3812
Providence	RI	160728	0.7024	0.0969	0.1455	0.0593	0.1477	58530	35367	0.4946	0.4720
Columbia	SC	98052	0.5383	0.0845	0.4361	0.0130	0.0207	33781	19091	0.4823	0.4646
Sioux Falls	SD	100814	0.9680	0.0900	0.0074	0.0073	0.0066	39923	26040	0.4245	0.3817
Knoxville	TN	166121	0.8234	0.1340	0.1551	0.0098	0.0059	69973	41229	0.4969	0.4620
Memphis	TN	610337	0.4398	0.0908	0.5488	0.0074	0.0066	229726	154881	0.4823	0.4629
Nashville-Davidson	TN	488518	0.7386	0.1315	0.2432	0.0124	0.0085	198643	125636	0.4333	0.4047
Abilene	TX	106665	0.8256	0.1201	0.0695	0.0120	0.1509	38298	27319	0.4417	0.4054
Amarillo	TX	157615	0.8289	0.1246	0.0581	0.0179	0.1445	61422	42736	0.4534	0.4235
Arlington	TX	261763	0.8270	0.1514	0.0844	0.0392	0.0846	101065	69227	0.3913	0.3562
Austin	TX	465557	0.7073	0.1029	0.1239	0.0293	0.2259	192136	105416	0.4608	0.4254
Beaumont	TX	114323	0.5499	0.1039	0.4123	0.0162	0.0444	43413	29853	0.4860	0.4527
Corpus Christi	TX	257453	0.7632	0.0794	0.0475	0.0087	0.5001	89307	66006	0.4564	0.4376
Dallas	TX	1006831	0.5542	0.0929	0.2950	0.0209	0.2033	160595	238696	0.5024	0.5146

City	St	Population	% Caucasian	% Northern European	% Black	% Asian	% Hispanic	1990 House-holds	1990 Families	HH GINI	Fam GINI
El Paso	TX	515342	0.7699	0.0516	0.0341	0.0112	0.6894	24180	127661	0.4492	0.4402
Galveston	TX	59072	0.6142	0.1084	0.2900	0.0235	0.2115	53578	24586	0.5077	0.4865
Garland	TX	180635	0.7980	0.1439	0.0895	0.0440	0.1133	617195	49500	0.3511	0.3321
Houston	TX	1630672	0.5276	0.0832	0.2806	0.0402	0.2716	53193	391833	0.4853	0.4813
Irving	TX	155037	0.7886	0.1362	0.0752	0.0449	0.1601	27224	39226	0.3978	0.3886
Longview	TX	70316	0.7662	0.1292	0.1984	0.0047	0.0426	59084	19120	0.4536	0.4186
Lubbock	TX	186281	0.7783	0.1164	0.0845	0.0126	0.2239	32813	45809	0.4749	0.4315
Odessa	TX	89783	0.7574	0.0995	0.0607	0.0030	0.3108	29421	24010	0.4538	0.4247
Tyler	TX	75450	0.6607	0.0964	0.2819	0.0049	0.0874	39405	19610	0.4913	0.4602
Waco	TX	103590	0.6761	0.0974	0.2318	0.0083	0.1614	35541	24186	0.5015	0.4572
Wichita Falls	TX	96259	0.8078	0.1318	0.1100	0.0174	0.0990	56653	24878	0.4506	0.4137
Salt Lake City	UT	159936	0.8717	0.0928	0.0164	0.0335	0.0952	53249	37638	0.4860	0.4638
Alexandria	VA	111183	0.6917	0.1663	0.2209	0.0415	0.0939	78745	24438	0.3874	0.3846
Arlington	VA	170936	0.7549	0.1793	0.1050	0.0668	0.1330	42113	37822	0.3928	0.3803
Chesapeake	VA	151976	0.7067	0.1319	0.2740	0.0118	0.0104	52287	42032	0.3521	0.3272
Hampton	VA	133793	0.5842	0.1036	0.3900	0.0167	0.0187	49699	35322	0.3753	0.3459
Lynchburg	VA	66049	0.7252	0.0979	0.2652	0.0065	0.0065	24923	16202	0.4644	0.4323
Newport News	VA	170045	0.6266	0.1126	0.3351	0.0220	0.0268	63940	45912	0.4066	0.3854
Norfolk	VA	261229	0.5571	0.1193	0.3910	0.0242	0.0277	89443	58246	0.4379	0.4239
Richmond	VA	203056	0.4330	0.0694	0.5536	0.0081	0.0086	85268	47322	0.4841	0.4814
Roanoke	VA	96397	0.7467	0.1040	0.2416	0.0081	0.0075	41064	25704	0.4422	0.4139
Virginia Beach	VA	393069	0.8047	0.1756	0.1394	0.0421	0.0309	135736	102963	0.3607	0.3477
Everett	WA	69961	0.9169	0.1307	0.0171	0.0374	0.0239	28614	17658	0.3901	0.3630

continued

Table 2, cont.

City	St	Population	% Caucasian	% Northern European	% Black	% Asian	% Hispanic	1990 House-holds	1990 Families	HH GINI	Fam GINI
Seattle	WA	516259	0.7541	0.1413	0.1001	0.1118	0.0330	236908	113856	0.4526	0.4103
Spokane	WA	177196	0.9347	0.1645	0.0190	0.0205	0.0159	75252	44976	0.4457	0.4018
Yakima	WA	54831	0.8252	0.1105	0.0252	0.0118	0.1587	21628	13844	0.4548	0.4314
Kenosha	WI	80375	0.8998	0.2317	0.0631	0.0061	0.0574	30008	20967	0.4300	0.3406
Madison	WI	191262	0.9081	0.1581	0.0414	0.0384	0.0189	76673	40247	0.3760	0.3723

Table 3: Organizational characteristics related to COP principles (1997 and 1999)

City	St	Geo Patrol 1997	Routine Foot Patrol 1997	Fixed Neigh Sub-stations 1997	Scale of Programs 1997	Encourage Sara 1997	COP Plan 1997	Geo Patrol 1999	Fixed Neigh Sub-stations 1999	Scale of Programs 1999	Encourage SARA 1999	COP Plan 1999	Officer Resources Devoted to COP 1999
Birmingham	AL	yes	yes	5	medium	no	formal	yes	5	high	no	yes, written	minimal
Mesa	AZ	yes	no	0	high	yes	informal	yes	0	high	yes	yes, not written	minimal
Phoenix	AZ	yes	yes	3	medium	yes	formal	yes	4	high	yes	yes, written	minimal
Tempe	AZ	yes	yes	0	low	yes	informal	yes	0	low	yes	yes, written	cop dept
Anaheim	CA	yes	no	2	low	yes	informal	yes	2	high	yes	yes, not written	minimal
Berkeley	CA	yes	no	1	high	yes	formal	yes	0	high	yes	yes, written	minimal
Beverly Hills	CA	no	yes	0	low	no	informal	no	0	low	no	yes, not written	minimal
Burbank	CA	no	yes	0	low	no	informal	yes	1	high	no	yes, not written	minimal
Concord	CA	yes	no	3	low	no	informal	yes	3	low	yes	yes, written	cop dept
Costa Mesa	CA	yes	no	1	low	yes	informal	yes	2	medium	yes	yes, written	minimal
Daly City	CA	yes	no	1	medium	yes	formal	yes	1	low	yes	yes, written	minimal
Fremont	CA	yes	no	1	medium	yes	formal	yes	1	high	yes	yes, written	medium
Fresno	CA	yes	no	0	medium	yes	formal	yes	10	medium	yes	yes, written	low
Garden Grove	CA	yes	yes	11	low	yes	formal	yes	2	medium	yes	yes, written	medium
Glendale	CA	yes	yes	3	high	yes	formal	yes	4	high	yes	yes, written	minimal
Hayward	CA	yes	no	2	medium	yes	formal	yes	2	medium	yes	yes, written	high
Inglewood	CA	no	no	4	low	yes	formal	yes	3	low	no	yes, not written	minimal
Long Beach	CA	yes	yes	3	high	yes	formal	yes	5	high	no	yes, not written	minimal
Los Angeles	CA	yes	yes	113	high	yes	formal	yes	10	high	yes	yes, written	high
Oakland	CA	yes	yes	5	high	no	formal	yes	11	high	yes	yes, written	minimal
Ontario	CA	no	yes	1	medium	yes	formal	yes	3	medium	yes	yes, written	minimal
Orange	CA	yes	no	0	medium	yes	formal	yes	0	medium	no	no	minimal

continued

Table 3, cont.

City	St	Geo Patrol 1997	Routine Foot Patrol 1997	Fixed Neigh Sub-stations 1997	Scale of Programs 1997	Encourage Sara 1997	COP Plan 1997	Geo Patrol 1999	Fixed Neigh Sub-stations 1999	Scale of Programs 1999	Encourage SARA 1999	COP Plan 1999	Officer Resources Devoted to COP 1999
Pasadena	CA	yes	no	3	high	yes	formal	yes	3	low	yes	yes, written	low
Pomona	CA	yes	no	2	low	yes	informal	yes	4	low	no	yes, written	minimal
Redondo Beach	CA	yes	yes	2	medium	yes	formal	yes	1	low	yes	yes, written	minimal
Richmond	CA	yes	yes	5	low	yes	formal	yes	4	low	yes	yes, written	low
Riverside	CA	yes	no	6	medium	yes	formal	yes	5	low	yes	yes, written	minimal
Sacramento	CA	yes	no	0	high	yes	formal	yes	8	low	yes	yes, written	low
Salinas	CA	yes	no	2	low	yes	formal	yes	2	medium	no	yes, written	minimal
San Bernardino	CA	yes	no	7	low	yes	formal	yes	7	medium	yes	yes, written	medium
San Diego	CA	yes	yes	0	medium	yes	formal	yes	26	low	yes	yes, written	cop dept
San Francisco	CA	yes	yes	0	medium	yes	formal	yes	1	low	yes	yes, written	medium
San Jose	CA	yes	no	0	medium	no	no cop plan	yes	0	medium	yes	yes, not written	cop dept
San Mateo	CA	yes	no	0	low	yes	formal	yes	0	medium	yes	yes, written	minimal
Santa Ana	CA	yes	no	4	medium	yes	formal	yes	4	medium	yes	yes, written	minimal
Santa Barbara	CA	yes	yes	0	medium	yes	formal	yes	0	high	yes	yes, not written	high
Santa Clara	CA	yes	no	0	medium	yes	formal	yes	0	low	yes	yes, written	minimal
Stockton	CA	yes	yes	1	low	yes	formal	yes	3	high	yes	yes, written	minimal
Sunnyvale	CA	yes	no	0	medium	no	informal	yes	0	high	yes	yes, written	minimal
Torrance	CA	yes	yes	3	medium	no	formal	yes	3	medium	yes	yes, not written	minimal
Vallejo	CA	yes	no	3	low	yes	informal	yes	3	medium	yes	yes, not written	minimal
West Covina	CA	yes	no	1	medium	no	formal	yes	1	high	no	yes, written	minimal
Aurora	CO	yes	yes	0	medium	yes	informal	yes	0	medium	yes	yes, written	minimal

City	St	Geo Patrol 1997	Routine Foot Patrol 1997	Fixed Neigh Sub-stations 1997	Scale of Programs 1997	Encourage Sara 1997	COP Plan 1997	Geo Patrol 1995	Fixed Neigh Sub-stations 1999	Scale of Programs 1999	Encourage SARA 1999	COP Plan 1999	Officer Resources Devoted to COP 1999
Colorado Springs	CO	yes	no	3	medium	yes	formal	yes	0	medium	yes	yes, written	minimal
Denver	CO	no	yes	6	medium	no	formal	yes	12	low	yes	yes, written	minimal
Fort Collins	CO	yes	yes	1	medium	yes	formal	yes	1	medium	yes	yes, written	low
Bridgeport	CT	yes	yes	6	medium	yes	informal	yes	0	medium	yes	yes, not written	low
Bristol	CT	yes	yes	1	low	no	no cop plan	yes	1	low	yes	no	minimal
Hartford	CT	yes	yes	3	medium	yes	formal	yes	3	medium	no	yes, written	minimal
New Britain	CT	no	yes	1	medium	no	formal	yes	1	medium	yes	yes, written	low
West Hartford	CT	no data	no data	no data	no data	no data	no data	yes	0	high	yes	no	minimal
Washington	DC	yes	yes	5	high	yes	formal	yes	2	high	yes	yes, written	low
Coral Gables	FL	yes	no	4	medium	no	informal	no	2	low	no	no	minimal
Fort Lauderdale	FL	yes	yes	0	high	yes	formal	yes	6	medium	no	yes, written	minimal
Fort Meyers	FL	yes	no	5	low	yes	formal	yes	0	high	yes	yes, written	minimal
Gainesville	FL	yes	no	2	low	no	informal	no	2	medium	yes	yes, not written	minimal
Hollywood	FL	yes	yes	1	medium	yes	formal	yes	2	high	yes	yes, written	minimal
Jacksonville	FL	yes	yes	0	high	yes	formal	yes	5	high	yes	yes, written	minimal
Lakeland	FL	no	no	16	medium	no	formal	yes	15	low	no	yes, written	low
Miami	FL	yes	yes	12	high	yes	formal	yes	13	high	yes	yes, written	minimal
Orlando	FL	yes	yes	4	medium	no	informal	yes	9	low	yes	yes, written	minimal
Pensacola	FL	yes	yes	3	low	yes	formal	no	0	low	yes	no	minimal
St. Petersburg	FL	yes	no	0	medium	yes	formal	yes	7	low	yes	yes, written	low
Tallahassee	FL	no	yes	2	low	yes	formal	yes	0	low	yes	yes, written	minimal
West Palm Beach	FL	yes	yes	8	medium	yes	formal	yes	14	high	yes	yes, written	minimal
Atlanta	GA	yes	yes	7	high	no	informal	yes	13	high	no	yes, written	minimal

continued

Table 3, cont.

City	St	Geo Patrol 1997	Routine Foot Patrol 1997	Fixed Neigh Sub-stations 1997	Scale of Programs 1997	Encourage Sara 1997	COP Plan 1997	Geo Patrol 1999	Fixed Neigh Sub-stations 1999	Scale of Programs 1999	Encourage SARA 1999	COP Plan 1999	Officer Resources Devoted to COP 1999
Augusta	GA	yes	yes	12	medium	no	informal	yes	23	low	yes	yes, not written	low
Columbus	GA	yes	yes	0	medium	no	informal	yes	0	low	no	yes, not written	minimal
Macon	GA	yes	no	14	medium	no	informal	yes	0	high	no	yes, written	minimal
Marietta	GA	yes	no	0	low	no	informal	yes	1	medium	yes	yes, written	minimal
Honolulu	HI	yes	no	5	medium	no	informal	yes	5	high	yes	yes, not written	minimal
Chicago	IL	yes	yes	0	high	yes	formal	no	0	high	no	yes, written	high
Elgin	IL	yes	no	1	low	yes	informal	yes	9	high	yes	yes, written	medium
Oak Park Village	IL	yes	yes	4	low	yes	formal	yes	4	low	yes	yes, written	low
Peoria	IL	yes	yes	1	medium	yes	formal	yes	5	medium	no	yes, written	minimal
Rockford	IL	yes	no	0	medium	no	informal	yes	0	medium	yes	yes, not written	minimal
Skokie Village	IL	yes	yes	1	low	yes	informal	yes	1	low	yes	yes, not written	no officer resources
Springfield	IL	yes	yes	5	medium	yes	formal	yes	0	low	yes	yes, written	minimal
Anderson	IN	yes	no	1	medium	no	informal	yes	1	low	no	yes, not written	minimal
Gary	IN	yes	yes	1	low	yes	formal	yes	4	low	yes	yes, written	minimal
Hammond	IN	yes	yes	1	medium	no	formal	yes	3	medium	no	yes, not written	minimal
Kokomo	IN	yes	no	3	low	yes	formal	yes	2	low	yes	yes, written	medium
Muncie	IN	yes	no	2	medium	yes	informal	yes	7	low	no	yes, not written	minimal
South Bend	IN	yes	yes	0	medium	no	informal	yes	0	medium	no	yes, not written	minimal
Davenport	IA	yes	no	2	medium	no	informal	yes	0	medium	no	yes, written	minimal
Des Moines	IA	yes	yes	0	medium	yes	formal	yes	0	high	yes	yes, written	minimal
Sioux City	IA	yes	yes	3	low	yes	formal	yes	5	low	yes	yes, not written	minimal

City	St	Geo Patrol 1997	Routine Foot Patrol 1997	Fixed Neigh Sub-stations 1997	Scale of Programs 1997	Encourage Sara 1997	COP Plan 1997	Geo Patrol 1999	Fixed Neigh Sub-stations 1999	Scale of Programs 1999	Encourage SARA 1999	COP Plan 1999	Officer Resources Devoted to COP 1999
Waterloo	IA	yes	no	0	low	yes	informal	yes	0	low	yes	yes, written	high
Overland Park	KS	yes	no	0	medium	no	formal	yes	1	high	yes	yes, not written	minimal
Wichita	KS	yes	no	4	high	yes	formal	yes	4	low	yes	yes, written	minimal
Lexington-Fayette	KY	yes	yes	2	medium	no	informal	yes	3	medium	yes	yes, not written	minimal
Louisville	KY	no	yes	0	medium	yes	formal	yes	5	medium	no	yes, written	minimal
Bossier City	LA	yes	no	1	low	no	informal	yes	1	medium	yes	yes, not written	minimal
Lafayette	LA	yes	no	0	medium	no	informal	yes	0	low	no	no	no officer resources
Shreveport	LA	yes	no	8	medium	yes	informal	yes	3	medium	yes	yes, written	minimal
Baltimore	MD	yes	yes	9	medium	yes	formal	yes	0	medium	no	yes, written	no officer resources
Boston	MA	yes	yes	1	medium	no	formal	yes	0	high	yes	yes, written	minimal
Newton	MA	yes	yes	0	low	yes	informal	yes	0	high	yes	yes, written	high
Quincy	MA	yes	yes	0	medium	yes	informal	yes	0	high	no	yes, written	minimal
Worcester	MA	yes	yes	0	medium	yes	formal	yes	0	low	no	yes, written	minimal
Ann Arbor	MI	yes	yes	4	medium	yes	formal	yes	4	low	yes	yes, written	low
Battle Creek	MI	yes	yes	3	low	yes	informal	yes	3	high	yes	yes, not written	minimal
Dearborn	MI	yes	no	0	medium	yes	formal	yes	2	high	yes	yes, written	minimal
Detroit	MI	yes	yes	38	medium	no	formal	yes	35	high	no	yes, written	minimal
Flint	MI	yes	no	4	high	yes	formal	yes	6	high	yes	yes, not written	low
Grand Rapids	MI	no	yes	4	low	yes	formal	yes	0	low	yes	yes, written	minimal
Kalamazoo	MI	yes	yes	2	low	no	formal	yes	3	high	no	yes, written	minimal
Pontiac	MI	no	yes	1	low	no	formal	yes	3	low	no	yes, written	minimal

195

continued

Table 3, cont.

City	St	Geo Patrol 1997	Routine Foot Patrol 1997	Fixed Neigh Sub-stations 1997	Scale of Programs 1997	Encourage Sara 1997	COP Plan 1997	Geo Patrol 1999	Fixed Neigh Sub-stations 1999	Scale of Programs 1999	Encourage SARA 1999	COP Plan 1999	Officer Resources Devoted to COP 1999
Saginaw	MI	no	yes	9	medium	no	formal	yes	10	low	no	yes, written	low
Warren	MI	yes	no	2	low	no	informal	yes	0	medium	no	yes, not written	minimal
Duluth	MN	yes	no	8	medium	yes	formal	yes	8	low	no	yes, written	low
Minneapolis	MN	yes	yes	15	high	yes	formal	yes	10	medium	yes	yes, not written	minimal
St. Paul	MN	yes	yes	3	medium	yes	informal	yes	7	medium	yes	yes, written	low
Kansas City	MO	yes	yes	9	medium	yes	informal	yes	0	high	yes	yes, written	minimal
Springfield	MO	yes	yes	5	medium	yes	informal	yes	5	low	yes	yes, not written	minimal
St. Louis	MO	yes	yes	0	high	yes	formal	yes	0	high	yes	yes, not written	minimal
Omaha	NE	yes	no	0	low	yes	formal	yes	0	high	yes	yes, written	high
Las Vegas	NV	yes	yes	5	medium	yes	informal	yes	7	high	yes	yes, not written	medium
North Las Vegas	NV	no	no	0	low	no	informal	yes	1	low	no	yes, not written	minimal
Reno	NV	no	yes	3	medium	yes	formal	yes	4	low	yes	yes, written	minimal
Manchester	NH	no	no	2	medium	no	formal	no	3	high	yes	yes, written	minimal
Bayonne	NJ	yes	yes	0	medium	yes	formal	yes	1	low	no	yes, not written	minimal
Clifton	NJ	yes	no	3	low	no	informal	yes	3	medium	no	yes, not written	low
Edison	NJ	yes	no	1	medium	no	formal	no	0	high	no	yes, written	minimal
Elizabeth	NJ	yes	yes	3	low	yes	formal	yes	0	medium	yes	yes, written	minimal
Irvington	NJ	no	yes	1	low	no	informal	yes	0	medium	yes	yes, written	minimal
Jersey City	NJ	yes	yes	5	medium	no	formal	yes	2	low	yes	yes, written	low
Linden	NJ	yes	yes	1	medium	yes	formal	yes	1	high	no	yes, written	minimal
Newark	NJ	yes	yes	2	high	yes	formal	yes	2	high	yes	yes, not written	minimal

City	St	Geo Patrol 1997	Routine Foot Patrol 1997	Fixed Neigh Sub-stations 1997	Scale of Programs 1997	Encourage Sara 1997	COP Plan 1997	Geo Patrol 1999	Fixed Neigh Sub-stations 1999	Scale of Programs 1999	Encourage SARA 1999	COP Plan 1999	Officer Resources Devoted to COP 1999
Paterson	NJ	no data	no data	no data	no data	no data	no data	no	0	high	no	yes, written	minimal
Woodbridge	NJ	no	no	1	high	no	informal	yes	1	medium	no	yes, written	minimal
Albuquerque	NM	yes	no	1	medium	yes	formal	no	5	medium	yes	yes, written	medium
Santa Fe	NM	yes	no	5	high	yes	formal	no	3	low	yes	yes, written	minimal
Albany	NY	yes	yes	1	medium	yes	formal	yes	18	high	yes	yes, written	minimal
Rochester	NY	yes	yes	3	medium	yes	informal	yes	9	medium	no	yes, not written	minimal
Syracuse	NY	yes	yes	3	high	no	formal	yes	2	high	yes	yes, written	low
Yonkers	NY	no	yes	1	medium	no	informal	yes	1	high	no	yes, not written	minimal
Charlotte	NC	yes	no	10	medium	yes	informal	yes	2	high	yes	yes, not written	cop dept
Durham	NC	no	no	3	high	no	formal	yes	6	low	no	yes, written	low
Greensboro	NC	yes	yes	2	low	yes	formal	yes	6	high	yes	yes, written	minimal
High Point	NC	yes	no	6	medium	no	informal	yes	4	medium	yes	yes, not written	minimal
Raleigh	NC	yes	yes	4	medium	yes	informal	yes	4	medium	yes	yes, written	minimal
Wilmington	NC	yes	yes	0	medium	no	formal	yes	0	low	yes	yes, not written	minimal
Akron	OH	yes	yes	1	medium	no	informal	no	0	high	no	yes, not written	minimal
Cincinnati	OH	yes	yes	26	high	no	formal	yes	20	low	yes	yes, written	minimal
Cleveland	OH	yes	yes	21	medium	no	formal	yes	21	high	no	yes, written	minimal
Columbus	OH	yes	yes	0	high	no	formal	yes	4	high	yes	yes, written	minimal
Dayton	OH	yes	no	6	medium	no	formal	yes	4	medium	yes	yes, written	minimal
Springfield	OH	no data	no data	no data	no data	no data	no data	yes	1	low	yes	yes, written	minimal
Toledo	OH	yes	yes	11	medium	yes	formal	yes	7	high	yes	yes, written	cop dept
Lawton	OK	yes	no	3	low	no	informal	yes	3	low	no	yes, not written	minimal

continued

Table 3, cont.

City	St	Geo Patrol 1997	Routine Foot Patrol 1997	Fixed Neigh Sub-stations 1997	Scale of Programs 1997	Encourage Sara 1997	COP Plan 1997	Geo Patrol 1999	Fixed Neigh Sub-stations 1999	Scale of Programs 1999	Encourage SARA 1999	COP Plan 1999	Officer Resources Devoted to COP 1999
Norman	OK	yes	no	0	medium	no	formal	yes	0	medium	yes	yes, not written	minimal
Oklahoma City	OK	yes	yes	0	medium	no	formal	yes	1	medium	no	yes, written	minimal
Tulsa	OK	yes	yes	0	medium	yes	formal	yes	0	medium	yes	yes, written	no officer resources
Eugene	OR	yes	yes	2	low	no	formal	yes	3	high	yes	yes, written	high
Portland	OR	yes	no	10	high	yes	formal	yes	10	medium	yes	yes, written	minimal
Salem	OR	yes	yes	0	low	yes	formal	yes	4	medium	yes	yes, written	minimal
Erie	PA	yes	no	0	medium	yes	informal	yes	0	high	yes	yes, written	minimal
Philadelphia	PA	yes	yes	19	high	no	formal	yes	18	high	yes	yes, not written	minimal
Pittsburgh	PA	yes	yes	42	medium	no	formal	yes	44	medium	yes	yes, not written	minimal
Reading	PA	yes	yes	2	low	no	informal	yes	1	low	yes	no	minimal
Providence	RI	yes	yes	11	medium	no	informal	yes	12	medium	yes	yes, not written	minimal
Columbia	SC	yes	yes	0	low	yes	formal	yes	0	low	no	yes, written	minimal
Sioux Falls	SD	yes	no	17	medium	yes	informal	yes	0	low	yes	yes, not written	minimal
Knoxville	TN	yes	yes	1	high	yes	formal	yes	0	high	yes	yes, not written	high
Memphis	TN	yes	no	10	high	no	informal	yes	15	high	no	yes, written	minimal
Nashville-Davidson	TN	yes	yes	3	high	no	formal	yes	3	low	no	yes, written	minimal
Abilene	TX	yes	no	0	low	yes	informal	yes	0	low	yes	yes, not written	minimal
Amarillo	TX	no	no	4	medium	yes	informal	yes	3	medium	yes	yes, not written	minimal
Arlington	TX	yes	yes	4	medium	yes	formal	yes	1	low	yes	yes, written	medium
Austin	TX	yes	yes	2	medium	yes	formal	yes	10	high	no	yes, written	minimal

City	St	Geo Patrol 1997	Routine Foot Patrol 1997	Fixed Neigh Sub-stations 1997	Scale of Programs 1997	Encourage Sara 1997	COP Plan 1997	Geo Patrol 1999	Fixed Neigh Sub-stations 1999	Scale of Programs 1999	Encourage SARA 1999	COP Plan 1999	Officer Resources Devoted to COP 1999
Beaumont	TX	yes	no	3	medium	yes	formal	yes	6	low	yes	yes, written	minimal
Corpus Christi	TX	no	no	0	low	no	informal	no	0	medium	no	yes, not written	no officer resources
Dallas	TX	yes	yes	14	high	no	formal	yes	14	medium	yes	yes, written	minimal
El Paso	TX	yes	yes	7	high	yes	informal	yes	10	medium	yes	yes, not written	low
Galveston	TX	yes	no	0	low	no	no cop plan	yes	2	medium	yes	yes, not written	minimal
Garland	TX	yes	no	3	high	yes	informal	yes	3	medium	no	yes, not written	minimal
Houston	TX	yes	yes	27	high	no	informal	yes	30	high	no	yes, not written	medium
Irving	TX	yes	yes	0	medium	no	informal	yes	1	high	no	yes, not written	minimal
Longview	TX	yes	no	6	low	no	informal	yes	6	low	no	yes, not written	minimal
Lubbock	TX	yes	no	0	low	yes	informal	yes	0	medium	yes	yes, not written	cop dept
Odessa	TX	yes	no	3	medium	no	formal	no	4	low	no	yes, not written	minimal
Tyler	TX	yes	no	1	low	yes	formal	yes	2	low	yes	yes, written	minimal
Waco	TX	yes	no	2	medium	no	informal	yes	9	low	yes	yes, written	high
Wichita Falls	TX	yes	no	0	low	no	no cop plan	no	1	medium	yes	yes, not written	minimal
Salt Lake City	UT	yes	no	11	medium	yes	formal	yes	12	low	yes	yes, written	minimal
Alexandria	VA	yes	yes	7	medium	no	formal	yes	0	high	yes	yes, written	minimal
Arlington	VA	yes	yes	0	medium	no	formal	yes	0	low	yes	yes, written	high
Chesapeake	VA	yes	yes	6	medium	yes	formal	yes	5	high	yes	yes, written	low
Hampton	VA	yes	yes	1	low	no	formal	yes	10	medium	yes	yes, not written	minimal
Lynchburg	VA	yes	no	0	low	yes	formal	yes	0	medium	yes	yes, not written	high
Newport News	VA	yes	no	4	high	yes	formal	yes	2	low	yes	yes, written	minimal
Norfolk	VA	yes	no	2	high	yes	formal	yes	4	high	yes	yes, written	cop dept

199

continued

Table 3, cont.

City	St	Geo Patrol 1997	Routine Foot Patrol 1997	Fixed Neigh Sub-stations 1997	Scale of Programs 1997	Encourage Sara 1997	COP Plan 1997	Geo Patrol 1999	Fixed Neigh Sub-stations 1999	Scale of Programs 1999	Encourage SARA 1999	COP Plan 1999	Officer Resources Devoted to COP 1999
Richmond	VA	yes	yes	2	medium	yes	formal	yes	0	medium	yes	yes, written	no officer resources
Roanoke	VA	yes	yes	0	medium	yes	informal	yes	4	low	yes	yes, written	low
Virginia Beach	VA	yes	yes	1	medium	yes	informal	yes	2	high	yes	yes, written	low
Everett	WA	yes	no	1	low	no	formal	yes	0	low	no	yes, not written	high
Seattle	WA	yes	yes	2	high	yes	formal	yes	0	high	yes	yes, not written	minimal
Spokane	WA	yes	no	9	medium	no	formal	yes	10	low	yes	yes, not written	minimal
Yakima	WA	yes	yes	0	medium	yes	formal	yes	0	low	yes	yes, written	low
Kenosha	WI	yes	no	0	low	no	no cop plan	yes	0	high	no	no	minimal
Madison	WI	yes	yes	12	low	yes	formal	yes	12	low	yes	yes, written	minimal

Table 4: Community connectivity data—type of surveys conducted

City	St	1997				1999			
		Public Satisfaction	Public Perceptions	Crime Experiences	Other	Public Satisfaction	Public Perceptions	Crime Experiences	Other
Birmingham	AL	Yes	No	No	No	Yes	Yes	Yes	No
Mesa	AZ	Yes	Yes	Yes	No	Yes	Yes	No	No
Phoenix	AZ	Yes	Yes	Yes	Yes	Yes	Yes	Yes	No
Tempe	AZ	Yes	Yes	Yes	No	No	No	No	No
Anaheim	CA	Yes	Yes	Yes	No	Yes	Yes	No	No
Berkeley	CA	Yes	Yes	No	No	Yes	Yes	No	No
Beverly Hills	CA	No	No	No	No	No	No	No	No
Burbank	CA	Yes	No	Yes	No	Yes	No	No	No
Concord	CA	Yes	Yes	Yes	No	Yes	Yes	Yes	Yes
Costa Mesa	CA	Yes	No	No	No	Yes	No	Yes	No
Daly City	CA	No	No	No	No	No	No	No	No
Fremont	CA	Yes	No	Yes	No	Yes	No	No	No
Fresno	CA	Yes	Yes	No	No	No	Yes	No	No
Garden Grove	CA	Yes	Yes	No	No	Yes	No	No	No
Glendale	CA	Yes	Yes	Yes	No	Yes	Yes	Yes	No
Hayward	CA	No	Yes	Yes	No	No	No	No	No
Inglewood	CA	No	No	No	No	No	Yes	No	No
Long Beach	CA	Yes	Yes	Yes	No	No	No	No	No
Oakland	CA	Yes	Yes	No	No	Yes	Yes	No	No

continued

Table 4, cont.

City	St	1997				1999			
		Public Satisfaction	Public Perceptions	Crime Experiences	Other	Public Satisfaction	Public Perceptions	Crime Experiences	Other
Ontario	CA	Yes	No	Yes	No	Yes	No	No	No
Orange	CA	No	No	No	No	No	No	No	No
Pasadena	CA	Yes	Yes	No	No	Yes	Yes	Yes	No
Pomona	CA	Yes	Yes	Yes	No	Yes	Yes	Yes	No
Redondo Beach	CA	Yes	Yes	Yes	No	Yes	No	No	Yes
Richmond	CA	No	No	No	No	Yes	Yes	No	No
Riverside	CA	Yes	Yes	Yes	No	No	No	No	No
Sacramento	CA	Yes	Yes	No	No	No	No	No	No
Salinas	CA	No	No	No	No	No	No	No	No
San Diego	CA	Yes	Yes	No	No	Yes	Yes	Yes	No
San Francisco	CA	No	No	No	No	No	No	No	No
San Jose	CA	No	No	No	No	No	No	No	No
San Mateo	CA	Yes	No	No	No	Yes	No	No	No
Santa Ana	CA	Yes	Yes	No	No	No	No	No	No
Santa Barbara	CA	Yes	No	No	No	No	No	No	No
Santa Clara	CA	Yes	Yes	Yes	No	Yes	Yes	Yes	No
Stockton	CA	No	No	No	No	No	No	No	No
Sunnyvale	CA	Yes	Yes	No	No	No	No	No	No
Vallejo	CA	No	No	No	No	Yes	No	No	No

City	St	1997				1999			
		Public Satisfaction	Public Perceptions	Crime Experiences	Other	Public Satisfaction	Public Perceptions	Crime Experiences	Other
West Covina	CA	No	No	No	No	No	No	No	No
Aurora	CO	Yes	No	No	No	No	No	No	No
Colorado Springs	CO	Yes	Yes	No	No	Yes	Yes	Yes	No
Denver	CO	No	No	No	No	No	No	No	No
Fort Collins	CO	Yes	Yes	Yes	No	Yes	Yes	Yes	No
Bridgeport	CT	No	No	No	No	No	No	No	No
Bristol	CT	No	No	No	No	Yes	Yes	Yes	No
Hartford	CT	Yes	No	No	No	No	No	No	No
New Britain	CT	Yes	Yes	No	No	No	No	No	No
West Hartford	CT	No Data	No Data	No Data	No Data	No	No	No	No
Washington	DC	No	No	No	No	Yes	Yes	No	No
Coral Gables	FL	Yes	Yes	Yes	No	Yes	No	No	No
Fort Lauderdale	FL	Yes	Yes	Yes	No	Yes	Yes	Yes	No
Fort Meyers	FL	Yes	Yes	No	No	No	No	No	No
Gainesville	FL	Yes	No	No	No	Yes	Yes	No	No
Hollywood	FL	No	No	No	No	No	No	No	No
Jacksonville	FL	Yes	Yes	Yes	No	Yes	Yes	Yes	No
Lakeland	FL	Yes	Yes	Yes	No	No	Yes	No	No
Orlando	FL	No	No	No	No	Yes	Yes	No	No
Pensacola	FL	Yes	Yes	Yes	No	No	No	No	No
St. Petersburg	FL	Yes	Yes	Yes	Yes	Yes	Yes	Yes	Yes

continued

Table 4, cont.

City	St	1997				1999			
		Public Satisfaction	Public Perceptions	Crime Experiences	Other	Public Satisfaction	Public Perceptions	Crime Experiences	Other
Tallahassee	FL	Yes	Yes	Yes	No	Yes	Yes	Yes	No
West Palm Beach	FL	Yes	Yes	No	No	No	No	No	Yes
Atlanta	GA	No	No	No	No	No	No	No	Yes
Augusta	GA	No	No	No	No	Yes	No	No	No
Columbus	GA	Yes	No	Yes	No	Yes	Yes	Yes	No
Macon	GA	Yes	Yes	Yes	No	Yes	Yes	Yes	No
Marietta	GA	No	No	No	No	Yes	Yes	No	No
Honolulu	HI	No	No	No	No	No	No	No	No
Chicago	IL	No	No	No	Yes	No	No	No	Yes
Elgin	IL	No	No	No	No	No	No	No	No
Oak Park Village	IL	Yes	Yes	Yes	No	Yes	Yes	No	No
Peoria	IL	No	No	No	No	No	No	No	No
Rockford	IL	No	No	No	No	No	No	No	No
Skokie Village	IL	Yes	Yes	Yes	No	Yes	Yes	Yes	No
Springfield	IL	Yes	Yes	Yes	No	No	No	No	No
Anderson	IN	Yes	Yes	Yes	No	No Data	No Data	No Data	No Data
Hammond	IN	Yes	Yes	Yes	No	No	No	No	No
Kokomo	IN	Yes	Yes	No	No	Yes	Yes	No	No
Muncie	IN	No	No	No	No	No	No	No	No

City	St	1997				1999			
		Public Satisfaction	Public Perceptions	Crime Experiences	Other	Public Satisfaction	Public Perceptions	Crime Experiences	Other
South Bend	IN	Yes	Yes	Yes	No	Yes	Yes	Yes	No
Davenport	IA	No	No	No	No	Yes	Yes	No	No
Des Moines	IA	No	Yes	No	No	Yes	Yes	Yes	No
Sioux City	IA	Yes	Yes	Yes	Yes	No	No	Yes	No
Waterloo	IA	No	No	Yes	No	Yes	Yes	Yes	No
Overland Park	KS	Yes	Yes	No	No	Yes	Yes	No	No
Wichita	KS	No	No	No	No	No	No	No	No
Lexington-Fayette	KY	Yes	Yes	No	No	Yes	Yes	No	No
Louisville	KY	No	No	No	No	Yes	Yes	Yes	No
Bossier City	LA	No	No	No	No	Yes	Yes	Yes	No
Lafayette	LA	No	No	No	No	No	No	No	No
Shreveport	LA	Yes	No	No	No	Yes	Yes	Yes	No
Baltimore	MD	Yes	No	Yes	No	No	No	No	No
Boston	MA	Yes	Yes	Yes	Yes	Yes	Yes	Yes	No
Newton	MA	Yes	Yes	Yes	No	Yes	Yes	Yes	No
Quincy	MA	Yes	Yes	No	No	Yes	No	No	No
Ann Arbor	MI	Yes	Yes	Yes	No	Yes	Yes	No	No
Battle Creek	MI	No	No	No	No	Yes	Yes	Yes	Yes
Dearborn	MI	Yes	No	No	No	No	No	No	No
Detroit	MI	No	No	No	No	Yes	Yes	No	No
Flint	MI	Yes	Yes	Yes	No	Yes	Yes	Yes	No

continued

Table 4, cont.

City	St	1997				1999			
		Public Satisfaction	Public Perceptions	Crime Experiences	Other	Public Satisfaction	Public Perceptions	Crime Experiences	Other
Grand Rapids	MI	Yes	Yes	No	No	No	No	No	No
Kalamazoo	MI	No	No	No	No	No	No	No	No
Pontiac	MI	No	No	No	No	Yes	Yes	No	No
Saginaw	MI	No	No	No	No	No	Yes	Yes	No
Warren	MI	No	No	No	No	Yes	Yes	No	No
Duluth	MN	No	No	No	No	No	No	No	No
Minneapolis	MN	Yes	Yes	Yes	No	Yes	Yes	Yes	No
St. Paul	MN	No	No	No	No	Yes	No	Yes	No
Kansas City	MO	No	Yes	Yes	No	Yes	Yes	Yes	No
Springfield	MO	Yes	Yes	Yes	No	Yes	Yes	Yes	No
St. Louis	MO	No	No	No	Yes	Yes	Yes	Yes	No
Omaha	NE	No	No	No	No	No	No	No	No
Las Vegas	NV	Yes	Yes	Yes	No	Yes	Yes	Yes	No
North Las Vegas	NV	Yes	Yes	No	No	Yes	Yes	No	No
Manchester	NH	Yes	Yes	Yes	No	Yes	Yes	Yes	No
Bayonne	NJ	No	No	No	No	No	No	No	No
Clifton	NJ	No	No	No	No	No	No	No	No
Edison	NJ	No	No	No	No	No	No	No	No
Elizabeth	NJ	No	No	No	No	Yes	No	No	No

City	St	1997				1999			
		Public Satisfaction	Public Perceptions	Crime Experiences	Other	Public Satisfaction	Public Perceptions	Crime Experiences	Other
Irvington	NJ	No	No	No	No	Yes	Yes	Yes	No
Jersey City	NJ	No	No	No	No	No	No	No	No
Linden	NJ	No	No	No	No	No	No	No	No
Newark	NJ	Yes	Yes	Yes	No	Yes	No	No	No
Paterson	NJ	No Data	No Data	No Data	No Data	No	No	No	No
Woodbridge	NJ	No	No	No	No	Yes	Yes	Yes	No
Albuquerque	NM	Yes	Yes	Yes	Yes	No	No	No	No
Santa Fe	NM	Yes	Yes	Yes	No	Yes	Yes	Yes	No
Albany	NY	No	No	Yes	No	No	No	No	No
Rochester	NY	Yes	Yes	No	No	No	No	No	No
Syracuse	NY	No	Yes	No	No	No	No	No	No
Yonkers	NY	No	No	No	No	No	No	No	No
Charlotte	NC	Yes	Yes	Yes	No	Yes	No	No	No
Durham	NC	No	No	No	No	No	No	No	No
High Point	NC	No	No	No	No	Yes	Yes	No	No
Raleigh	NC	Yes	Yes	No	No	No	No	No	No
Wilmington	NC	No	No	No	No	Yes	No	No	No
Akron	OH	No	No	No	No	Yes	Yes	No	Yes
Cincinnati	OH	Yes	No	No	No	No	No	No	No
Cleveland	OH	Yes	No	No	No	No	No	No	No
Columbus	OH	Yes	Yes	Yes	No	Yes	No	No	No

continued

Table 4, cont.

City	St	1997				1999			
		Public Satisfaction	Public Perceptions	Crime Experiences	Other	Public Satisfaction	Public Perceptions	Crime Experiences	Other
Dayton	OH	No	No	No	No	Yes	Yes	Yes	No
Springfield	OH	No Data	No Data	No Data	No Data	No Data	No Data	No Data	No Data
Toledo	OH	Yes	No	No	No	Yes	No	Yes	No
Lawton	OK	No	No	No	No	Yes	Yes	Yes	No
Norman	OK	No	No	No	No	No	No	No	No
Oklahoma City	OK	No	No	No	No	No	No	No	No
Tulsa	OK	No	No	No	No	No	No	No	No
Eugene	OR	Yes	Yes	No	No	No	No	No	No
Portland	OR	Yes	Yes	Yes	No	No	No	No	No
Salem	OR	Yes	Yes	Yes	No	Yes	Yes	Yes	No
Erie	PA	No	No	No	No	No	No	No	No
Philadelphia	PA	Yes	Yes	Yes	Yes	No	No	No	No
Reading	PA	No	No	No	No	Yes	No	No	No
Providence	RI	No	Yes	No	No	No	No	No	No
Columbia	SC	Yes	Yes	Yes	No	Yes	No	No	No
Sioux Falls	SD	No	No	No	No	No	No	No	No
Knoxville	TN	Yes	Yes	No	No	Yes	Yes	Yes	No
Memphis	TN	No	No	No	No	Yes	Yes	Yes	No
Nashville-Davidson	TN	Yes	No	No	No	Yes	Yes	No	No

City	St	1997				1999			
		Public Satisfaction	Public Perceptions	Crime Experiences	Other	Public Satisfaction	Public Perceptions	Crime Experiences	Other
Abilene	TX	No	Yes	No	No	No	No	No	No
Amarillo	TX	No	No	No	No	No	No	No	No
Arlington	TX	Yes	Yes	Yes	No	Yes	Yes	Yes	No
Austin	TX	Yes	Yes	Yes	No	Yes	Yes	Yes	No
Beaumont	TX	Yes	Yes	No	No	No	No	No	No
Corpus Christi	TX	No	No	No	No	No	No	No	No
Dallas	TX	No	No	No	No	No	No	No	No
El Paso	TX	Yes	Yes	No	No	No	No	No	No
Galveston	TX	No	No	No	No	No	No	Yes	No
Garland	TX	Yes	Yes	Yes	No	Yes	Yes	Yes	No
Houston	TX	Yes	No	No	No	Yes	No	No	No
Irving	TX	No	No	No	No	No	No	No	No
Lubbock	TX	No	No	No	No	Yes	Yes	Yes	No
Odessa	TX	No	No	No	No	Yes	Yes	Yes	Yes
Tyler	TX	No	No	No	No	No	No	No	No
Waco	TX	No	No	No	No	No	No	No	No
Wichita Falls	TX	Yes	Yes	Yes	No	Yes	Yes	No	No
Salt Lake City	UT	Yes	Yes	Yes	No	Yes	Yes	Yes	No
Alexandria	VA	Yes	Yes	Yes	No	Yes	Yes	Yes	No
Arlington	VA	Yes	Yes	No	No	No	No	No	No
Chesapeake	VA	Yes	Yes	Yes	No	Yes	Yes	Yes	No

continued

Table 4, cont.

City	St	1997				1999			
		Public Satisfaction	Public Perceptions	Crime Experiences	Other	Public Satisfaction	Public Perceptions	Crime Experiences	Other
Hampton	VA	No	No	No	No	Yes	Yes	Yes	No
Lynchburg	VA	No	No	No	No	Yes	No	No	No
Newport News	VA	Yes	Yes	No	No	No	No	No	No
Norfolk	VA	Yes	Yes	Yes	No	Yes	Yes	Yes	No
Richmond	VA	Yes	No	Yes	No	Yes	Yes	Yes	No
Roanoke	VA	Yes	Yes	No	No	Yes	Yes	No	No
Virginia Beach	VA	Yes	Yes	No	No	Yes	Yes	Yes	No
Everett	WA	No	No	No	No	No	Yes	No	No
Seattle	WA	No	No	No	No	No	No	No	No
Spokane	WA	No	No	No	No	Yes	Yes	Yes	No
Kenosha	WI	Yes	Yes	Yes	No	No	No	No	No
Madison	WI	Yes	Yes	No	No	Yes	Yes	Yes	No

Table 5: 911 system calls and differences in Type 1 offenses, 1993-1999

City	ST	911 in 1993	911 in 1997	Total Calls 1997	911 in 1999	Total Calls 1999	Murder	Rape	Robbery	Aggravated Assault	Burglary	Larceny	Auto Theft
Birmingham	AL	yes, enhanced	yes, expanded	1,347,185	yes, enhanced	no data	-43	-85	-767	-2940	-2773	-2891	-1567
Mesa	AZ	yes, enhanced	yes, basic	806,000	yes, enhanced	1,116,000	3	23	-40	-189	-748	-597	134
Phoenix	AZ	yes, enhanced	yes, expanded	2,030,140	yes, enhanced	no data	56	-44	382	-2106	-4690	2174	2393
Tempe	AZ	yes, enhanced	yes, expanded	125,491	yes, enhanced	284,101	2	3	73	-37	-143	1297	587
Anaheim	CA	yes, enhanced	yes, basic	542,400	yes, enhanced	no data	-17	15	441	no data	-2302	-3693	-2234
Berkeley	CA	yes, basic	yes, basic	no data	yes, basic	no data	-5	-3	-424	-357	-1186	-2456	-316
Beverly Hills	CA	yes, enhanced	yes, expanded	78,207	yes, enhanced	67,213	0	-1	-197	-7	-241	-812	-144
Burbank	CA	yes, enhanced	yes, expanded	no data	yes, enhanced	no data	-3	-8	-114	-56	-303	-964	-444
Concord	CA	yes, basic	yes, basic	60,000	yes, basic	no data	-3	-7	-32	79	-860	-290	-247
Costa Mesa	CA	yes, basic	yes, basic	200,701	yes, enhanced	no data	-1	-1	-78	-45	-761	-2498	-595
Daly City	CA	yes, basic	yes, basic	70,000	yes, enhanced	55,088	0	8	-67	-231	-108	-308	-252
Fremont	CA	yes, enhanced	yes, expanded	no data	yes, enhanced	270,000	-3	-16	-20	-430	-591	36	-255
Fresno	CA	yes, basic	yes, expanded	388,055	yes, enhanced	no data	-61	-56	-1611	225	-4053	1245	-8440
Garden Grove	CA	yes, enhanced	yes, expanded	297,835	yes, enhanced	no data	-2	-7	-225	27	-961	-2093	-808
Glendale	CA	yes, basic	yes, expanded	67,428	yes, enhanced	no data	-6	-10	-173	52	-873	-1506	-704
Hayward	CA	yes, enhanced	yes, expanded	172,000	yes, enhanced	no data	3	11	-91	-351	-939	-1301	157
Inglewood	CA	yes, enhanced	yes, expanded	145,463	yes, enhanced	74,312	-29	-29	-728	-165	-870	1161	-1365
Long Beach	CA	yes, enhanced	yes, expanded	570,062	yes, enhanced	927,469	-80	-81	-2151	-1547	-3423	-5929	-4265
Los Angeles	CA	yes, enhanced	yes, expanded	3,728,425	yes, enhanced	no data	-651	-485	-24004	-11721	-28711	-44635	-35087
Oakland	CA	yes, enhanced	yes, expanded	911,708	yes, enhanced	443,979	-94	-48	-2369	-1544	-3261	-3554	-2984
Ontario	CA	yes, enhanced	yes, expanded	149,884	yes, enhanced	no data	-10	-22	-357	-178	-1297	-623	-585

Difference in Type 1 Offenses 1993-1999 (Negative numbers indicate a reduction and boldface numbers indicate an increase)

911 System 1993, 1997, and 1999 and Total Calls for Service 1997 and 1999

continued

211

Table 5, cont.

		911 System 1993, 1997, and 1999 and Total Calls for Service 1997 and 1999					Difference in Type 1 Offenses 1993-1999 (Negative numbers indicate a reduction and boldface numbers indicate an increase)						
City	ST	911 in 1993	911 in 1997	Total Calls 1997	911 in 1999	Total Calls 1999	Murder	Rape	Robbery	Aggravated Assault	Burglary	Larceny	Auto Theft
Orange	CA	yes, enhanced	yes, expanded	no data	yes, enhanced	47,011	-2	-16	-133	**70**	-927	-877	-502
Pasadena	CA	yes, basic	yes, expanded	146,000	yes, enhanced	58,000	-25	-14	-484	-378	-1002	-1895	-901
Pomona	CA	yes, enhanced	yes, basic	266,941	yes, basic	no data	-14	-33	-614	-246	-1113	-884	-682
Redondo Beach	CA	yes, basic	yes, expanded	72,371	yes, enhanced	71,561	-3	-4	-75	-139	-535	-863	-366
Richmond	CA	yes, enhanced	yes, expanded	137,057	yes, enhanced	41,000	-21	-35	-566	-1016	-913	-82	-510
Riverside	CA	yes, enhanced	yes, expanded	164,938	yes, enhanced	541,561	-3	-54	-659	-1195	-2725	-3902	-1944
Sacramento	CA	yes, enhanced	yes, expanded	793,577	yes, enhanced	889,449	-31	-24	-860	-851	-3275	-3909	-3425
Salinas	CA	yes, enhanced	yes, expanded	107,387	yes, enhanced	no data	-3	**10**	-214	-107	-598	-1080	-134
San Bernardino	CA	yes, enhanced	yes, basic	103,000	yes, basic	no data	-59	-48	-841	-2598	-2170	-2886	-1801
San Diego	CA	yes, enhanced	yes, expanded	1,488,251	yes, enhanced	1,694,539	-76	-41	-2839	-3096	-8015	-11745	-9828
San Francisco	CA	yes, enhanced	yes, expanded	1,133,007	yes, enhanced	no data	-65	-168	-4979	-1598	-5627	-9294	-5079
San Jose	CA	yes, basic	yes, expanded	1,617,884	yes, enhanced	no data	-16	-44	-460	**291**	-3329	-6247	-1154
San Mateo	CA	yes, enhanced	yes, expanded	406,500	yes, enhanced	no data	-3	-3	-46	-59	-276	-337	-189
Santa Ana	CA	yes, enhanced	yes, expanded	479,257	yes, enhanced	184,785	-63	**20**	-1021	-298	-1724	-3147	-1671
Santa Barbara	CA	yes, basic	yes, expanded	146,000	yes, enhanced	no data	-3	-20	-85	-40	-465	-1542	-78
Santa Clara	CA	yes, enhanced	yes, expanded	166,663	yes, enhanced	no data	-1	-20	-39	-137	-463	-1661	-234
Stockton	CA	yes, enhanced	yes, expanded	412,321	yes, enhanced	572,229	-13	-27	-650	-2	-2886	-3169	-1556
Sunnyvale	CA	yes, enhanced	yes, expanded	120,860	yes, enhanced	175,534	-2	**4**	-60	42	-300	-1622	-312
Torrance	CA	yes, enhanced	yes, basic	76,835	yes, enhanced	no data	-9	-7	-242	-161	-797	-1460	-957
Vallejo	CA	yes, enhanced	yes, expanded	58,706	yes, enhanced	116,205	-4	-17	-166	-139	-479	-798	-371

911 System 1993, 1997, and 1999 and Total Calls for Service 1997 and 1999

Difference in Type 1 Offenses 1993-1999
(Negative numbers indicate a reduction and boldface numbers indicate an increase)

City	ST	911 in 1993	911 in 1997	Total Calls 1997	911 in 1999	Total Calls 1999	Murder	Rape	Robbery	Aggravated Assault	Burglary	Larceny	Auto Theft
West Covina	CA	yes, basic	yes, expanded	46,905	yes, enhanced	92,653	-2	-14	-96	-131	-506	-552	-701
Aurora	CO	yes, enhanced	yes, expanded	318,477	yes, enhanced	140,436	-8	**12**	-276	-2704	-759	-2791	**462**
Colorado Springs	CO	yes, enhanced	yes, expanded	429,724	yes, enhanced	434,416	**6**	-13	**164**	**221**	-712	-423	**86**
Denver	CO	yes, enhanced	yes, expanded	no data	yes, enhanced	no data	-11	-144	-825	-1363	-3719	-4383	-2565
Fort Collins	CO	yes, enhanced	yes, expanded	149,648	yes, enhanced	179,343	**2**	**4**	**9**	-15	-26	**57**	**50**
Bridgeport	CT	yes, enhanced	yes, expanded	109,832	yes, enhanced	no data	-30	-6	-835	**151**	-1768	-1115	-1711
Bristol	CT	yes, enhanced	yes, expanded	no data	yes, enhanced	no data	-1	**17**	-30	no data	-188	-256	-109
Hartford	CT	yes, enhanced	yes, expanded	no data	yes, enhanced	251,402	-9	-47	-478	-823	-2086	-2994	-1229
New Britain	CT	yes, enhanced	yes, expanded	47,869	yes, enhanced	no data	-3	-11	-81	-74	-85	-623	-317
West Hartford	CT	yes, enhanced	no data	no data	yes, enhanced	71,319	-1	**5**	-26	-24	-264	-200	-89
Washington	DC	yes, enhanced	yes, expanded	2,117,312	yes, enhanced	no data	-213	-76	-3763	-4388	-6465	-9793	-1408
Coral Gables	FL	yes, enhanced	yes, expanded	108,769	yes, enhanced	no data	-1	-1	-169	-56	-525	-1541	-492
Fort Lauderdale	FL	yes, enhanced	yes, basic	649,193	yes, enhanced	no data	-9	-16	-557	-197	-2808	-6542	-1337
Fort Meyers	FL	yes, enhanced	yes, expanded	125,307	yes, enhanced	no data	**2**	-12	-44	-237	-616	-881	-80
Gainesville	FL	yes, enhanced	yes, expanded	130,460	yes, enhanced	no data	**2**	-27	-129	-328	-933	-1436	-208
Hollywood	FL	yes, enhanced	yes, basic	147,352	yes, basic	no data	0	-7	-115	**23**	-811	-873	-8
Jacksonville	FL	yes, enhanced	yes, expanded	no data	yes, enhanced	1,901,192	-42	-240	-1901	-1969	-5476	-3491	-4156
Lakeland	FL	yes, enhanced	yes, expanded	86,757	yes, enhanced	no data	-6	-3	-133	-371	-935	-1333	-936
Miami	FL	yes, enhanced	yes, expanded	532,025	yes, enhanced	no data	-64	-91	-4006	-2480	-4948	-12736	-5455
Orlando	FL	yes, enhanced	yes, expanded	662,135	yes, enhanced	no data	**4**	-40	-11	-171	-669	**3637**	**292**
Pensacola	FL	yes, enhanced	yes, expanded	106,190	yes, enhanced	260,484	no data	no data	no data	no data	no data	no data	no data
St. Petersburg	FL	yes, enhanced	yes, basic	no data	yes, enhanced	no data	**1**	**5**	-487	-582	-862	-693	**774**

213

continued

Table 5, cont.

City	ST	911 in 1993	911 in 1997	Total Calls 1997	911 in 1999	Total Calls 1999	Murder	Rape	Robbery	Aggravated Assault	Burglary	Larceny	Auto Theft
Tallahassee	FL	yes, enhanced	yes, expanded	462,574	yes, enhanced	no data	-4	5	-321	-418	-1748	-2893	-1142
West Palm Beach	FL	yes, enhanced	yes, expanded	481,082	yes, enhanced	no data	no data	no data	no data	no data	no data	no data	no data
Atlanta	GA	yes, enhanced	yes, expanded	1,443,196	yes, enhanced	no data	-60	-171	-1973	-2851	-4597	-2897	-1888
Augusta	GA	yes, enhanced	yes, expanded	365,000	yes, enhanced	no data	no data	no data	no data	no data	no data	no data	no data
Columbus	GA	yes, enhanced	yes, expanded	188,675	yes, enhanced	no data	-16	-22	8	-145	-698	**835**	**117**
Macon	GA	yes, basic	yes, expanded	192,605	yes, enhanced	no data	**8**	-21	**21**	**139**	**660**	-350	**800**
Marietta	GA	yes, enhanced	yes, expanded	no data	yes, enhanced	no data	**5**	-51	-43	-43	-226	-1940	-62
Honolulu	HI	yes, enhanced	yes, expanded	653,491	yes, enhanced	no data	**6**	-51	-178	-80	-3209	-9752	-463
Chicago	IL	yes, enhanced	yes, expanded	4,198,663	yes, enhanced	4,900,103	-203	no data	-14728	-6950	-15351	-9682	-8914
Elgin	IL	yes, enhanced	yes, expanded	64,484	yes, enhanced	no data	no data	no data	no data	no data	no data	no data	no data
Oak Park Village	IL	yes, enhanced	yes, basic	47,288	yes, basic	no data	no data	no data	no data	no data	no data	no data	no data
Peoria	IL	yes, enhanced	yes, expanded	92,073	yes, enhanced	no data	no data	no data	no data	no data	no data	no data	no data
Rockford	IL	yes, enhanced	yes, expanded	184,467	yes, enhanced	187,000	-5	no data	-301	-585	-1060	-491	-231
Skokie Village	IL	yes, enhanced	yes, expanded	34,216	yes, enhanced	no data	no data	no data	no data	no data	no data	no data	no data
Springfield	IL	yes, enhanced	yes, expanded	125,952	yes, enhanced	no data	no data	no data	no data	no data	no data	no data	no data
Anderson	IN	yes, enhanced	yes, expanded	83,062	yes, enhanced	no data	no data	no data	no data	no data	no data	no data	no data
Gary	IN	yes, enhanced	yes, basic	131,000	yes, basic	no data	-30	-144	-450	-930	-444	-1388	-1242
Hammond	IN	yes, enhanced	yes, basic	111,714	yes, enhanced	108,000	**5**	-31	-1	-232	-236	-62	-417
Kokomo	IN	yes, enhanced	yes, expanded	59,343	yes, enhanced	64,209	0	-19	**5**	-21	**31**	**67**	**13**

911 System 1993, 1997, and 1999 and Total Calls for Service 1997 and 1999

Difference in Type 1 Offenses 1993-1999 (Negative numbers indicate a reduction and boldface numbers indicate an increase)

911 System 1993, 1997, and 1999 and Total Calls for Service 1997 and 1999

City	ST	911 in 1993	911 in 1997	Total Calls 1997	911 in 1999	Total Calls 1999	Murder	Rape	Robbery	Aggravated Assault	Burglary	Larceny	Auto Theft
Muncie	IN	yes, enhanced	yes, expanded	55,505	yes, enhanced	no data	no data	no data	no data	no data	no data	no data	no data
South Bend	IN	yes, enhanced	yes, expanded	352,423	yes, enhanced	128,395	-2	-28	-102	-243	-348	-765	-72
Davenport	IA	yes, enhanced	yes, expanded	109,092	yes, enhanced	no data	-2	-11	-105	-21	-398	-1225	23
Des Moines	IA	yes, enhanced	yes, expanded	246,888	yes, enhanced	no data	4	**8**	-5	-164	-377	-3271	-21
Sioux City	IA	yes, enhanced	yes, expanded	no data	yes, enhanced	no data	-3	**62**	-60	-571	-185	-302	**133**
Waterloo	IA	yes, enhanced	yes, expanded	62,541	yes, enhanced	67,000	no data	-15	-22	-83	-150	-203	31
Overland Park	KS	yes, enhanced	yes, expanded	165,520	yes, enhanced	no data	no data	no data	no data	no data	no data	no data	no data
Wichita	KS	yes, enhanced	yes, expanded	158,126	yes, enhanced	no data	-21	-96	-627	-72	-1857	-2876	-1211
Lexington-Fayette	KY	yes, basic	yes, basic	293,954	yes, enhanced	524,168	**16**	**4**	-28	-239	-704	-162	**314**
Louisville	KY	yes, basic	yes, basic	752,518	yes, enhanced	345,581	0	-73	-235	-200	-786	-393	-325
Bossier City	LA	no	yes, expanded	62,290	yes, enhanced	73,572	-7	**8**	**3**	-98	**184**	**134**	**67**
Lafayette	LA	yes, enhanced	yes, expanded	70,022	yes, enhanced	no data	-11	**1**	-35	-30	**31**	-221	**248**
Shreveport	LA	yes, enhanced	yes, expanded	no data	yes, enhanced	794,708	-45	**15**	-334	-238	-1055	-2217	-461
Baltimore	MD	yes, enhanced	yes, expanded	1,082,190	yes, enhanced	no data	no data	no data	no data	no data	no data	no data	no data
Boston	MA	yes, basic	yes, expanded	600,000	yes, enhanced	no data	-67	-143	-1614	-1756	-4568	-7161	-5168
Newton	MA	yes, basic	yes, expanded	35,799	yes, enhanced	34,600	0	-5	-18	-124	-232	-452	-192
Quincy	MA	yes, basic	no	56,476	yes, enhanced	no data	no data	-4	-19	-57	**18**	**109**	-331
Worcester	MA	yes, basic	yes, expanded	98,220	yes, enhanced	130,806	-4	**71**	-287	no data	-1847	**53**	-529
Ann Arbor	MI	yes, enhanced	yes, expanded	52,256	yes, enhanced	no data	1	no data	-29	-93	-242	-1451	-54
Battle Creek	MI	yes, basic	yes, expanded	no data	yes, enhanced	no data	1	no data	-61	-33	-242	-395	**83**
Dearborn	MI	yes, enhanced	yes, expanded	no data	yes, enhanced	no data	0	no data	-57	**306**	-162	-1133	-113
Detroit	MI	yes, enhanced	yes, basic	1,599,174	yes, enhanced	no data	-164	no data	-5768	-51	-4814	-8281	-1291

Difference in Type 1 Offenses 1993-1999 (Negative numbers indicate a reduction and boldface numbers indicate an increase)

continued

215

Table 5, cont.

		911 System 1993, 1997, and 1999 and Total Calls for Service 1997 and 1999					Difference in Type 1 Offenses 1993-1999 (Negative numbers indicate a reduction and boldface numbers indicate an increase)						
City	ST	911 in 1993	911 in 1997	Total Calls 1997	911 in 1999	Total Calls 1999	Murder	Rape	Robbery	Aggravated Assault	Burglary	Larceny	Auto Theft
Flint	MI	yes, enhanced	yes, basic	no data	yes, enhanced	no data	-9	no data	-299	-327	-306	-1735	-511
Grand Rapids	MI	yes, enhanced	yes, expanded	325,067	yes, enhanced	no data	no data	no data	no data	no data	no data	no data	no data
Kalamazoo	MI	yes, basic	yes, expanded	82,272	yes, enhanced	no data	-2	no data	-72	-634	-289	-842	25
Pontiac	MI	yes, enhanced	yes, expanded	75,728	yes, expanded	82,000	-14	no data	-152	-549	-506	-181	-285
Saginaw	MI	yes, basic	yes, expanded	166,000	yes, expanded	no data	-12	no data	-264	-769	-717	-1546	68
Warren	MI	yes, enhanced	yes, expanded	74,100	yes, expanded	no data	no data	no data	no data	no data	no data	no data	no data
Duluth	MN	yes, enhanced	yes, expanded	58,408	yes, expanded	68,000	-1	no data	15	-42	-382	-531	-47
Minneapolis	MN	yes, enhanced	yes, expanded	no data	yes, expanded	no data	-11	-67	-1082	-378	-3796	-3586	-806
St. Paul	MN	yes, enhanced	yes, expanded	190,000	yes, expanded	no data	-8	-42	-180	-266	-468	-624	-426
Kansas City	MO	yes, enhanced	yes, expanded	759,173	yes, expanded	923,522	-36	-185	-1412	-1562	-3495	4902	-1737
Springfield	MO	yes, enhanced	yes, expanded	no data	yes, expanded	161,868	-3	-12	-12	-90	-286	712	283
St. Louis	MO	yes, basic	yes, expanded	903,092	yes, expanded	no data	-137	-175	-3431	-3644	-4544	-1376	-3420
Omaha	NE	yes, enhanced	yes, expanded	512,879	yes, expanded	no data	no data	no data	no data	no data	no data	no data	no data
Las Vegas	NV	yes, enhanced	yes, expanded	2,121,835	yes, expanded	no data	18	97	-451	-812	347	-2062	2326
North Las Vegas	NV	yes, enhanced	yes, basic	264,317	yes, expanded	189,901	no data	no data	no data	no data	no data	no data	no data
Reno	NV	yes, enhanced	yes, expanded	331,834	yes, expanded	no data	-2	-41	-74	-73	-280	-1740	55
Manchester	NH	yes, basic	yes, basic	no data	yes, expanded	no data	-3	2	-18	24	-517	-869	-14
Bayonne	NJ	yes, basic	yes, basic	no data	yes, expanded	no data	2	-2	-31	-77	-85	-371	-73
Clifton	NJ	no	yes, expanded	160,000	yes, expanded	162,000	1	0	14	3	-12	102	-45
Edison	NJ	yes, enhanced	yes, expanded	no data	yes, expanded	no data	no data	9	-21	107	-364	-443	-2

Difference in Type 1 Offenses 1993-1999
(Negative numbers indicate a reduction and boldface numbers indicate an increase)

911 System 1993, 1997, and 1999 and Total Calls for Service 1997 and 1999

City	ST	911 in 1993	911 in 1997	Total Calls 1997	911 in 1999	Total Calls 1999	Murder	Rape	Robbery	Aggravated Assault	Burglary	Larceny	Auto Theft
Elizabeth	NJ	yes, basic	yes, expanded	140,704	yes, enhanced	117,991	-8	-23	-260	-183	-825	-915	-172
Irvington	NJ	yes, enhanced	yes, expanded	62,517	yes, enhanced	56,860	**5**	-20	-152	**238**	-180	-610	-1035
Jersey City	NJ	yes, basic	yes, expanded	443,895	yes, enhanced	440,000	-5	-21	-969	-309	-1638	-1125	-1293
Linden	NJ	yes, enhanced	yes, expanded	no data	yes, enhanced	47,670	no data	-3	-27	-16	-150	-10	-69
Newark	NJ	yes, enhanced	yes, expanded	816,680	yes, enhanced	737,971	-27	-154	-3460	-1714	-3792	-2492	-5726
Paterson	NJ	yes, enhanced	no data	no data	yes, enhanced	no data	-10	-44	-517	-403	-1688	-1650	-481
Woodbridge	NJ	yes, enhanced	yes, expanded	76,243	yes, enhanced	no data	**1**	**15**	**56**	**232**	**396**	**1686**	**372**
Albuquerque	NM	yes, basic	yes, expanded	no data	yes, enhanced	no data	-2	-39	**115**	-1515	-1390	**3725**	**1115**
Santa Fe	NM	yes, enhanced	yes, expanded	254,306	yes, enhanced	no data	no data	no data	no data	no data	no data	no data	no data
Albany	NY	no	yes, expanded	434,908	yes, enhanced	no data	**6**	-13	-105	-229	-237	**294**	-43
Rochester	NY	yes, enhanced	yes, expanded	458,360	yes, enhanced	no data	-37	-42	-820	-283	-3330	-4001	-907
Syracuse	NY	yes, enhanced	yes, expanded	189,806	yes, enhanced	no data	-9	-32	-78	**197**	-808	-1695	**178**
Yonkers	NY	yes, enhanced	yes, expanded	150,943	yes, enhanced	no data	-15	-1	-352	-68	-743	-1688	-594
Charlotte	NC	yes, enhanced	yes, expanded	601,034	yes, enhanced	885,839	-38	-94	-710	-745	-377	**3746**	**1873**
Durham	NC	yes, basic	yes, expanded	241,769	yes, enhanced	289,232	-12	-26	**255**	**92**	-707	**2424**	**703**
Greensboro	NC	yes, enhanced	yes, expanded	216,742	yes, enhanced	781,819	-8	0	-33	**141**	**21**	-483	**590**
High Point	NC	yes, enhanced	yes, expanded	126,826	yes, enhanced	196,644	-8	**8**	-15	-43	-399	**203**	**57**
Raleigh	NC	yes, enhanced	yes, expanded	292,919	yes, enhanced	no data	-11	-2	-56	**70**	**512**	**2452**	**452**
Wilmington	NC	no	yes, basic	no data	yes, enhanced	no data	**4**	**6**	**84**	-87	**258**	**440**	**332**
Akron	OH	yes, enhanced	yes, expanded	267,310	yes, enhanced	no data	-3	-38	-159	no data	-500	**725**	-606
Cincinnati	OH	yes, enhanced	yes, expanded	585,932	yes, enhanced	700,000	-10	-213	-2120	-1803	-1822	-4081	-405
Cleveland	OH	yes, basic	yes, expanded	783,284	yes, enhanced	1,558,851	-91	-328	-1259	-583	-785	-626	-2760

continued

Table 5, cont.

City	ST	911 in 1993	911 in 1997	Total Calls 1997	911 in 1999	Total Calls 1999	Murder	Rape	Robbery	Aggravated Assault	Burglary	Larceny	Auto Theft
Columbus	OH	yes, enhanced	yes, expanded	863,187	yes, enhanced	1,632,000	-34	-20	-861	-476	1035	5574	-248
Dayton	OH	yes, enhanced	yes, expanded	no data	yes, enhanced	633,523	-22	-88	-504	-519	-650	-1844	-13
Springfield	OH	yes, enhanced	no data	no data	yes, enhanced	no data	-2	10	-18	-109	272	-77	62
Toledo	OH	yes, enhanced	yes, basic	347,448	yes, enhanced	no data	-30	-202	-684	-117	-781	-1680	-1739
Lawton	OK	yes, basic	yes, expanded	261,744	yes, enhanced	no data	-6	-14	-59	-313	-200	-532	-128
Norman	OK	yes, enhanced	yes, expanded	no data	yes, enhanced	57,645	no data	-7	-10	-34	-332	-776	-79
Oklahoma City	OK	yes, enhanced	yes, expanded	974,921	yes, enhanced	966,800	-24	-117	-660	-1608	-1962	-902	-1909
Tulsa	OK	yes, enhanced	yes, expanded	296,003	yes, enhanced	800,030	-13	-104	-256	3	-638	1280	-1219
Eugene	OR	yes, basic	yes, expanded	120,747	yes, enhanced	347,417	-1	-16	3	174	394	674	277
Portland	OR	yes, enhanced	yes, expanded	610,491	yes, enhanced	455,953	-23	-139	-887	-1102	-1738	-2708	-3769
Salem	OR	yes, enhanced	yes, expanded	154,971	yes, enhanced	no data	-5	16	-64	-51	-299	292	-60
Erie	PA	yes, enhanced	yes, expanded	45,798	yes, enhanced	no data	no data	no data	-379	-331	-839	-2258	-261
Philadelphia	PA	yes, enhanced	yes, expanded	no data	yes, enhanced	no data	-147	149	-427	3880	-1075	10693	-6074
Pittsburgh	PA	yes, enhanced	yes, expanded	no data	yes, enhanced	no data	-31	-88	-1203	-111	-1496	-1122	-3309
Reading	PA	yes, enhanced	yes, expanded	no data	yes, enhanced	no data	5	1	-100	43	-21	-315	-117
Providence	RI	yes, enhanced	yes, expanded	no data	yes, enhanced	no data	4	-34	-173	-29	-2139	204	-839
Columbia	SC	yes, enhanced	yes, expanded	no data	yes, enhanced	no data	-8	-20	-156	-562	-800	no data	-5
Sioux Falls	SD	yes, enhanced	yes, expanded	no data	yes, enhanced	no data	3	-28	-1	-84	-115	-297	25
Knoxville	TN	yes, enhanced	yes, expanded	no data	yes, enhanced	no data	6	-36	-29	-1461	-1436	-691	-249
Memphis	TN	yes, basic	yes, expanded	805,453	yes, enhanced	no data	-80	-37	-1651	257	-2309	-1678	-5619

911 System 1993, 1997, and 1999 and Total Calls for Service 1997 and 1999

Difference in Type 1 Offenses 1993-1999 (Negative numbers indicate a reduction and boldface numbers indicate an increase)

218

911 System 1993, 1997, and 1999 and Total Calls for Service 1997 and 1999

Difference in Type 1 Offenses 1993-1999
(Negative numbers indicate a reduction and boldface numbers indicate an increase)

City	ST	911 in 1993	911 in 1997	Total Calls 1997	911 in 1999	Total Calls 1999	Murder	Rape	Robbery	Aggravated Assault	Burglary	Larceny	Auto Theft
Nashville-Davidson	TN	yes, enhanced	yes, expanded	1,211,061	yes, enhanced	3,119,263	-19	-117	-749	126	-2187	-6356	**258**
Abilene	TX	yes, enhanced	yes, expanded	192,629	yes, enhanced	no data	4	-39	-11	-349	-66	-116	**83**
Amarillo	TX	yes, enhanced	yes, expanded	127,592	yes, enhanced	no data	-1	-33	26	100	-967	**301**	**54**
Arlington	TX	yes, enhanced	yes, expanded	no data	yes, enhanced	no data	4	-37	-164	-111	-797	**1042**	-732
Austin	TX	yes, enhanced	yes, expanded	no data	yes, enhanced	777,716	-10	-32	-533	**529**	-1445	-8374	-1562
Beaumont	TX	yes, enhanced	yes, expanded	165,864	yes, enhanced	no data	-11	-40	-332	**240**	-559	-1036	-757
Corpus Christi	TX	yes, basic	yes, expanded	no data	yes, enhanced	no data	-19	0	-121	**400**	-1079	-6060	-162
Dallas	TX	yes, enhanced	yes, expanded	1,632,530	yes, enhanced	2,657,507	-126	-337	-1063	-1215	-1346	-2157	**389**
El Paso	TX	yes, enhanced	yes, expanded	no data	yes, enhanced	632,668	-33	-96	-846	-852	-3147	-2388	-3239
Galveston	TX	yes, enhanced	yes, expanded	no data	yes, enhanced	no data	-17	-22	-122	-431	-39	-543	-214
Garland	TX	yes, enhanced	yes, expanded	146,273	yes, enhanced	no data	-11	-66	-142	no data	-743	-1910	-203
Houston	TX	yes, enhanced	yes, expanded	2,464,396	yes, enhanced	no data	-205	-361	no data	no data	-2278	**4499**	-8074
Irving	TX	yes, enhanced	yes, expanded	146,868	yes, enhanced	no data	-3	-11	-1	77	-372	-1440	**144**
Longview	TX	yes, enhanced	yes, expanded	85,648	yes, enhanced	79,072	-4	-11	-77	-137	-428	-606	-97
Lubbock	TX	yes, enhanced	yes, expanded	no data	yes, enhanced	262,420	-3	-12	**25**	**1109**	-189	-517	**86**
Odessa	TX	yes, enhanced	yes, expanded	no data	yes, enhanced	no data	-5	-29	-64	-115	-1038	-2583	-234
Tyler	TX	yes, enhanced	yes, expanded	66,147	yes, enhanced	63,691	no data	no data	no data	no data	no data	no data	no data
Waco	TX	yes, enhanced	yes, expanded	109,893	yes, enhanced	no data	-17	-48	-195	-368	-526	-263	-48
Wichita Falls	TX	yes, enhanced	yes, expanded	no data	yes, enhanced	no data	-6	-13	-67	-135	-433	-1441	no data
Salt Lake City	UT	yes, enhanced	yes, expanded	210,300	yes, enhanced	no data	-4	-57	-13	-71	-579	**91**	**448**
Alexandria	VA	yes, enhanced	yes, expanded	535,047	yes, enhanced	no data	-7	-11	-218	-128	-365	-1646	-267
Arlington	VA	yes, enhanced	yes, expanded	602,562	yes, enhanced	612,500	no data	no data	no data	no data	no data	no data	no data

continued

Table 5, cont.

City	ST	911 in 1993	911 in 1997	911 in 1999	Total Calls 1997	Total Calls 1999	Murder	Rape	Robbery	Aggravated Assault	Burglary	Larceny	Auto Theft
Chesapeake	VA	no	yes, expanded	yes, enhanced	130,431	135,049	no data	no data	no data	no data	no data	no data	no data
Hampton	VA	yes, enhanced	yes, expanded	yes, enhanced	448,892	no data	-3	-13	-92	-54	-3	-1566	-99
Lynchburg	VA	yes, enhanced	yes, expanded	yes, enhanced	no data	no data	3	-22	-49	-140	-204	-311	-62
Newport News	VA	yes, enhanced	yes, expanded	yes, enhanced	339,418	no data	-6	3	-292	-391	-562	-1205	465
Norfolk	VA	yes, enhanced	yes, expanded	yes, enhanced	no data	no data	no data	no data	no data	no data	no data	no data	no data
Richmond	VA	yes, enhanced	yes, expanded	yes, enhanced	970,009	no data	-40	-63	-543	-385	-2201	-3232	-114
Roanoke	VA	yes, basic	yes, expanded	yes, enhanced	78,540	79,322	-4	16	7	68	492	-1333	-11
Virginia Beach	VA	no	yes, expanded	yes, enhanced	650,000	no data	-10	-74	-124	4	-1227	-2519	-477
Everett	WA	yes, enhanced	yes, expanded	yes, enhanced	144,074	157,572	1	24	-26	86	29	-1326	711
Seattle	WA	yes, enhanced	yes, expanded	yes, enhanced	no data	no data	-22	-168	-1028	-2053	-2778	-8691	1821
Spokane	WA	yes, enhanced	yes, expanded	yes, enhanced	217,831	no data	-7	-30	10	-159	453	-1481	238
Yakima	WA	yes, basic	yes, expanded	yes, enhanced	25,745	no data	4	-34	-81	-313	-164	-917	271
Kenosha	WI	yes, enhanced	yes, expanded	yes, enhanced	85,685	88,317	-7	-29	-62	72	-325	-1237	-106
Madison	WI	yes, enhanced	yes, expanded	yes, enhanced	120,775	no data	2	-23	-52	148	-251	-2247	-311

911 System 1993, 1997, and 1999 and Total Calls for Service 1997 and 1999

Difference in Type 1 Offenses 1993-1999 (Negative numbers indicate a reduction and boldface numbers indicate an increase)

Table 6: List of cities and COP hiring awards

CITY	ST	AHEAD	CIS	DNP	MORE 1995	MORE 1996	MORE 1998	MORE 2000	MORE 2001	Renewal	PHASE1	PHSP	UHP	Total	Total COPS
Birmingham	AL	0	0	$2,865,400	0	0	$59,130	0	0	0	0	$1,039,773	0	$3,964,303	41.20
Mesa	AZ	$975,000	$2,125,000	0	0	0	0	0	$753,448	0	0	0	$4,725,000	$8,578,448	122.40
Phoenix	AZ	$3,900,000	$125,000	0	$524,246	$324,042	$73,248	$150,000	0	$1,083,774	0	$2,100,000	$45,000,000	$53,280,310	751.30
Tempe	AZ	$375,000	0	0	0	0	$203,784	0	0	0	0	$525,000	$3,525,000	$4,628,784	65.70
Anaheim	CA	$675,000	0	0	0	0	$122,026	0	0	0	0	0	0	$1,097,026	25.90
Berkeley	CA	0	0	0	0	0	$500,000	0	0	0	0	$501,748	$450,000	$1,451,748	31.00
Beverly Hills	CA	0	$375,000	0	0	0	0	0	0	0	0	0	0	$375,000	6.00
Burbank	CA	0	$125,000	0	0	0	0	0	0	0	0	0	$675,000	$800,000	10.00
Concord	CA	0	0	0	0	$269,850	0	0	0	0	$994,080	0	0	$1,263,930	20.80
Costa Mesa	CA	0	$250,000	0	0	0	0	0	0	0	0	0	0	$250,000	1.00
Daly City	CA	0	$250,000	0	0	$35,074	0	0	0	$70,148	0	0	0	$355,222	2.40
Fremont	CA	$375,000	$125,000	0	0	0	$109,678	$25,000	0	$64,578	0	0	$675,000	$1,374,356	20.40
Fresno	CA	$75,000	0	$13,727,100	$1,500,000	$1,665,663	$296,694	$251,979	0	$256,694	$1,016,625	0	$6,000,000	$24,829,755	314.00
Garden Grove	CA	$300,000	0	0	$201,972	0	$1,348,803	0	0	0	0	$593,533	0	$2,444,308	74.00
Glendale	CA	$375,000	0	0	0	0	0	0	0	0	0	0	$1,350,000	$1,725,000	23.00
Hayward	CA	$75,000	$250,000	0	$93,750	$112,500	$205,440	0	0	0	0	0	$1,050,000	$1,786,690	49.70
Inglewood	CA	$375,000	0	0	$75,000	0	0	0	0	0	0	$1,000,000	0	$1,450,000	30.00
Long Beach	CA	0	0	0	$58,875	0	$6,776,679	0	0	0	$1,980,357	0	$8,847,708	$17,663,619	313.90
Los Angeles	CA	0	0	0	$18,349,735	$14,613,210	$6,706,599	0	0	$17,183,700	0	$4,000,000	$235,284,156	$296,137,400	370.80
Oakland	CA	$1,275,000	$2,500,000	0	0	0	$6,188,466	0	$298,791	$223,570	0	$1,687,684	$13,164,512	$25,348,023	335.70

221

continued

Table 6, cont.

CITY	ST	AHEAD	CIS	DNP	MORE 1995	MORE 1996	MORE 1998	MORE 2000	MORE 2001	Renewal	PHASE1	PHSP	UHP	Total	Total COPS
Ontario	CA	0	$125,000	0	0	0	0	0	0	0	$374,524	0	$750,000	$1,249,524	15.00
Orange	CA	$300,000	0	0	$74,470	0	$1,022,680	0	0	$148,940	0	0	$375,000	$1,921,090	53.00
Pasadena	CA	$450,000	0	0	0	0	0	0	0	0	0	0	0	$450,000	6.00
Redondo Beach	CA	$150,000	0	0	$105,000	0	0	0	0	0	0	0	0	$255,000	8.40
Richmond	CA	$300,000	$625,000	0	$11,547	$136,060	0	0	0	0	0	$944,883	$825,000	$2,842,490	38.90
Riverside	CA	$75,000	$875,000	0	$412,500	$50,730	$396,499	0	0	0	$553,245	0	0	$2,362,974	50.40
Sacramento	CA	0	0	0	$813,728	$9,401,500	0	0	0	$1,627,456	$1,985,665	0	$29,562,235	$43,390,584	468.00
Salinas	CA	$225,000	$625,000	0	$97,000	$802,500	0	$98,068	0	$194,000	0	0	0	$2,041,568	48.00
San Bernardino	CA	0	0	$1,656,712	0	$229,008	$155,046	0	0	$155,046	0	$1,493,195	$4,093,136	$7,782,143	59.20
San Diego	CA	$1,080,000	$0	$0	$3,241,485	$4,494,631	$14,897,248	$0	$0	$219,868	$0	$0	$6,450,000	$30,353,232	1013.80
San Francisco	CA	$1,950,000	$3,250,000	$0	$3,522,980	$1,558,717	$878,925	$0	$0	$1,883,017	$2,000,000	$0	$4,650,000	$19,693,639	675.70
San Jose	CA	$2,325,000	$0	$0	$1,888,892	$1,492,310	$0	$0	$0	$0	$0	$0	$5,550,000	$11,256,202	260.90
San Mateo	CA	$225,000	$125,000	$0	$0	$0	$0	$0	$359,939	$0	$0	$0	$0	$709,939	18.40
Santa Ana	CA	$0	$0	$0	$228,910	$1,838,407	$1,082,875	$0	$0	$116,614	$2,000,000	$0	$0	$5,266,806	115.30
Santa Barbara	CA	$150,000	$0	$0	$0	$0	$0	$0	$0	$0	$0	$0	$0	$150,000	2.00
Santa Clara	CA	$0	$125,000	$0	$0	$0	$0	$0	$0	$0	$0	$0	$0	$125,000	1.00
Stockton	CA	$675,000	$625,000	$0	$373,125	$710,250	$2,748,100	$25,000	$0	$165,000	$0	$1,377,264	$1,575,000	$8,273,739	179.10
Vallejo	CA	$0	$125,000	$0	$0	$0	$0	$0	$500,000	$0	$475,204	$0	$627,429	$1,727,633	35.00
West Covina	CA	$0	$250,000	$0	$0	$0	$35,357	$0	$0	$32,424	$0	$0	$0	$317,781	3.40

222

CITY	ST	AHEAD	CIS	DNP	MORE 1995	MORE 1996	MORE 1998	MORE 2000	MORE 2001	Renewal	PHASE1	PHSP	UHP	Total	Total COPS
Aurora	CO	$0	$1,000,000	$0	$0	$0	$963,993	$0	$0	$0	$0	$0	$250,000	$4,213,993	76.40
Colorado Springs	CO	$0	$1,000,000	$0	$239,953	$53,069	$0	$0	$0	$90,000	$0	$0	$4,050,000	$5,433,022	115.60
Denver	CO	$0	$0	$0	$1,357,182	$0	$0	$0	$1,000,000	$0	$1,950,000	$0	$3,750,000	$8,057,182	222.00
Fort Collins	CO	$225,000	$0	$0	$0	$0	$0	$0	$0	$0	$0	$0	$184,410	$409,410	9.00
Bridgeport	CT	$150,000	$625,000	$0	$0	$208,575	$0	$0	$0	$0	$600,000	$0	$2,850,000	$4,433,575	61.30
Bristol	CT	$0	$125,000	$0	$253,763	$7,888	$74,730	$0	$0	$74,730	$450,000	$0	$450,000	$1,436,111	33.40
Hartford	CT	$900,000	$625,000	$1,830,765	$222,255	$0	$2,825,416	$0	$0	$0	$0	$975,000	$0	$7,378,436	139.80
New Britain	CT	$300,000	$0	$0	$150,000	$0	$0	$50,000	$0	$0	$0	$0	$0	$500,000	14.30
West Hartford	CT	$225,000	$0	$0	$0	$0	$127,500	$0	$0	$0	$0	$0	$0	$352,500	8.10
Washington	DC	$0	$0	$0	$6,061,806	$4,798,878	$0	$0	$996,250	$0	$0	$0	$15,000,000	$26,857,434	761.30
Coral Gables	FL	$0	$0	$0	$0	$0	$1,323,250	$75,000	$0	$0	$0	$0	$375,000	$1,773,250	64.90
Fort Lauderdale	FL	$225,000	$750,000	$0	$185,820	$300,000	$775,769	$0	$0	$164,384	$675,000	$0	$450,000	$3,525,973	88.70
Fort Meyers	FL	$0	$0	$0	$15,000	$0	$1,766,250	$0	$0	$0	$0	$600,000	$600,000	$2,981,250	92.00
Gainesville	FL	$438,165	$349,974	$0	$0	$19,615	$0	$0	$0	$39,230	$0	$0	$600,000	$1,446,984	18.10
Hollywood	FL	$150,000	$625,000	$0	$163,850	$0	$0	$324,781	$0	$0	$0	$0	$675,000	$1,938,631	47.40
Jacksonville	FL	$2,325,000	$0	$0	$0	$1,847,250	$0	$0	$0	$0	$0	$0	$8,775,000	$12,947,250	221.90
Lakeland	FL	$375,000	$873,988	$0	$80,000	$247,315	$242,978	$26,053	$0	$455,434	$0	$0	$2,175,000	$4,475,768	66.70
Miami	FL	$450,000	$0	$25,672,505	$0	$9,537,933	$12,668,336	$0	$0	$1,090,378	$0	$1,950,000	$22,048,029	$83,417,181	1183.50
Orlando	FL	$1,125,000	$625,000	$0	$0	$0	$0	$192,354	$710,664	$0	$0	$1,950,000	$4,650,000	$9,253,018	144.10
Pensacola	FL	$0	$0	$0	$0	$0	$0	$0	$0	$0	$0	$0	$823,590	$823,590	10.00
St. Petersburg	FL	$0	$0	$0	$825,000	$0	$0	$100,000	$0	$0	$1,350,000	$0	$1,575,000	$3,850,000	89.20

223

continued

Table 6, cont.

CITY	ST	AHEAD	CIS	DNP	MORE 1995	MORE 1996	MORE 1998	MORE 2000	MORE 2001	Renewal	PHASE1	PHSP	UHP	Total	Total COPS
Tallahassee	FL	$0	$0	$0	$0	$0	$0	$0	$0	$0	$0	$900,000	$0	$900,000	12.00
West Palm Beach	FL	$0	$0	$0	$0	$0	$1,577,458	$0	$0	$0	$0	$0	$1,950,000	$3,527,458	102.40
Atlanta	GA	$2,787,385	$0	$0	$2,662,238	$705,082	$0	$0	$0	$639,380	$0	$1,500,000	$6,300,000	$14,594,185	286.20
Columbus	GA	$600,358	$0	$0	$0	$0	$0	$0	$0	$0	$0	$0	$0	$600,358	9.00
Marietta	GA	$0	$0	$0	$0	$0	$732,525	$0	$0	$0	$297,558	$0	$975,000	$2,005,083	46.30
Honolulu	HI	$0	$0	$0	$0	$0	$9,332,500	$0	$0	$0	$3,000,000	$0	$0	$12,332,500	413.50
Chicago	IL	$24,075,000	$0	$27,412,650	$1,175,156	$765,579	$2,785,500	$0	$0	$0	$0	$4,000,000	$63,125,314	$123,339,199	1593.10
Elgin	IL	$225,000	$0	$0	$0	$121,230	$0	$0	$0	$242,460	$0	$0	$1,200,000	$1,788,690	23.90
Oak Park Village	IL	$225,000	$0	$0	$20,000	$19,035	$90,462	$0	$0	$19,035	$0	$0	$0	$373,532	8.10
Peoria	IL	$0	$0	$0	$0	$0	$445,302	$45,348	$0	$0	$600,000	$0	$1,575,000	$2,665,650	48.60
Rockford	IL	$0	$0	$0	$0	$0	$0	$0	$0	$0	$580,469	$0	$600,000	$1,180,469	16.00
Skokie Village	IL	$0	$250,000	$0	$0	$0	$119,700	$0	$0	$0	$0	$0	$75,000	$444,700	7.80
Springfield	IL	$375,000	$1,500,000	$0	$65,242	$0	$37,800	$50,000	$0	$0	$0	$0	$600,000	$2,628,042	34.00
Anderson	IN	$150,000	$0	$0	$38,394	$20,452	$187,500	$0	$0	$38,394	$0	$150,000	$0	$584,740	15.80
Gary	IN	$450,000	$0	$0	$1,155,204	$0	$0	$0	$0	$0	$0	$749,982	$2,625,000	$4,980,186	101.50
Hammond	IN	$375,000	$0	$0	$75,973	$0	$0	$0	$0	$151,946	$0	$0	$375,000	$977,919	14.00
Kokomo	IN	$0	$0	$0	$0	$0	$0	$0	$0	$0	$375,000	$0	$0	$375,000	5.00
Muncie	IN	$0	$0	$0	$0	$0	$121,350	$0	$0	$0	$0	$0	$0	$121,350	4.90
South Bend	IN	$0	$0	$0	$799,750	$0	$0	$0	$0	$0	$0	$750,000	$300,000	$1,849,750	72.70

224

CITY	ST	AHEAD	CIS	DNP	MORE 1995	MORE 1996	MORE 1998	MORE 2000	MCRE 2001	Renewal	PHASE1	PHSP	UHP	Total	Total COPS
Davenport	IA	$300,000	$0	$0	$0	$0	$0	$100,000	$0	$0	$0	$0	$375,000	$775,000	13.00
Des Moines	IA	$300,000	$0	$0	$0	$0	$550,000	$0	$0	$0	$66,312	$0	$1,350,000	$2,904,812	50.70
Sioux City	IA	$0	$250,000	$0	$37,500	$0	$0	$0	$0	$93,300	$0	$750,000	$0	$1,139,500	14.20
Waterloo	IA	$0	$0	$0	$46,500	$0	$0	$0	$0	$0	$0	$975,000	$0	$975,000	13.00
Overland Park	KS	$300,000	$250,000	$0	$0	$0	$0	$0	$0	$0	$0	$0	$1,050,000	$1,600,000	20.00
Wichita	KS	$975,000	$985,283	$0	$0	$0	$0	$0	$0	$0	$0	$1,028,372	$8,025,000	$11,013,655	143.00
Lexington-Fayette	KY	$683,925	$530,970	$0	$109,105	$66,000	$0	$0	$0	$2 8210	$0	$0	$1,816,032	$3,424,242	48.10
Louisville	KY	$1,200,000	$0	$0	$0	$0	$2,014,500	$0	$0	$0	$0	$0	$2,625,000	$5,839,500	138.60
Bossier City	LA	$0	$0	$0	$0	$0	$0	$0	$0	$0	$0	$0	$252,713	$252,713	4.00
Lafayette	LA	$284,613	$0	$0	$0	$0	$0	$0	$0	$0	$0	$0	$895,246	$1,179,889	20.00
Shreveport	LA	$694,790	$0	$0	$0	$963,750	$0	$0	$0	$0	$0	$1,084,766	$0	$2,743,306	79.00
Baltimore	MD	$5,700,000	$0	$10,123,830	$376,550	$1,779,672	$2,005,323	$0	$0	$2,229,224	$0	$2,000,000	$30,857,220	$55,071,419	599.80
Boston	MA	$3,525,000	$0	$0	$276,150	$0	$0	$225,000	$0	$0	$0	$0	$4,875,000	$8,901,150	148.10
Newton	MA	$0	$0	$0	$135,000	$0	$0	$0	$0	$0	$0	$0	$0	$135,000	6.30
Quincy	MA	$375,000	$0	$0	$0	$0	$0	$0	$0	$0	$0	$900,000	$0	$1,275,000	17.00
Worcester	MA	$0	$0	$0	$199,708	$126,735	$0	$0	$0	$399,416	$1,950,000	$0	$2,175,000	$4,850,889	70.90
Ann Arbor	MI	$300,000	$0	$0	$0	$0	$0	$68,800	$0	$0	$0	$0	$825,000	$1,193,800	17.70
Battle Creek	MI	$225,000	$250,000	$0	$25,129	$0	$0	$0	$0	$24,518	$0	$0	$150,000	$674,647	8.00
Dearborn	MI	$0	$0	$0	$0	$0	$351,561	$0	$0	$0	$0	$0	$0	$351,561	14.10
Detroit	MI	$7,200,000	$0	$0	$134,034	$4,604,197	$0	$0	$0	$0	$0	$1,500,000	$18,000,000	$31,438,231	550.60
Flint	MI	$600,000	$0	$1,659,636	$0	$0	$0	$0	$0	$0	$0	$1,000,000	$1,125,000	$4,384,636	49.00

225

continued

Table 6, cont.

CITY	ST	AHEAD	CIS	DNP	MORE 1995	MORE 1996	MORE 1998	MORE 2000	MORE 2001	Renewal	PHASE1	PHSP	UHP	Total	Total COPS
Grand Rapids	MI	$0	$0	$0	$0	$0	$825,000	$0	$0	$0	$1,275,000	$0	$0	$2,100,000	50.00
Kalamazoo	MI	$0	$0	$0	$0	$0	$253,946	$0	$0	$0	$0	$0	$300,000	$553,946	15.20
Pontiac	MI	$300,000	$0	$0	$50,000	$0	$267,181	$95,124	$0	$348,799	$0	$0	$600,000	$1,661,104	27.30
Saginaw	MI	$0	$0	$0	$0	$0	$0	$0	$0	$0	$0	$975,000	$0	$975,000	13.00
Warren	MI	$450,000	$500,000	$0	$0	$0	$0	$0	$0	$0	$0	$0	$0	$950,000	10.00
Duluth	MN	$225,000	$0	$0	$0	$47,000	$0	$29,375	$0	$94,000	$0	$0	$750,000	$1,145,375	16.10
Minneapolis	MN	$1,575,000	$500,000	$0	$0	$501,841	$1,218,360	$0	$0	$0	$0	$750,000	$3,750,000	$8,295,201	153.70
St. Paul	MN	$1,050,000	$250,000	$0	$658,082	$677,945	$190,875	$0	$0	$0	$0	$750,000	$0	$3,576,902	88.10
Kansas City	MO	$0	$0	$0	$604,233	$0	$0	$746,045	$679,125	$1,113,536	$0	$1,950,000	$6,900,000	$11,992,939	194.20
Springfield	MO	$447,610	$0	$0	$120,783	$0	$0	$0	$0	$225,066	$0	$0	$1,200,000	$1,993,459	26.80
St. Louis	MO	$1,723,728	$0	$0	$881,085	$0	$1,834,251	$0	$0	$0	$0	$1,725,000	$3,675,000	$9,839,064	246.70
Omaha	NE	$0	$2,375,000	$0	$1,189,382	$519,750	$0	$0	$635,829	$1,082,283	$2,000,000	$0	$4,021,280	$11,823,524	200.20
Las Vegas	NV	$300,000	$0	$0	$0	$99,754	$0	$0	$0	$0	$1,990,885	$0	$0	$2,390,639	34.00
North Las Vegas	NV	$0	$0	$0	$0	$0	$0	$24,221	$0	$0	$0	$0	$0	$24,221	1.00
Reno	NV	$525,000	$0	$0	$455,310	$144,753	$193,665	$0	$59,795	$348,171	$0	$0	$450,000	$2,176,694	56.40
Manchester	NH	$300,000	$500,000	$0	$59,593	$0	$173,220	$0	$307,243	$73,886	$0	$0	$600,000	$2,013,942	38.50
Bayonne	NJ	$300,000	$3,250,000	$0	$161,391	$150,000	$178,761	$288,923	$0	$214,128	$0	$450,000	$2,925,000	$7,918,203	106.60
Clifton	NJ	$225,000	$0	$0	$0	$0	$0	$0	$0	$0	$0	$0	$675,000	$900,000	12.00
Edison	NJ	$300,000	$0	$0	$0	$325,561	$0	$0	$0	$0	$0	$0	$1,725,000	$2,350,561	39.90
Elizabeth	NJ	$225,000	$0	$0	$117,975	$0	$73,890	$0	$0	$235,950	$375,000	$0	$2,250,000	$3,277,815	46.00

CITY	ST	AHEAD	CIS	DNP	MORE 1995	MORE 1996	MORE 1998	MORE 2000	MORE 2001	Renewal	PHASE1	PHSP	UHP	Total	Total COPS
Irvington	NJ	$375,000	$1,875,000	$0	$82,755	$0	$0	$498,750	$0	$0	$0	$385,366	$3,741,297	$6,958,168	65.00
Jersey City	NJ	$1,575,000	$0	$0	$211,242	$261,206	$908,339	$1,140,522	$1,013,400	$1,384,863	$0	$1,350,000	$2,925,000	$10,769,572	198.30
Linden	NJ	$0	$250,000	$0	$42,081	$59,803	$75,000	$0	$0	$96,162	$450,000	$0	$0	$973,046	18.70
Newark	NJ	$2,175,000	$0	$0	$332,461	$1,544,325	$0	$0	$750,000	$1,899,872	$0	$2,000,000	$16,500,000	$25,201,658	380.50
Paterson	NJ	$0	$0	$0	$270,515	$0	$247,320	$0	$0	$540,630	$1,000,000	$0	$4,500,000	$6,558,265	92.90
Woodbridge	NJ	$375,000	$0	$0	$53,788	$0	$0	$0	$0	$45,000	$0	$0	$150,000	$623,788	11.60
Albuquerque	NM	$0	$1,209,170	$0	$392,670	$0	$667,321	$0	$0	$986,255	$1,906,536	$0	$6,457,770	$11,619,722	127.00
Santa Fe	NM	$225,000	$495,264	$0	$0	$0	$0	$25,000	$0	$0	$0	$0	$0	$745,264	8.00
Albany	NY	$0	$375,000	$0	$130,071	$194,669	$108,375	$320,173	$0	$505,592	$0	$999,309	$1,043,546	$3,676,935	62.90
Rochester	NY	$0	$3,000,000	$0	$0	$0	$315,680	$0	$0	$241,420	$1,350,000	$0	$0	$5,107,100	53.00
Syracuse	NY	$900,000	$0	$0	$0	$193,128	$0	$0	$0	$0	$1,500,000	$0	$2,850,000	$3,943,128	57.70
Yonkers	NY	$0	$1,500,000	$0	$0	$0	$0	$50,000	$877,756	$0	$1,500,000	$0	$0	$3,927,756	67.10
Charlotte	NC	$0	$0	$0	$3,559,961	$4,120,920	$4,033,592	$0	$0	$682,372	$0	$1,799,478	$13,800,000	$27,996,633	734.60
Durham	NC	$0	$1,103,470	$0	$0	$0	$0	$0	$0	$0	$0	$0	$750,000	$1,853,470	20.00
Greensboro	NC	$824,505	$0	$0	$0	$0	$0	$191,385	$597,277	$0	$0	$0	$0	$1,613,267	42.60
High Point	NC	$267,663	$0	$0	$0	$0	$0	$0	$0	$0	$0	$0	$362,981	$630,644	9.00
Raleigh	NC	$907,277	$0	$0	$193,579	$44,640	$0	$102,701	$685,248	$476,058	$0	$0	$3,921,875	$6,331,158	102.00
Wilmington	NC	$0	$0	$0	$65,593	$0	$49,665	$0	$0	$181,151	$476,840	$0	$1,387,988	$2,161,137	32.20
Akron	OH	$225,000	$0	$0	$24,000	$451,687	$0	$0	$0	$48,000	$647,860	$0	$2,025,000	$3,421,547	57.00
Cincinnati	OH	$0	$0	$0	$725,000	$0	$0	$0	$0	$1,450,000	$0	$0	$3,450,000	$5,625,000	75.00
Cleveland	OH	$1,875,000	$2,500,000	$15,852,200	$430,077	$0	$0	$0	$0	$875,368	$0	$2,000,000	$4,950,000	$28,482,645	258.50
Columbus	OH	$2,850,000	$0	$0	$199,531	$43,499	$0	$0	$0	$0	$0	$0	$1,350,000	$4,443,030	83.70
Dayton	OH	$0	$0	$0	$0	$0	$68,696	$0	$0	$0	$615,925	$0	$150,000	$934,621	15.70

227

continued

Table 6, cont.

CITY	ST	AHEAD	CIS	DNP	MORE 1995	MORE 1996	MORE 1998	MORE 2000	MORE 2001	Renewal	PHASE1	PHSP	UHP	Total	Total COPS
Springfield	OH	$225,000	$500,000	$0	$0	$0	$0	$0	$0	$0	$0	$0	$0	$725,000	7.00
Toledo	OH	$1,275,000	$0	$0	$885,198	$198,923	$300,000	$100,000	$579,130	$0	$0	$1,476,347	$375,000	$5,189,598	123.10
Lawton	OK	$0	$0	$0	$0	$0	$0	$0	$0	$0	$0	$0	$292,899	$292,899	4.00
Orman	OK	$0	$0	$0	$87,524	$0	$0	$0	$0	$175,048	$0	$600,000	$0	$862,572	12.00
Tulsa	OK	$0	$0	$0	$0	$0	$0	$0	$0	$0	$1,935,687	$0	$0	$1,935,687	26.00
Eugene	OR	$300,000	$0	$0	$39,438	$0	$0	$0	$0	$0	$0	$0	$0	$339,438	6.00
Portland	OR	$0	$1,875,000	$0	$30,000	$1,035,463	$3,609,451	$0	$0	$2,258,734	$0	$0	$8,066,280	$16,874,928	258.20
Salem	OR	$0	$250,000	$0	$0	$0	$905,418	$0	$0	$0	$0	$0	$0	$1,155,418	40.90
Erie	PA	$0	$0	$0	$116,988	$0	$0	$0	$0	$0	$0	$0	$0	$116,988	9.60
Philadelphia	PA	$11,475,000	$0	$0	$2,065,301	$2,024,056	$0	$0	$495,000	$155,124	$0	$0	$45,000,000	$59,149,180	853.80
Pittsburgh	PA	$0	$0	$0	$0	$2,253,021	$0	$0	$0	$0	$0	$0	$0	$4,318,322	196.00
Reading	PA	$375,000	$125,000	$0	$0	$0	$0	$0	$0	$0	$0	$750,000	$0	$1,250,000	16.00
Providence	RI	$0	$0	$0	$108,423	$0	$3,317,283	$0	$0	$108,423	$0	$1,213,156	$1,050,000	$5,797,285	175.50
Columbia	SC	$506,774	$599,994	$0	$0	$0	$0	$0	$0	$0	$0	$0	$0	$1,103,768	13.00
Sioux Falls	SD	$30,000	$625,000	$0	$0	$0	$0	$0	$0	$0	$0	$0	$0	$925,000	9.00
Knoxville	TN	$553,397	$0	$0	$56,116	$675,000	$150,000	$0	$0	$112,232	$0	$0	$4,462,780	$6,009,525	194.90
Memphis	TN	$1,500,000	$0	$0	$0	$0	$851,677	$216,573	$0	$0	$0	$1,500,000	$7,500,000	$11,568,250	184.50
Nashville-Davidson	TN	$2,025,000	$1,199,140	$0	$280,904	$1,139,859	$2,660,625	$0	$0	$0	$0	$0	$13,266,200	$20,571,728	387.40
Abilene	TX	$129,013	$0	$0	$33,911	$58,763	$0	$0	$0	$116,350	$0	$0	$746,573	$1,084,610	16.00
Amarillo	TX	$427,936	$685,326	$0	$0	$0	$868,500	$0	$0	$0	$0	$0	$450,000	$2,431,762	52.70

CITY	ST	AHEAD	CIS	DNP	MORE 1995	MORE 1996	MORE 1998	MORE 2000	MORE 2001	Renewal	PHASE1	PHSP	UHP	Total	Total COPS
Arlington	TX	$750,000	$750,000	$0	$0	$0	$0	$75,000	$0	$0	$0	$0	$4,875,000	$6,450,000	84.00
Austin	TX	$0	$0	$0	$621,561	$217,409	$-59,478	$200,000	$0	$1,281,800	$1,875,000	$0	$16,350,000	$20,996,248	317.90
Beaumont	TX	$450,000	$0	$0	$0	$0	$765,893	$0	$0	$0	$0	$600,200	$0	$1,815,893	44.60
Corpus Christi	TX	$750,000	$0	$0	$0	$1,201,500	$0	$0	$468,750	$0	$0	$0	$750,000	$3,170,250	86.80
Dallas	TX	$2,400,000	$0	$0	$0	$0	$94,500	$0	$187,500	$0	$0	$2,100,000	$0	$4,782,000	71.40
El Paso	TX	$825,000	$0	$687,566	$390,905	$937,500	$823,302	$150,071	$0	$1,455,120	$975,000	$0	$19,981,630	$26,125,898	317.30
Galveston	TX	$300,000	$0	$0	$0	$0	$0	$0	$0	$0	$0	$0	$0	$300,000	4.00
Garland	TX	$525,000	$0	$0	$0	$0	$0	$0	$0	$0	$0	$0	$0	$525,000	7.00
Houston	TX	$9,225,000	$0	$0	$5,435,390	$2,662,500	$2,448,557	$0	$0	$9,400,000	$0	$2,100,000	$13,875,000	$45,146,447	889.00
Irving	TX	$0	$0	$0	$0	$0	$150,592	$0	$0	$0	$0	$0	$0	$150,592	6.10
Longview	TX	$217,854	$0	$0	$0	$0	$0	$0	$375,000	$0	$0	$0	$0	$592,854	18.00
Lubbock	TX	$447,114	$0	$0	$0	$142,511	$0	$0	$0	$187,522	$0	$0	$0	$777,147	11.90
Tyler	TX	$300,000	$0	$0	$64,060	$0	$0	$0	$0	$30,963	$0	$0	$750,000	$1,145,023	18.90
Waco	TX	$0	$0	$0	$0	$0	$0	$0	$0	$0	$975,000	$0	$216,110	$1,191,110	20.00
Wichita Falls	TX	$0	$0	$0	$0	$0	$103,065	$0	$0	$0	$0	$0	$300,000	$403,065	8.10
Salt Lake City	UT	$675,000	$0	$0	$82,287	$152,212	$1,955,000	$0	$0	$146,480	$0	$1,050,000	$2,250,000	$6,308,979	142.60
Alexandria	VA	$450,000	$0	$0	$198,276	$207,862	$187,500	$0	$0	$0	$0	$0	$450,000	$1,493,638	18.40
Arlington	VA	$0	$0	$0	$0	$0	$355,970	$0	$625,600	$88,427	$425,475	$0	$2,310,426	$3,803,898	71.70
Chesapeake	VA	$510,662	$330,408	$0	$128,201	$141,750	$150,000	$313,514	$0	$256,402	$0	$0	$4,475,812	$6,306,749	100.50
Hampton	VA	$395,613	$561,140	$0	$0	$30,810	$0	$0	$0	$0	$0	$4,000,000	$897,227	$2,884,790	45.40
Lynchburg	VA	$0	$0	$0	$0	$0	$138,956	$0	$0	$109,351	$0	$0	$399,640	$647,927	11.50

continued

Table 6, cont.

CITY	ST	AHEAD	CIS	DNP	MORE 1995	MORE 1996	MORE 1998	MORE 2000	MORE 2001	Renewal	PHASE1	PHSP	UHP	Total	Total COPS
Newport News	VA	$0	$0	$0	$0	$1,552,500	$0	$0	$0	$0	$0	$1,500,000	$2,400,000	$5,452,500	1179.0
Norfolk	VA	$1,195,134	$0	$0	$373,964	$495,000	$540,000	$0	$0	$747,928	$0	$0	$2,789,880	$6,141,906	1139.0
Richmond	VA	$0	$0	$0	$0	$0	$4,244,707	$0	$0	$142,805	$1,997,514	$0	$3,415,430	$9,800,456	2172.0
Virginia Beach	VA	$1,264,448	$0	$0	$60,125	$81,314	$0	$0	$0	$0	$0	$1,991,415	$6,750,000	$10,147,302	1444.0
Everett	WA	$300,000	$375,000	$0	$0	$0	$0	$0	$0	$0	$0	$0	$525,000	$1,200,000	140.0
Seattle	WA	$300,000	$1,250,000	$0	$300,000	$0	$0	$0	$0	$0	$0	$1,452,390	$0	$3,302,390	590.0
Spokane	WA	$0	$0	$0	$0	$853,513	$0	$0	$0	$810,786	$1,950,000	$0	$2,250,000	$5,864,299	911.0
Yakima	WA	$225,000	$0	$0	$0	$0	$0	$0	$0	$0	$0	$0	$225,000	$450,000	60.0
Kenosha	WI	$0	$500,000	$0	$0	$0	$0	$0	$0	$0	$0	$0	$500,000	$1,000,000	80.0
Madison	WI	$0	$0	$0	$0	$0	$0	$51,725	$0	$0	$1,500,000	$0	$2,400,000	$3,951,725	540.0
TOTALS		$136,579,964	$52,799,127	$101,488,164	$70,829,111	$89,368,654	$122,196,153	$6,426,486	$12,956,345	$60,174,485	$49,096,761	$69,593,861	$881,864,354	$1,653,373,465	269,832

No funds granted, omitted from table: Pomona, CA; Sunnyvale, CA; Torrance, CA; Augusta, GA; Macon, GA; Oklahoma City, OK; Odessa, TX; Roanoke, VA

230

Table 7: Innovative grants

Advancing COP, Comprehensive Communities, CICP, Methamphetamine, Demonstration Sites, Domestic Violence, Integrity, Justice Based After School Program, Problem Solving Partnership, Problem Solving Partnership Evaluation, Problem Solver Peace Maker, Regional

City	St	ACP	CCP	CICP	COPS METH	DEMO	DV	DVTS	DVWA	INTEG-RITY	JBAS	PSP	PSP EVAL	PSPM	RCPI
							Community Policing Institute Grant Programs								
Birmingham	AL	$0	$0	$0	$0	$0	$199,950	$0	$0	$0	$0	$0	$0	$0	$0
Mesa	AZ	$0	$0	$0	$0	$0	$0	$0	$0	$0	$0	$114,390	$0	$0	$0
Phoenix	AZ	$0	$999,000	$0	$750,000	$0	$222,208	$0	$0	$0	$0	$149,897	$0	$0	$0
Tempe	AZ	$250,000	$0	$0	$0	$399,978	$0	$0	$0	$0	$0	$91,103	$0	$0	$0
Berkeley	CA	$0	$0	$0	$0	$0	$195,033	$0	$0	$0	$0	$91,103	$0	$0	$0
Concord	CA	$500,000	$0	$0	$0	$0	$161,410	$0	$0	$0	$0	$65,853	$0	$0	$0
Fremont	CA	$0	$0	$0	$0	$0	$250,000	$0	$0	$0	$0	$0	$0	$0	$0
Fresno	CA	$0	$0	$0	$0	$0	$199,355	$0	$0	$0	$0	$0	$0	$0	$0
Hayward	CA	$0	$0	$0	$0	$387,616	$0	$0	$0	$0	$0	$0	$0	$0	$0
Inglewood	CA	$0	$0	$0	$0	$0	$0	$0	$0	$0	$0	$0	$0	$0	$0
Long Beach	CA	$0	$0	$0	$0	$0	$200,000	$0	$0	$0	$0	$150,000	$0	$0	$0
Los Angeles	CA	$240,996	$0	$0	$0	$0	$200,000	$450,000	$0	$163,492	$0	$149,998	$0	$0	$0
Oakland	CA	$250,000	$0	$0	$0	$0	$199,669	$0	$0	$200,000	$0	$149,647	$0	$0	$0
Ontario	CA	$0	$0	$0	$0	$0	$0	$0	$0	$0	$0	$0	$0	$0	$0
Redondo Beach	CA	$0	$0	$0	$0	$0	$56,508	$0	$0	$0	$0	$86,534	$0	$0	$0
Richmond	CA	$0	$0	$0	$0	$0	$200,000	$0	$0	$0	$0	$149,981	$0	$0	$0
Riverside	CA	$159,695	$0	$0	$0	$0	$0	$0	$0	$0	$0	$53,990	$0	$0	$0
Sacramento	CA	$250,000	$0	$0	$0	$0	$120,337	$100,000	$0	$434,000	$0	$0	$0	$200,000	$2,500,000

continued

231

Table 7, cont.

City	St	ACP	CCP	CICP	COPS METH	DEMO	DV	DVTS	DVWA	INTEG-RITY	JBAS	PSP	PSP EVAL	PSPM	RCPI
Salinas	CA	$198,824	$0	$0	$0	$0	$0	$0	$0	$0	$0	$0	$0	$0	$0
San Diego	CA	$1,000,000	$0	$0	$0	$200,000	$200,000	$489,000	$0	$400,000	$0	$123,060	$50,000	$0	$2,500,000
San Francisco	CA	$0	$0	$0	$0	$0	$200,000	$0	$0	$0	$0	$0	$0	$0	$0
San Jose	CA	$248,359	$0	$0	$0	$0	$149,239	$0	$0	$0	$0	$0	$0	$0	$0
Santa Ana	CA	$1,000,000	$0	$0	$0	$0	$0	$0	$0	$0	$0	$104,049	$0	$0	$0
Santa Barbara	CA	$99,930	$0	$0	$0	$0	$64,480	$0	$0	$0	$0	$0	$0	$0	$0
Vallejo	CA	$0	$0	$0	$0	$0	$0	$0	$0	$0	$0	$138,097	$0	$0	$0
West Covina	CA	$0	$0	$0	$0	$0	$0	$300,000	$0	$0	$0	$0	$0	$0	$0
Aurora	CO	$0	$0	$0	$0	$0	$3,954	$0	$0	$0	$0	$124,377	$0	$0	$0
Colorado Springs	CO	$988,641	$0	$0	$0	$0	$199,646	$490,000	$0	$34,000	$0	$124,377	$0	$200,000	$0
Denver	CO	$0	$0	$0	$0	$0	$198,800	$0	$0	$200,000	$0	$0	$0	$0	$0
Bridgeport	CT	$177,231	$0	$0	$0	$0	$196,500	$0	$0	$0	$0	$149,998	$0	$0	$0
Bristol	CT	$0	$0	$0	$0	$0	$124,860	$0	$0	$0	$0	$31,733	$0	$0	$0
Hartford	CT	$250,000	$0	$0	$0	$0	$200,000	$0	$0	$0	$0	$146,712	$0	$0	$0
Washington	DC	$228,000	$999,000	$0	$0	$0	$250,000	$0	$0	$0	$0	$146,712	$0	$0	$0
Fort Lauderdale	FL	$500,000	$0	$0	$0	$0	$113,197	$0	$0	$0	$0	$0	$0	$0	$0
Fort Meyers	FL	$0	$0	$0	$0	$0	$185,747	$0	$0	$0	$0	$100,099	$0	$0	$0
Gainesville	FL	$0	$0	$0	$0	$0	$194,071	$0	$0	$0	$0	$0	$0	$0	$924,000
Hollywood	FL	$0	$0	$0	$0	$0	$198,647	$0	$0	$0	$0	$61,700	$0	$0	$0
Jacksonville	FL	$185,000	$0	$0	$0	$0	$200,000	$0	$0	$0	$0	$0	$0	$0	$0

City	St	ACP	CCP	CICP	COPS METH	DEMO	DV	DVTS	DVWA	INTEG-RITY	JBAS	PSP	PSP EVAL	PSPM	RCPI
Lakeland	FL	$0	$0	$0	$0	$0	$0	$0	$0	$0	$0	$95,254	$0	$0	$0
Miami	FL	$1,000,000	$0	$0	$0	$0	$149,985	$0	$0	$0	$0	$56,388	$49,950	$0	$0
Pensacola	FL	$0	$0	$0	$0	$0	$0	$0	$0	$0	$0	$147,373	$0	$0	$0
St Petersburg	FL	$0	$0	$0	$0	$399,850	$192,783	$0	$0	$0	$0	$150,000	$43,889	$0	$0
Atlanta	GA	$0	$0	$0	$0	$0	$219,172	$0	$0	$0	$0	$0	$0	$0	$0
Honolulu	HI	$1,000,000	$0	$0	$0	$0	$0	$0	$0	$0	$0	$0	$0	$0	$0
Chicago	IL	$0	$0	$0	$0	$200,000	$200,000	$0	$0	$0	$0	$0	$0	$0	$0
Peoria	IL	$0	$0	$0	$0	$0	$155,504	$0	$0	$0	$0	$0	$0	$0	$0
Springfield	IL	$0	$0	$0	$0	$0	$194,490	$0	$0	$0	$0	$108,672	$0	$0	$0
Anderson	IN	$0	$0	$0	$0	$0	$0	$0	$0	$0	$0	$115,984	$0	$0	$0
Hammond	IN	$0	$0	$0	$0	$0	$89,328	$0	$0	$0	$0	$0	$0	$0	$0
South Bend	IN	$0	$0	$0	$0	$0	$200,000	$0	$0	$0	$0	$0	$0	$0	$0
Des Moines	IA	$0	$0	$0	$237,818	$0	$175,608	$0	$0	$0	$0	$0	$0	$0	$0
Sioux City	IA	$153,981	$0	$0	$0	$0	$0	$0	$0	$0	$0	$0	$0	$0	$0
Waterloo	IA	$0	$0	$0	$0	$0	$0	$0	$0	$0	$0	$80,011	$0	$0	$0
Wichita	KS	$0	$999,000	$0	$0	$0	$0	$0	$0	$0	$0	$0	$0	$0	$0
Lexington-Fayette	KY	$0	$0	$0	$0	$0	$0	$0	$0	$0	$0	$150,000	$0	$0	$0
Louisville	KY	$144,164	$0	$0	$0	$0	$0	$0	$0	$0	$0	$0	$0	$0	$0
Lafayette	LA	$0	$0	$0	$0	$0	$0	$0	$0	$0	$0	$130,532	$0	$0	$0
Shreveport	LA	$248,500	$0	$0	$0	$0	$0	$0	$0	$0	$0	$0	$0	$0	$0
Baltimore	MD	$999,998	$0	$0	$0	$0	$198,632	$0	$0	$0	$0	$0	$0	$0	$0
Boston	MA	$245,200	$0	$0	$0	$0	$200,000	$289,000	$0	$575,570	$0	$148,525	$0	$0	$2,407,353

continued

233

Table 7, cont.

City	St	ACP	CCP	CICP	COPS METH	DEMO	DV	DVTS	DVWA	INTEG-RITY	JBAS	PSP	PSP EVAL	PSPM	RCPI
Newton	MA	$0	$0	$0	$0	$0	$200,000	$0	$0	$0	$0	$0	$0	$0	$0
Worcester	MA	$0	$0	$0	$0	$0	$141,719	$0	$0	$0	$0	$81,486	$0	$0	$0
Ann Arbor	MI	$0	$0	$0	$0	$400,000	$134,381	$0	$0	$0	$0	$0	$0	$0	$0
Detroit	MI	$0	$0	$0	$0	$0	$175,059	$0	$0	$0	$0	$0	$0	$0	$0
Flint	MI	$0	$0	$0	$0	$0	$73,616	$0	$0	$0	$0	$45,297	$0	$0	$0
Kalamazoo	MI	$0	$0	$0	$0	$0	$249,315	$0	$0	$0	$0	$0	$0	$0	$0
Warren	MI	$0	$0	$0	$0	$0	$0	$0	$0	$0	$0	$149,655	$0	$0	$0
Duluth	MN	$192,732	$0	$0	$750,000	$0	$197,076	$0	$0	$0	$0	$72,671	$0	$0	$0
Minneapolis	MN	$0	$0	$0	$0	$0	$177,221	$0	$0	$0	$0	$0	$0	$0	$0
St Paul	MN	$1,000,000	$0	$0	$0	$199,885	$0	$0	$0	$199,946	$233,051	$89,250	$0	$0	$0
Kansas City	MO	$205,682	$0	$0	$300,000	$0	$0	$0	$0	$200,000	$277,782	$0	$0	$0	$0
St Louis	MO	$847,702	$0	$0	$0	$0	$0	$0	$0	$0	$0	$0	$0	$0	$0
Omaha	NE	$0	$999,000	$0	$267,377	$0	$200,000	$0	$0	$0	$0	$63,501	$0	$0	$0
Reno	NV	$0	$0	$0	$0	$0	$0	$0	$0	$0	$0	$0	$0	$0	$0
Jersey City	NJ	$201,037	$0	$0	$0	$0	$182,650	$0	$0	$200,000	$0	$125,241	$0	$0	$0
Newark	NJ	$250,000	$0	$0	$0	$0	$249,717	$0	$0	$0	$0	$0	$0	$0	$0
Woodbridge	NJ	$0	$0	$0	$0	$0	$0	$0	$0	$0	$0	$149,974	$0	$0	$0
Albuquerque	NM	$173,219	$0	$0	$0	$0	$0	$0	$0	$0	$0	$0	$0	$0	$0
Santa Fe	NM	$0	$0	$375,000	$0	$0	$0	$0	$0	$0	$0	$0	$0	$0	$0
Albany	NY	$0	$0	$0	$0	$0	$131,116	$0	$0	$0	$0	$0	$0	$0	$0
Rochester	NY	$0	$0	$0	$0	$200,000	$0	$0	$0	$0	$0	$0	$0	$0	$0

City	St	ACP	CCP	CICP	COPS METH	DEMO	DV	DVTS	DVWA	INTEG-RITY	JBAS	PSP	PSP EVAL	PSPM	RCPI
Syracuse	NY	$0	$0	$0	$0	$0	$190,776	$0	$0	$0	$0	$0	$0	$0	$0
Yonkers	NY	$0	$0	$75,000	$0	$0	$0	$0	$0	$0	$0	$0	$0	$0	$0
Charlotte	NC	$153,588	$0	$0	$0	$0	$0	$550,000	$0	$551,193	$0	$0	$0	$0	$1,940,000
Akron	OH	$172,507	$0	$0	$0	$0	$250,000	$0	$0	$0	$0	$0	$0	$0	$0
Cleveland	OH	$0	$0	$0	$0	$0	$0	$0	$0	$0	$0	$128,418	$0	$0	$0
Toledo	OH	$98,338	$0	$0	$0	$0	$198,741	$0	$0	$0	$0	$0	$0	$0	$0
Lawton	OK	$0	$0	$0	$0	$0	$0	$0	$0	$0	$0	$86,940	$0	$0	$0
Oklahoma City	OK	$0	$0	$0	$750,000	$0	$0	$0	$0	$0	$0	$0	$0	$0	$0
Tulsa	OK	$0	$0	$0	$0	$0	$54,909	$0	$0	$0	$0	$0	$0	$0	$0
Eugene	OR	$0	$0	$0	$0	$382,159	$0	$0	$0	$0	$0	$0	$0	$0	$0
Portland	OR	$247,223	$0	$0	$300,000	$0	$0	$0	$0	$0	$386,678	$93,592	$0	$0	$0
Philadelphia	PA	$0	$0	$0	$0	$0	$0	$0	$0	$0	$0	$0	$0	$0	$0
Pittsburgh	PA	$0	$0	$0	$0	$0	$200,000	$0	$0	$0	$0	$0	$0	$0	$0
Providence	RI	$208,184	$0	$0	$0	$0	$190,000	$0	$0	$0	$0	$0	$0	$0	$0
Columbia	SC	$0	$999,000	$0	$0	$0	$0	$0	$0	$0	$0	$0	$0	$0	$0
Knoxville	TN	$935,015	$0	$0	$0	$420,000	$190,632	$550,000	$0	$415,315	$0	$80,041	$0	$200,000	$2,847,692
Memphis	TN	$0	$0	$0	$0	$0	$143,289	$0	$0	$0	$0	$150,000	$0	$0	$0
Nashville-Davidson	TN	$0	$0	$0	$0	$0	$490,000	$0	$0	$0	$0	$104,037	$49,986	$0	$0
Arlington	TX	$129,870	$0	$0	$0	$0	$197,934	$0	$0	$129,658	$0	$63,359	$48,180	$0	$0
Austin	TX	$1,000,000	$0	$0	$0	$398,744	$191,688	$0	$0	$0	$0	$56,939	$0	$0	$0
Dallas	TX	$248,400	$0	$0	$749,999	$0	$197,907	$0	$0	$0	$0	$0	$0	$0	$0
El Paso	TX	$0	$0	$0	$0	$0	$148,480	$0	$0	$0	$0	$0	$0	$0	$0

235

continued

Table 7, cont.

City	St	ACP	CCP	CICP	COPS METH	DEMO	DV	DVTS	DVWA	INTEG-RITY	JBAS	PSP	PSP EVAL	PSPM	RCPI
Waco	TX	$126,112	$0	$0	$0	$0	$189,548	$0	$0	$0	$0	$0	$0	$0	$0
Salt Lake City	UT	$1,000,000	$0	$0	$750,000	$0	$200,000	$0	$0	$0	$0	$47,713	$0	$0	$0
Alexandria	VA	$0	$0	$0	$0	$0	$197,582	$0	$0	$0	$0	$0	$0	$0	$0
Hampton	VA	$0	$0	$0	$0	$0	$200,000	$0	$0	$0	$0	$0	$0	$0	$0
Lynchburg	VA	$0	$0	$0	$0	$0	$77,267	$0	$0	$0	$0	$0	$0	$0	$0
Newport News	VA	$0	$0	$0	$0	$0	$149,700	$0	$0	$0	$0	$0	$0	$0	$0
Norfolk	VA	$0	$0	$0	$0	$0	$234,307	$0	$0	$0	$0	$0	$0	$0	$0
Richmond	VA	$0	$0	$0	$0	$0	$136,910	$0	$0	$0	$0	$0	$0	$0	$0
Seattle	WA	$1,000,000	$0	$0	$0	$0	$200,000	$0	$185,000	$200,000	$0	$107,911	$50,000	$0	$0
Spokane	WA	$1,000,000	$999,000	$0	$0	$399,997	$0	$0	$0	$200,000	$0	$0	$0	$0	$0
Madison	WI	$0	$0	$0	$0	$0	$209,527	$0	$0	$0	$0	$0	$0	$0	$0
TOTALS		$19,508,128	$5,594,000	$450,000	$4,905,194	$3,988,229	$13,120,880	$3,708,000	$185,000	$4,103,174	$897,511	$5,144,360	$292,005	$600,000	$13,119,045

Table 8: Innovative awards

School Based Partnerships, Targeted, Training, Troops, TTA, Value Based Initiative, Youth Firearms Violence Initiative, Other Methamphetamine, Technical Assistance, Alternative to 911

City	St	SBP	TARGETED	TRAINING	TROOPS	TTA	VBI	YFVI	OTMETH	OTTECH	ALTEMERG
Birmingham	AL	$152,915	$0	$0	$0	$0	$0	$748,396	$0	$350,000	$434,080
Mesa	AZ	$0	$0	$0	$91,140	$0	$0	$0	$0	$0	$0
Phoenix	AZ	$0	$0	$0	$46,000	$49,700	$0	$0	$0	$0	$0
Anaheim	CA	$0	$0	$0	$5,000	$0	$0	$0	$0	$0	$0
Concord	CA	$0	$0	$0	$4,243	$0	$0	$0	$0	$0	$0
Fresno	CA	$0	$0	$0	$0	$0	$0	$0	$0	$1,500,000	$0
Glendale	CA	$0	$0	$0	$0	$0	$0	$0	$0	$229,494	$0
Inglewood	CA	$0	$0	$0	$0	$0	$0	$787,201	$0	$599,780	$0
Los Angeles	CA	$150,000	$0	$0	$0	$0	$0	$0	$0	$0	$912,270
Oakland	CA	$0	$0	$0	$80,120	$0	$0	$0	$0	$0	$0
Ontario	CA	$0	$0	$0	$5,000	$0	$0	$0	$0	$0	$0
Orange	CA	$0	$0	$0	$5,000	$0	$0	$0	$0	$0	$0
Pasadena	CA	$0	$0	$0	$0	$0	$0	$0	$0	$3,060,246	$0
Pomona	CA	$122,966	$0	$0	$0	$0	$0	$0	$0	$0	$0
Riverside	CA	$0	$0	$0	$0	$0	$200,000	$0	$0	$0	$0
Sacramento	CA	$0	$50,000	$0	$0	$0	$0	$0	$0	$250,000	$0
Salinas	CA	$0	$0	$0	$0	$0	$0	$989,524	$0	$0	$0

continued

237

Table 8, cont.

City	St	SBP	TARGETED	TRAINING	TROOPS	TTA	VBI	YFVI	OTMETH	OTTECH	ALTEMERG
San Bernardino	CA	$0	$0	$0	$0	$0	$125,000	$0	$0	$0	$0
San Diego	CA	$129,720	$0	$0	$135,354	$47,947	$0	$0	$0	$0	$0
San Jose	CA	$172,990	$0	$0	$32,328	$0	$0	$0	$0	$0	$0
Santa Ana	CA	$0	$0	$0	$0	$0	$0	$0	$0	$563,406	$0
West Covina	CA	$152,370	$0	$0	$0	$0	$0	$0	$0	$0	$0
Aurora	CO	$0	$0	$0	$25,166	$0	$0	$0	$0	$0	$0
Colorado Springs	CO	$218,877	$0	$0	$0	$0	$0	$0	$0	$700,000	$0
Bridgeport	CT	$0	$0	$0	$0	$0	$0	$916,748	$0	$0	$0
Hartford	CT	$149,056	$0	$0	$0	$0	$0	$0	$0	$0	$0
Washington	DC	$168,649	$0	$0	$0	$0	$0	$0	$0	$0	$0
Fort Lauderdale	FL	$131,196	$0	$0	$0	$0	$0	$0	$0	$0	$0
Gainesville	FL	$0	$0	$0	$0	$0	$0	$0	$0	$1,000,000	$0
Hollywood	FL	$69,746	$0	$0	$17,383	$0	$0	$0	$0	$0	$0
Jacksonville	FL	$0	$0	$0	$15,000	$350,000	$0	$0	$0	$0	$0
Lakeland	FL	$65,542	$0	$0	$22,051	$0	$0	$0	$0	$0	$0
Miami	FL	$402,868	$0	$0	$51,957	$0	$0	$0	$0	$0	$423,737
Tallahassee	FL	$0	$0	$0	$0	$0	$0	$0	$0	$750,000	$0
West Palm Beach	FL	$0	$0	$0	$21,562	$0	$0	$0	$0	$0	$0

City	St	SBP	TARGETED	TRAINING	TROOPS	TTA	VBI	YFVI	OTMETH	OTTECH	ALTEMERG
Atlanta	GA	$0	$0	$0	$25,000	$0	$0	$0	$0	$0	$0
Columbus	GA	$94,597	$0	$0	$0	$0	$0	$0	$0	$0	$0
Macon	GA	$0	$0	$0	$0	$0	$0	$0	$0	$748,350	$0
Chicago	IL	$164,476	$0	$0	$10,000	$200,000	$0	$0	$0	$0	$0
Hammond	IN	$0	$0	$0	$10,000	$0	$0	$0	$0	$0	$0
Kokomo	IN	$0	$0	$0	$5,000	$0	$0	$0	$0	$0	$0
Muncie	IN	$0	$0	$0	$0	$0	$0	$0	$0	$125,000	$0
South Bend	IN	$0	$0	$0	$0	$0	$0	$0	$0	$500,000	$0
Davenport	IA	$0	$0	$0	$4,850	$0	$0	$0	$0	$0	$0
Sioux City	IA	$0	$0	$0	$0	$0	$0	$0	$7,895,158	$0	$0
Overland Park	KS	$0	$0	$0	$20,000	$0	$0	$0	$0	$500,000	$0
Wichita	KS	$0	$0	$0	$20,000	$0	$0	$0	$0	$1,496,700	$0
Lexington-Fayette	KY	$0	$0	$0	$15,000	$0	$0	$0	$0	$100,000	$0
Louisville	KY	$0	$0	$0	$0	$0	$0	$0	$0	$1,248,900	$0
Shreveport	LA	$0	$0	$0	$60,000	$0	$0	$0	$0	$0	$0
Baltimore	MD	$298,980	$0	$0	$45,000	$0	$0	$949,907	$0	$0	$0
Boston	MA	$109,175	$109,850	$0	$25,000	$68,579	$323,261	$0	$0	$0	$796,153
Battle Creek	MI	$114,177	$0	$0	$0	$0	$0	$0	$0	$0	$0
Detroit	MI	$0	$0	$0	$3,350	$0	$0	$0	$0	$0	$0

continued

Table 8, cont.

City	St	SBP	TARGETED	TRAINING	TROOPS	TTA	VBI	YFVI	OTMETH	OTTECH	ALTEMERG
Grand Rapids	MI	$0	$0	$0	$0	$0	$0	$0	$0	$299,340	$0
St Paul	MN	$162,640	$0	$0	$0	$0	$300,000	$0	$0	$210,000	$0
Kansas City	MO	$130,136	$0	$0	$0	$0	$200,000	$0	$0	$0	$0
Springfield	MO	$0	$0	$0	$0	$0	$0	$0	$0	$250,000	$0
St Louis	MO	$0	$0	$0	$15,000	$0	$0	$0	$0	$0	$0
Omaha	NE	$0	$0	$0	$165,656	$0	$0	$0	$0	$2,200,000	$0
Las Vegas	NV	$0	$0	$0	$0	$0	$0	$0	$0	$3,420,600	$0
Reno	NV	$0	$0	$495,592	$0	$0	$0	$0	$0	$0	$0
Manchester	NH	$0	$0	$0	$15,402	$0	$0	$0	$0	$0	$0
Jersey City	NJ	$352,483	$0	$0	$0	$0	$0	$0	$0	$1,750,000	$0
Newark	NJ	$0	$0	$0	$10,000	$0	$0	$0	$0	$0	$0
Albuquerque	NM	$0	$0	$0	$35,000	$0	$0	$0	$0	$0	$0
Albany	NY	$131,437	$0	$0	$0	$0	$0	$0	$0	$0	$0
Rochester	NY	$0	$0	$0	$0	$0	$0	$0	$0	$0	$383,900
Syracuse	NY	$163,108	$0	$0	$0	$0	$0	$0	$0	$0	$0
Charlotte	NC	$169,660	$0	$0	$0	$0	$0	$0	$0	$0	$0
Greensboro	NC	$0	$0	$0	$15,000	$0	$0	$0	$0	$0	$0
Raleigh	NC	$0	$0	$0	$20,000	$0	$0	$0	$0	$0	$0

City	St	SBP	TARGETED	TRAINING	TROOPS	TTA	VBI	YFVI	OTMETH	OTTECH	ALTEMERG
Akron	OH	$111,058	$0	$0	$0	$0	$0	$0	$0	$0	$0
Cincinnati	OH	$0	$0	$0	$13,312	$0	$0	$0	$0	$0	$0
Cleveland	OH	$92,972	$0	$0	$80,764	$0	$0	$634,842	$0	$0	$0
Columbus	OH	$0	$0	$0	$5,000	$0	$0	$0	$0	$0	$0
Tulsa	OK	$0	$0	$0	$2,907	$0	$0	$0	$0	$0	$0
Portland	OR	$0	$0	$0	$0	$0	$200,000	$0	$0	$0	$0
Knoxville	TN	$0	$0	$0	$8,120	$0	$0	$0	$0	$250,000	$0
Memphis	TN	$0	$0	$0	$24,345	$0	$0	$0	$0	$0	$0
Nashville-Davidson	TN	$218,541	$0	$0	$0	$0	$0	$0	$0	$0	$0
Abilene	TX	$0	$0	$0	$5,000	$0	$0	$0	$0	$0	$0
Arlington	TX	$122,369	$0	$0	$5,000	$0	$0	$0	$0	$0	$0
Austin	TX	$0	$0	$0	$220,260	$0	$0	$0	$0	$0	$381,710
Corpus Christi	TX	$0	$0	$0	$77,284	$0	$0	$0	$0	$0	$0
Dallas	TX	$0	$0	$0	$40,000	$0	$0	$0	$0	$0	$0
El Paso	TX	$0	$0	$0	$45,000	$0	$0	$0	$0	$0	$0
Houston	TX	$0	$0	$0	$180,000	$0	$0	$0	$0	$0	$637,464
Lubbock	TX	$0	$0	$0	$10,000	$0	$0	$0	$0	$0	$0
Waco	TX	$0	$0	$0	$15,000	$0	$0	$0	$0	$0	$0
Salt Lake City	UT	$128,631	$0	$0	$14,572	$0	$0	$0	$0	$0	$0

241

continued

Table 8, cont.

City	St	SBP	TARGETED	TRAINING	TROOPS	TTA	VBI	YFVI	OTMETH	OTTECH	ALTEMERG
Chesapeake	VA	$0	$0	$0	$212,670	$0	$0	$0	$0	$0	$0
Norfolk	VA	$0	$0	$0	$15,000	$0	$0	$0	$0	$0	$0
Richmond	VA	$0	$0	$0	$35,000	$0	$200,000	$692,605	$0	$0	$0
Roanoke	VA	$111,429	$0	$0	$0	$0	$0	$0	$0	$0	$0
Virginia Beach	VA	$0	$0	$0	$45,533	$0	$0	$0	$0	$0	$0
Seattle	WA	$306,862	$0	$0	$20,000	$100,000	$0	$981,380	$0	$2,498,900	$0
Yakima	WA	$0	$0	$0	$10,459	$0	$0	$0	$0	$0	$0
Madison	WI	$0	$0	$0	$20,051	$0	$0	$0	$0	$1,998,900	$0
TOTALS		$5,069,626	$159,850	$495,592	$2,170,841	$816,326	$1,548,261	$6,700,603	$7,895,158	$26,599,616	$3,969,314

Index

Printed in the United States
23964LVS00001B/439-456

9 781593 320966